Get Real about Sex:
The Politics and Practice of Sex Education

Get Real about Sex: The Politics and Practice of Sex Education

Pam Alldred and Miriam E. David

Open University Press

Open University Press
McGraw-Hill Education
McGraw-Hill House
Shoppenhangers Road
Maidenhead, Berkshire
England SL6 2QL

email: enquiries@openup.co.uk
world wide web: www.openup.co.uk

and Two Penn Plaza, New York, NY 10122289, USA

A catalogue record of this book is available from the British Library

ISBN   13: 9780335214105 (pb) 9780335214099 hb)
        10: 033521410X (pb)   0335214096 (hb)

Library of Congress Cataloging-in-Publication Data
CIP data has been applied for

Typeset by BookEns Ltd, Royston, Herts.
Printed and bound in Poland by OZGraf. S.A.
www.polskabook.pl

Contents

Acknowledgements

We would especially like to thank Pat Smith, the third member of our project team during its two years of project funding, for her insights, knowledge of the local schools, teachers and PSHE coordinators and without whose work the project might not have developed. We would also like to thank the team that devised the project, particularly Lyn Frith, the LEA's Social Inclusion Officer. The generous support of Tracey Kirk, the Schools Reintegration Officer, and Jane Henry of the Young People's Health and Wellbeing project was vital in facilitating the project. We are hugely grateful to all the young men and women and all the professionals who spent time talking to us and we hope that we have reflected their concerns in this book.

Colleagues in the then Department of Education at Keele University were very generous in hosting the project, providing general support and membership of the project's advisory group: in particular, Nafsika Alexiadou, Ken Jones, Angela Packwood, Farzana Shain and, especially, Gladys Pye for her administrative care and support. Other members of our advisory group included colleagues in the Law Department at the time, Daniel Monk and Davina Cooper, whose contributions were much appreciated, as were those of colleagues in Criminology, Susanne Karstedt, Ian Loader, Richard Sparks and Anne Worrall, and in Social Relations, Ian Butler, Nick Lee and Graham Allan.

There are many other people we would both like to thank. For Pam, this includes her Brunel University colleagues, especially Simon Bradford, Nic Crowe, Valerie Hey, Yvonne McNamara, Kyoko Murakami and Evie Xinos; her previous colleagues and students in the School of Education and Training at Greenwich University; colleagues and friends in Psychosocial Studies, Sociology and Cultural Studies at University of East London; and members of Manchester Metropolitan University's Discourse Unit, especially Erica Burman. Thanks to members of the Feminist Review Collective for their personal support and encouragement, as well as for a period of leave from the journal. And for all those times when work breached the boundaries of home, huge thanks (and apologies) to Shaun Butler, and thanks to Vivienne, John and Jude Alldred for extra childminding and their continued loving support.

For Miriam, this includes colleagues at the Institute of Education, University of London, within the Teaching and Learning Research Programme, and those in and around Gender and Education and the GEA, especially Madeleine Arnot, Becky Francis, Carolyn Jackson, Diana Leonard, Heidi Mirza, Diane Reay and Gaby Weiner. Colleagues in the USA and Canada such as Sandra Acker, Michael Apple, Mimi Bloch, Jane Gaskell, Wendy Luttrell, Tom Popkewitz and Amy Stambach have also been influential, as have colleagues in Australia and New Zealand, including Jill Blackmore, Alison Jones, Jane Kenway, Julie McLeod, Sue Middleton and Lyn Yates.

Last but by no means least, we both especially want to thank all of our former colleagues at London South Bank University where we first met in the Social Science Research Centre. Ros Edwards, Robert Bell, Clare Farquhar, Jane Franklin, Philip Gatter, Val Gillies, Brian Heaphy, Janet Holland, Sheena McGrellis, Rajni Naidoo, Sue Sharpe, Rachel Thomson, Matthew Waites and Jeffrey Weeks need especially warm thanks for their academic influence and personal support.

For critical comments on some of the chapters, thanks to Jamie Heckert, Mary James, Yvonne McNamara, Kyoko Murakami, Alan White, and for sharing rants, Barbara Alldred, Lisa Blackman, Collette Jones and Lucy Russell of YWCA. Debbie Epstein provided the most critical and yet friendly help in reviewing the final manuscript and helping us to put it to bed, so to speak. Finally, we thank Fiona Richman at Open University Press for her patience as the book's progress was interrupted by a maternity leave and various other life events.

This book is dedicated to our children, Millie Butler Alldred and Charlotte and Toby Reiner, in the hope that future generations manage to loosen the ties around gender and lose some of the baggage around sex.

List of abbreviations

CE	citizenship education
CIB	Clinic in a Box
C of E	Church of England
CRE	Commission for Racial Equality
DfEE	Department for Education and Employment
DfES	Department for Education and Skills
DH	Department of Health
EET	education, employment or training
ERA	Education Reform Act
FPA	Family Planning Association
GCSE	General Certificate of Secondary Education
IVF	*in vitro* fertilisation
LEA	local education authority
MD	Miriam David
NC	National Curriculum
NEET	not in education, employment or training
OfSTED	Office for Standards in Education
ONS	Office for National Statistics
PA	Pam Alldred
PS	Pat Smith
PSE	personal and social education
PSHCE	personal, social, health and citizenship education
PSHE	personal, social and health education
RC	Roman Catholic
RE	religious education
SEF	Sex Education Forum
SEU	Social Exclusion Unit
SMT	senior management team
SRE	sex and relationship education
SRO	Schools Reintegration Officer
STI	sexually transmitted infection
TPS	Teenage Pregnancy Strategy
UNCRC	United Nations Convention on the Rights of the Child
YWCA	Young Women's Christian Association

chapter / **one**

Introduction: 'Get *Real* about Sex!'

Sex education is political in two respects: it invokes party political conflicts over policy, and, in the wider sense, it reinforces particular meanings and power relations. This book explores the cultural politics of contemporary *understandings* of sex education, and the political and cultural *consequences* of sex education practices. We examine the multiple perspectives on the delivery of school sex education that exist in any school by presenting the views of teachers, head-teachers, school nurses, boys and girls in school and young mothers and young men not attending school. These are drawn from accounts we gathered during a two-year study of sex education in all the secondary schools of one local education authority (LEA) in the North of England.

Our title, *Get Real about Sex*, comes from a remark by a young mother we interviewed when asked what schools ought to do to improve sex education. It encapsulates a widely held sentiment, expressed by many of the young people we spoke to, particularly those who were not in school, and many of the teachers and school nurses we interviewed. Adults need to 'get real' about teenagers and sex – meaning that parents, those working with young people, and society more generally need to deal with their resistance to acknowledging and responding constructively to the sexualities and sexual relationships of boys and girls. Of course, claims about what is 'real' always rest on particular yet naturalised perspectives and produce particular 'truth effects' (Foucault 1980). Our two main concerns are to recognise the differing perspectives within policy and within actual schools, and to trace the consequences for practice of these differing discourses of sex education, particularly regarding their gendered normative assumptions.

The troublesome nature of sex

Sex is an object of fascination, anxiety and taboo in Western societies (Douglas 1966; Halstead and Reiss 2003). If it is an object of pleasure too, for a culture influenced by ancient Christianity, it can be a guilty pleasure (Aries and Bejin 1985). As Foucault (1987) argued, sexuality has become an ethical and problematic part of human existence. Some argue that there is a peculiarly British ambivalence about sex and sexuality, producing contradictions between the social licence granted innuendo and smutty humour and the moralistic censure of explicit discussion of sexuality or sexual practice. 'Sex' evokes strong disapproval, yet sells more British newspapers than any other issue: 'tits and tuts' alongside each other (Stronach *et al.* 2006). Frank discussion of heterosexual activity within socially recognised relationships evokes coyness, embarrassment, resistance or discomfort.

Admonishments of 'not in public' or 'not in front of the children' reveal the assumptions and cultural baggage about the private nature of such matters and about their unsuitability for children's eyes. Aries (1962) argued that hiding sex and bawdy humour from children produced our modern-day understanding of childhood as a phase distinct from adulthood. The school, as a public setting, is a troublesome site for the discussion of sex and yet one that carries the public duty to educate children on this 'private' matter. Not surprisingly, strong but implicit codes delimit acceptable classroom topics and conduct and contradictory impulses emerge. First, this separation of children and sexuality warrants some elaboration.

The non-sexual nature of children

In Western societies, sex represents a key cultural distinction between adulthood and childhood, and this constructs childhood as pre-sexual personhood (Jackson 1982; James and Prout 1990). Our collective attachment to the cultural construct of the child as non-sexual makes the task of sex education seem troublesome. It troubles this idealised notion of the child and can appear to conflict with protecting children – a view that we will contest. According to Jenks (2005: 124),

> an archaeology of the ideas which gave rise to the modern 'child' reveals a strong and continuous commitment to conceptions of childhood innocence ... from Rousseau, children are awarded a purity by virtue of their special nature ... from the Enlightenment, they are the Ideal immanence, and the messengers of

Reason. It is the experience of society which corrupts them. [And] from Locke: children are thought to be innocent, not innately, but like halfwits, as a consequence of their lack of social experience. Through time, the unknowing, unworldly child may become corrupted by society.

The association of sex with guilt reinforces the conflation of innocence with non-sexuality for the child. The idea of childhood *sexual* innocence inhibits progressive change regarding some of the oppressive aspects of adult–child relations in Western culture, producing culpability for children who fall short of this ideal, as Epstein and Johnson (1998) argued. Kitzinger (1988) showed the double-edged nature of childhood sexual innocence in creating the conditions for children's vulnerability and abuse, and attaching penalties to those children seen as sexually aware who forfeit their 'innocence'.

Discussing sexuality in schools threatens the assumption that schools deal with 'pupils', who are 'children' (not even, until very recently, 'young people') and are in the business of tending their minds. The educated mind is expected to exercise better, more rational control over the body – the troublesome side of the mind–body split (O'Flynn and Epstein 2005). The body's general lack of order, hygiene and predictability lies in the unruly nature of desire and sexuality. The ungendered nature of 'the pupil' in policy, and of 'the body' in Cartesian and modern Western thought, may well obscure more than they reveal for real, gendered and embodied young people in school today, as we shall see.

A key theme of the book is the construction of the child as non-sexual and how this idea obstructs sex education. There is also a gendered history to be told; this desexualised invention, 'the child', had exceptions. Firestone (1972: 43) described how, in the late seventeenth century, as special games and artefacts for the children of the bourgeoisie emerged:

> *childhood did not apply to women* [*sic*]. The female child went from swaddling clothes right into adult female dress. She did not go to school ... the institution that structured childhood. At the age of 9 or 10 she acted, literally, like a 'little lady' and as soon as she reached puberty, as early as ten or twelve, she was married off to a much older male.

The exclusion of girl children from the notion of childhood for the 'proper' education of 'men' makes the association of masculinity with reason and the mind, and femininity with emotion and the body. This remains significant, and girls' bodies are those 'marked' as different within schools. Whilst normative expectations of pupils' embodiment are interrupted by changing and sexual bodies whatever their gender, the peculiarly leaky, fertile or even pregnant body seems particularly 'unreliable' or inconvenient to a rational, bureaucratic system of schooling.

The non-sexual child remains a strikingly persistent notion despite its exceptions and, given the usual resistance to acknowledging the sexuality of the young, penalties attach to those whose sexuality is in evidence. In addition, discourses of deviancy among young people and deviant sexualities provide for subject positions that are gendered (Warner 1996; Griffin 1997, 2004). For instance, recent attempts to make sex education more engaging for boys, the hyperbole regarding teenage pregnancy and the treatment of school-aged mothers each illustrate the *normalised absence* – a concept we adopt from Phoenix (1987) – of pupils' sexuality and the anxiety surrounding it when present. They also evidence particularly gendered ideas about young people and the requisite professional responses. These two 'childhoods' – the 'non-sexual' child and its corollary the 'aberrant sexually active child' – construct each other, and arise out of a need to categorise and 'know' the child (Rose 1989), just as the two 'opposite' gender categories construct each other.

The sex/gender/sexuality matrix

If sex is a troublesome topic in public, sexuality is even more vexed. The term sexuality is used variously to mean desires, identities, psychic and physical activities, or, as a form of popular shorthand, sexual orientation. In our sexually normative culture, heterosexuality is sanctioned, sanctified, normalised and naturalised – meaning that any alternative is obscured by its presentation as if is the only and 'natural' form of sexuality. Homosexuality, as heterosexuality's Other, occupies a strikingly prominent role in the field of sex education, as it does in Western sexuality generally (Weeks 1981; Butler 1990; Dollimore 1991). As Daniel Monk (2001: 285) has argued: 'the persistent focus on [homosexuality] by moral authoritarians and the tabloid press has strategically served to problematise sex education as a whole and legitimised the restrictive legislative framework'.

Despite the denial and sanitising of young people's sexuality from the official culture of the school, recent studies in secondary schools by Mary Jane Kehily (e.g. Nayak and Kehily 2006), as well as in primary schools (Hey *et al.* 2001; Renold 2005), show that schools are highly sexualised spaces:

Researchers in this field have commented on the ways in which informal school-based cultures are saturated with sex – through humour, innuendo, double-entendre and explicit commentary – yet the official culture of the school frequently seeks to deny the sexual and desexualize schooling relations (Epstein and Johnson 1998; Jackson 1982). (Kehily 2002: 5)

Whilst we follow in the footsteps of writers such as Mac an Ghaill (1994a) in viewing young people as active in producing their own identities and we recognise the powerful role of peer subcultures, after writers such as Kehily (2002), we are acutely aware of the fact that whatever creative space for play and resistance young people may carve out in their own relationships and cultures is against the force of hegemonic cultural meanings assigned gender and sexuality. Gender categories and normative expectations of their occupancy by 'appropriately' sexed bodies, with their associated expectations of behaviour and subjectivities, shore up particular categories of sexuality and sexual orientation. The binary gender system produces the 'heterosexual matrix' of desire and sexual relations across 'difference', a relation which confirms these two gender categories (Butler 1990, 1993). The intersections of gendered and sexual identities with race and class are particularly significant in recent research on peer and classroom relations (Mac an Ghaill 1994a, 1994b; Connolly 1998; Reay 2002; Renold 2005). The ever-present default nature of heterosexualised gender relations in school makes dominant sexualities available to young people and results in their alternatives – lesbian, gay, bisexual, queer or trans- or ambiguously gendered identities – being marginalised, stigmatised or persecuted (Epstein 1994; Epstein and Johnson 1998; Ellis and High 2004).

'Hegemonic masculinity' (Connell 1995) – the 'ascendant masculinity in a particular time and place' (Haywood and Mac an Ghaill 2003) – is usually associated with toughness, power, authority, competitiveness, and the subordination of its Others. Being 'acceptably' male in this dominant cultural mode can involve denigrating the feminine and/or the homosexual, and many boys, as well as girls, feel the brunt of this. It is an 'ideal' many boys and men do not match up to (Frosh *et al.* 2002), and it produces different kinds of masculinities (Mac an Ghaill 1994b; Connell 1995; Martino 1999), but this does not dent its power to devalue its Others. Boys in school work hard to perform socially valued masculinities, which can conflict with educational success, especially for working-class and/or black boys (Mac an Ghaill 1994b; Sewell 1997; O'Donnell and Sharpe 2000; Frosh *et al.* 2002; Reay 2002). Girls, on the other hand, may be able to identify with a female teacher and integrate educational success into socially valued feminine identities (Hey *et al.* 2001). If girls are criticised by their peers for working hard at school, the slurs are differently gendered and they are more likely to be called 'snobs', whereas boys who work hard are sometimes called 'gay' (Nayak and Kehily 1997). Some of the new, feminist-inflected femininities are feistier than classic 1950s-style femininity, but we remain cautious about them since they adopt the sexual aggression and occlusion of self-doubt of hegemonic masculinity. It is with the normative expectations of identity and behaviour at the peer group/ classroom, teacher professional/staffroom and societal level that all emergent gendered and sexual identities have to contend. So, therefore, should sex and relationship education.

This study is situated within gender studies and alongside critical masculinities work (Mac an Ghaill 1994b; Connell 1995; O'Donnell and Sharpe 2000; Skelton 2001; Frosh *et al.* 2002; Haywood and Mac an Ghaill 2003). We approach gender through the lens of feminist work in education and the social sciences over the past few decades. At a time of considerable popular concern and academic research about the problem of boys and boys' problems (Skelton 2001), as regards their education, we agree with Hey *et al.* (2001: 124) that 'as numerous feminist critics note (Epstein *et al.* 1998; Arnot *et al.* 1999; Lingard and Douglas 1999; Francis 2000), the rush to rewrite gender equity as the discourse of male disadvantage is misguided and premature'. A feminist critical stance on hegemonic masculinity does not limit our recognition of the difficulties boys face in struggling to perform a credible masculinity in the eyes of their peers, and the cost of succeeding or penalties of being judged lacking, explored in Chapter 7.

Femininity and masculinity are relational discourses and whilst boys and girls in our study each discuss gender, and give us some indication of the dominant and resistive discourses they have access to in school and classroom peer groups, some of the deeper currents of gendered discourses of adult male and female lives only became vivid when we analysed our interviews with young men and women who were not in school. Different themes, concerns and expectations characterised the boys' and the girls' accounts. The significance of motherhood for young women who do not go to school cannot be denied, whether this is a cause or effect of being outside of education. Parenting is a profoundly gendered and gendering experience irrespective of today's gender-neutral discourses of parenthood, childcare and earning (David *et al.* 1993, 1994; Alldred 1999). Within the context of young people's lives, the school and ideas about education may be a very powerful site for the production of gendered, classed and racialised identities. Within the domain of education, sex and relationship education represents one specific site for the construction of young people's gendered and sexual identities: a set of policies and practices steeped in assumptions about what men's and women's lives and loves are and ought to be.

The politics of sex education

Sex education is a contentious political topic and is described variously as a basic human right or as corrupting of children's innocence (Monk 2000; Osler 2005; Mirza 2006). It has been the site of highly politicised struggles in Britain between central and local government, right-wing moral traditionalists, the liberal left, conservative moralists and health promoters (David 1986; Durham 1991; Thomson 1994; Monk 1998) and over parental versus the state's responsibilities for children (David 1980, 1993; Rose 1989; Packer 2000). When the New Labour Government came into power in 1997, whilst there was a social and family policy framework, a new language was created: 'Where the focus of debate had previously been on boundaries of authority between the state, professionals and the family, new terms began to dominate the policy agenda: social exclusion, targets and effectiveness' (Thomson and Blake 2002: 188). Rachel Thomson and Simon Blake amongst others (Levitas 1998; Bullen *et al.* 2000; David 2003a, 2003b), offer the Teenage Pregnancy Strategy (Social Exclusion Unit (SEU) 1999) as the most vivid example of New Labour's social exclusion agenda:

> Teenage pregnancy is seen both as the result of social exclusion (occurring in deprived communities among young women who are educational underachievers) and as a central cause of social exclusion (associated with low birth weight and other negative social and health indicators). (Thomson and Blake 2002: 188)

Thomson (1994) had also shown the past schism between health and education approaches to sex education, whereas now there was a cross-departmental brief for 'joined up' government between the Department of Health (DH) and the Department for Education and Employment (DfEE), as it was then.

Recognising the politics of childhood makes us sceptical about public concern or panic about sexuality and childhood (Jackson 1982; Armstrong 1995). Concerns about 'the child' are sometimes about the notion of childhood, a cultural construct independent of those occupying the category, which is invested with our collective and personal hopes and fears for the future, and our nostalgia for past certainties. No wonder that debates about children attract powerful feelings and contributions from all 'sides' and perspectives. In passionate argument for or against sex education might be seen the last vestiges of a sense of collective 'ownership' or responsibility for children. In acknowledging the emotional and political investment in the category 'child' comes the recognition that public debates about sex education can be about maintaining the purity of idealised objects, rather than the well-being of actual, flesh-and-blood children. Placing sex on the school curriculum entails a perceived threat to the idea that pupils do not need such knowledge, and even if they do, it is the school's rather than parents' business to teach about sex or morality (Halstead and Reiss 2003). Talking about sexuality and schooling in the same breath is disturbing because schooling is on the public and sexuality on the private side of the public/private division (Epstein and Johnson 1998).

There is a particularly complex relationship between state regulation, provision and parental rights about schooling and education (David 1980, 1993). Since Margaret Thatcher's governments the consumerist approach in education has increasingly granted parents more power and control in education through the notion of parental choice. This notion is problematic in failing to recognise social and economic impediments to parents' exercise of free choice thus reproducing race and class hierarchies (Whitty 2001; Ball 2003) and it exacerbates educational inequalities by concentrating socially and economically advantaged children in what are seen as 'good' schools (David et al. 1993, 1994). School choice does not operate in a 'perfect' market, and the limits of 'free market ideology' in terms of social justice and equality are clear (Gewirtz et al. 1995; David et al. 1996; Stambach and David 2005). Schools tend to 'market' themselves to parents to attract the 'best' or highest-achieving pupils, ignoring children/young people's views. It is notable that whilst schools do not address children or young people as consumers, health care services do. The legal requirement to listen to children's views is a recent British policy development, and discussion of children's views is distinctly muted or circumscribed on the subject of sex education.

Children are not only the 'objects' of parental concern emotionally and legally. They are also the legitimate concern of teachers and other professionals or practitioners (Rose 1989; Halstead and Reiss 2003). Expert claims to know children's needs or what is in their best interest, on the basis of training and professional responsibilities, can be pitted against parents' claims to be best placed to know their own children's needs (Alldred 1996). The potential for competition between these two sets of claims has intensified in recent years as parental rights are increasingly claimed and parents no longer defer to professionals, yet practitioners have become more highly trained, regulated and professionalised. This is complicated by the colonisation of the hitherto 'private' parent–child relationship by psychological and educational discourses (Woollett and Phoenix 1991; Burman 1994a). There exists great potential for conflict between and within parental and professional opinions about sex education.

Two distinct principles that inform policy on children/young people are usually labelled 'protectionist' and 'empowerment' discourses. Either can claim the moral high ground: as either 'adults have a responsibility to protect children' or, alternatively, 'adults have a moral obligation not to limit the power that children could have'. Parents in Britain have frequently been seen as a conservative lobby for protection, not empowerment, and as invested in their own powerful position as parent, relative to their child. In the case of sex education, the discourse of protection has argued against provision, lest it 'corrupts' 'innocent minds' and makes sexual activity more likely. The discourse of empowerment tends to be mobilised by children's rights campaigners and public health pragmatists to argue for sex education on the grounds either that it is an entitlement or that being well informed will make children more able to protect themselves from infection or abuse (Thomson 1994). Even the, arguably, historically most progressive legislative framework for sex education that exists in Britain today still falls short of an empowerment approach that provides sex education on the basis of children's rights (Monk 2001; Halstead and Reiss 2003), despite the support this would find in the UN Convention on the Rights of the Child (Corteen 2006; Lyon 2007). In general, policy-makers and practitioners anticipate much resistance to sex education from parents, which in practice may not be as common as is imagined (Wyness 1992) and is certainly not unanimous (Halstead and Reiss 2003).

The dominant discourse or model of children as 'human becomings' (Alanen 1990; James and Prout 1990) has been criticised for constructing them as merely future persons and undermining attention to children's choices and well-being in the present. However, whilst less radical than a children's rights-informed approach to sex education, this understanding of the child as a future adult can support the conclusion that sex education is 'the responsible thing' to provide for children, arming them for their future sexual 'careers'. For example, cultural differences between Britain and The Netherlands have interested policy-makers looking to explain the differing current teenage pregnancy rates (Lewis and Knijn 2002). British newspapers, covering a study visit to The Netherlands by TV presenter Davina McCall and several head-teachers, report that Dutch parents look aghast when asked 'if they minded their children having these lessons'. 'They looked at me like I was crazy' one of the heads recounted, 'and said "You wouldn't put someone in a car without giving them driving lessons, would you?"'. Ignoring the ecological irresponsibility of constructing learning to drive as a rite of passage into adulthood, this shows how parental responsibility can be taken to include ensuring children are 'prepared' for sexual activity, and frank sex education can be framed within a discourse of protection. This has echoes in the

Government's current direction on sex education, but is contradicted by a moralising tendency.

The Family Planning Association (FPA), now in its 75th year of providing sexual health services, is currently lobbying the British Government on contraception and abortion, with an emphasis on education and services for young people. It recommends that: sex and relationship education (SRE) be delivered by trained specialist teachers; all young people have access to confidential sexual health advice and services; and SRE be made statutory within the National Curriculum (NC) as part of the personal social and health education (PSHE) framework before and certainly from Key Stage 1 (8-year-olds) onwards (FPA 2005). We agree and we discuss the obstacles to achieving these aims at a national policy level and in the local context and across one LEA. We examine what blocks these aims intentionally, for instance, by having agendas to the contrary, and forms of resistance that emerge from indirect pressures or differing values and cultures. We present the views of teachers, school nurses and young people themselves about who should deliver SRE and with what training; trace the effects of an LEA-wide attempt to raise the status of SRE in secondary schools; explore the difficulties that emerged in inter-agency working to bring sexual health services into schools; and examine the various priorities that work against the SRE agenda.

The politics of teenage motherhood

The British teenage pregnancy rate is not escalating, despite the SEU's (1999) claims, and is static and unremarkable, but over the last three decades it has not reduced as in other western European countries (David 2003b; Stronach *et al.* 2006). The only rising birth-rate is amongst the over-30s; whilst the birth-rate is static for the under-20s, is dropping for 20–29-year-olds, and increasing for 30–39-year-olds. According to the Office for National Statistics (ONS 2006a), in 2004 the fertility rate for women aged 30–34 overtook that for women aged 25–29, and in 2005 the average age for giving birth was 29.5 years. The year 1971 saw the peak birth-rate among mothers under 20 (MacIntyre and Cunningham-Burley 1987) so 'paradoxically, the focus on teen motherhood as an object of concern in the West has coincided with declining rates of teen birth' (Wilson and Huntington 2005: 1). The proportion of births outside marriage continues to rise: to 42.8 per cent in 2005, compared to 33 per cent in 1995 (ONS 2006a).

It is the governmental agendas with which teenage motherhood clashes that have changed. As generations of post-war women have gained educational and employment opportunities, women's expectations of employment have changed (Arnot *et al*. 1999). Most dramatic is New Labour's intensification of the individualisation of responsibility for financial security and the deconstruction of social welfare towards what Beck (1992) and Giddens (1998) have called the 'risk society'. Unlike under the post-war social democratic consensus, there are 'no excuses' for economic inactivity. The expectation is that all adults, including mothers and lone parents, are in paid work. The youngest mothers usually have least to offer, not having finished compulsory schooling, taken examinations or gained work experience. The problematisation of teenage pregnancy as underpinned by economic imperatives about women as workers (Bullen *et al*. 2000; Wilson and Huntington 2005) is apparent in the SEU's Teenage Pregnancy Report, with references to the cost of teenage parenthood to the young person, their child and the nation: 'The UK cannot afford high rates of teenage conception and parenthood at the end of the twentieth century' (SEU 1999: 7) and 'Our failure to tackle this problem has cost the teenagers, their children and the country dear' (SEU 1999: 4; see also David 2003b).

Leaving aside obstetric concerns, the key factor is the characterisation of the two groups of mothers at opposite ends of the age continuum as representing distinctly different social class cultures. The 'older' mothers typically have participated in post-compulsory education and the labour market, whereas the younger mothers are seen as lacking education and the potential to earn to support their children (David 2003b). Early mothering compounds their socio-economic disadvantage, increasing the risk of reliance on benefits, social housing and unemployment (Kiernan 1995; Botting *et al*. 1998; Allen and Bourke-Dowling 1999, all cited by McDermott and Graham 2005), but the model of combining earning simultaneously with mothering is neither ubiquitous nor 'blind' to race and class (Duncan and Edwards 1999; Duncan *et al*. 2003b). There are stark differences between the implications for individuals of living in communities that are work-rich, with women feeling they cannot step off the career ladder to have a baby (Bunting 2005), and those that are work-poor. There are also many who remain poor despite working long hours. In public policy debates about 'young' mothers, as Phoenix (1991) has shown, 'new' concerns recirculate older themes. Particular social values are asserted and presented as if uncontested, and those not sharing them are seen as morally lacking, resonating with Charles Murray's US-imported underclass theory (David 1990). We see the pathologisation or criminalisation of those whose choices and investments differ from those the government prefers, in the so-called responsibilisation of individuals in communitarian policy.

The racialisation of this debate has shifted. Under the Conservatives, rhetoric about young mothers racialised it as a problem of black young women, constructing black families as deviant for their dominant mothers and disengaged fathers. Today 'the problem' appears to have been mainstreamed, and the stereotypical images are of white working-class young women in the North of England. The SEU seeks to 'halv[e] the rate of conceptions among under 18s by 2010, and to get more teenage parents into education, training or employment, to reduce their risk of long term social exclusion' (SEU 1999: 8). It is this work agenda that leads to the construction of teenage pregnancy as a problem of white young women. Some sociological research has shown that black (African Caribbean) mothers in London expect to combine paid work and mothering, whereas white mothers are more likely to see paid work and mothering as incompatible or full-time motherhood as their ideal (Duncan and Edwards 1999; Duncan et al. 2003b).

Luttrell (2003) describes a 'campaign against teenage pregnancy' in the USA that translates what is a political problem into a problem of individual dependency, namely the social instability brought about by globalisation, economic restructuring and diminished forms of social welfare. The stigma contests that are waged in America's anxious 'war' on teen pregnancy deflect attention from the economic, political and social injustices that are the causes of intense feelings and conflicts about dependency, nurturance and protection. As Singer has argued: 'in order to represent a phenomenon as socially undesirable ... one need only call it an epidemic. ... An epidemic is a phenomenon that in its very representation calls for, indeed seems to demand, some form of managerial response, some mobilized effort of control' (1993: 27). Furthermore, as she suggests: 'An epidemic emerges as a product of a socially authoritative discourse in light of which bodies will be mobilized, resources will be dispensed, and tactics of surveillance and regulation will appear to be justified' (1993: 117).

Young people are actively governed through the teenage pregnancy strategy. Funds are released for, amongst other things, improving SRE and access to sexual health services, and for projects that engage young parents in education, employment or training. These will be evaluated strictly on the basis of their contribution to the agenda of reducing the teenage conception rate and getting existing young parents into or nearer to paid work. The model of the socially desirable young person is clearly someone who prioritises education, and sees it as instrumental in gaining employment (Bullen et al. 2000). The role of work in the model of the citizen means that women who are 'full-time' mothers are aberrant and, worse still, 'dependent' on benefits. The changing social contract sees citizenship as conditional on participation in paid work (Levitas 2005), and the labour market as the only response to social exclusion (Mizen 1987, cited in Mizen 2004). Young people are a key focus for the Government because they are important to the remaining areas a late modern government can control, labour and consumption (Mizen 2004). Young people are also valuable in the framing of social exclusion by New Labour and their production as flexible workers, familiar with insecure work, low wages and not expecting any state support (Levitas 2005).

The national guidance on SRE (DfEE 2000) argues that pupils should learn the positive benefits to be gained by avoiding teenage pregnancy. But what are young people's views on the Government's problematisation of teenage pregnancy? We asked young people what they consider to be 'young parenting' and at what age is it acceptable to start a family in their community. We reflect on the acceptable role for schools in implementing government policy, especially where it concerns contested values about reducing welfare, rather than an educational agenda.

The politics of education

Contemporary British education policy is preoccupied with 'raising standards', effective teaching and 'what works', reflecting a narrow agenda for schools and education and an impoverished model of the pupil. The overarching concern is with examination grades, hence a focus on the academic 'success' of young people, as opposed to their personal and social development, emotional well-being or happiness, or preparedness for adult life in today's society. Recently, however, this preoccupation has shifted and a new agenda of personalisation, linked with choice, has emerged. However, as we shall see, this is not the same personalisation as in PSHE, but rather a new, twenty-first-century term for what we call individualisation, linked with the revised and reinvigorated choice agenda, reasserting schools' right to choose their own values. This is emerging as a new educational policy in the recent Education Act 2006 and as reflected in the Chancellor of the Exchequer's 2006 Budget (HM Treasury 2006).

As New Labour took office in 1997 their priorities were to be 'Education, education, education' (David 1997), and in the Schools' Standards and Framework Act 1998 the rationale for strengthening home–school relations was that 'parents are a child's first and enduring teachers'. We already know that the way to sell anything to parents is to call it educational, but this is an example of what feminist theorists have described as happening to motherhood recently: its colonisation by professional discourses of education (David 2003b) and psychology

(Woollett and Phoenix 1991). Here the status of parents is bolstered by analogy with teachers (Edwards and Alldred 1999).

The significance of education in the New Labour project is one key theme of this book. Another theme is the reification of cultural tropes and expectations so that it becomes impossible to see any alternative to this increasingly consumerist culture, rampant individualism and how the market is getting its tentacles and logic into everything. As McRobbie (2000: 100) has argued, 'the main concern is narrowly "me and my family" and any notion of the social good is accessed through this prism of the family' in the new neoliberal common sense that is 'colonising' civil society (Hall 2003).

The effects of an acute pressure to improve grades have demoralised the teaching profession, and forced schools into a quasi-market in which they are required to compete with nearby schools in league tables to win pupils who carry with them *per capita* funding. Children and young people become sidelined in the education marketplace because schools address parents as consumers of education. But young people are far from passive, and truancy and exclusion rates tell other stories of the relationship between young people and their schools. These have no place in the new economy of schooling. The quality audit trail only measures rates to rank schools; their meanings and the individual stories behind them are lost.

The centralising control and regulation by central government that seeks to measure standards by the one ruler, has disciplined teachers, undermined their creativity, and implies a lack of trust in their judgement and abilities. For some, the recovery of professionalism from the malign forces of new managerialism 'can only occur if teaching and research are recovered as autonomous moral activities' (Ashley 2000: 6). The democratisation of educational visions does not seem possible within what the Government depicts as the chance for each school to assert its own values framework. We locate current debates in this recent history of education and struggles around social justice and equality – in particular, gender – and we examine the specific struggles around sex education through recent legislation. Then we explore the indirect consequences of the 'achievement agenda' for sex education.

The non-fixed nature of 'nature' or the 'real'

Our approach involves a scepticism about arguments over what is 'natural' or 'unnatural'. References to the 'natural' interest of girls in babies, the 'only natural' sexual harassment of girls by boys and 'unnatural' same-sex desire, for instance, abound in popular discussion of sexuality. We see these appeals to 'the natural' as a discursive manoeuvre that, whilst remaining powerful in popular and political debate, is not a guarantor of truth. What is seen as 'natural' or 'real' in one cultural time and place is not in another. Claims about the 'real' are attempts to privilege one version of the truth and undermine others. In our title the injunction to 'get real' represents an assertion that sex is everyday and all around, and that 'ignoring it won't make it go away'. This suggests a systematic non-recognition of young people's sexuality to avoid an uncomfortable truth. We have a great deal of sympathy with young people in this respect and are concerned to trace the suppression, evasion or idealisation of sexuality. However, we also try to see the 'problem' of young people's sexuality in schools at different times from the perspectives of teachers, head-teachers and school nurses, recognising that they are differently positioned in relation to young people and each other in terms of roles, responsibilities and investments. We also see differing imprints of common themes across their accounts.

Managing the various anxieties about breaching 'the symbolic boundaries that shape contemporary schooling' (Kehily 2002: 5) is one common theme. Kehily describes how the boundaries that stand to be scrutinised by attending to sex and sexuality inside schools are also broader: 'Constructions such as public/private, adult/child, teacher/pupil, male/female, proper/improper organize social relations within the school in ways that seek to demarcate and prescribe the domain of the sexual' (2002: 5). We also hear these tensions reverberate in all our participants' accounts. Kehily (2002: 5) notes this contradictory pull to contain and yet to speak of sexuality: 'The symbolic boundaries containing issues of sexuality in school juxtaposed with the simultaneous desire to speak the sexual, point to some ways of understanding the sexual politics of schooling'.

This book centres on the different perspectives on and hopes for sex education in schools. Sex education researchers such as the Women, Risk and Aids Project team, Linda Measor *et al.* (2000) and Halstead and Reiss (2003) have argued that sex education programmes fail because of their limited understanding of or respectful engagement with young people's own culture and values. This book explores the gender culture and dynamics of the school and the implicit gendering of pedagogic discourse, situated within the local culture and school ethos and national policy imperatives and rhetoric. Gender is both a topic and an analytic theme for us. We ask young women and young men in school about gender and the gendered dynamics of the classroom to think about how sex education practice might be improved, and then allow gender to become more central to our analysis. We felt it became almost impossible to write about young men and young women's experiences of education and schooling together.

The original study

The SEU (1999) identified improving sex education as one strand of its Teenage Pregnancy Strategy (TPS), and within a year the Government had published new guidance for schools on SRE (DfEE 2000). The SEU's report had also identified LEAs in England with the highest conception rates among 15–17-year-old girls. The DfEE – now the Department for Education and Science (DfES) – allocated targeted monies from the School Standards fund to conduct what it called action research projects in schools to implement the strategy and the new SRE guidance. The LEA that commissioned us was within the top 10 per cent of LEAs (SEU 1999: 20) with around 65 conceptions per thousand 15–17-year-old girls. It pooled the money allocated to schools to have us conduct one study across all its 17 state secondary schools. Our study was action research (Halsey 1972; Taylor 1994) in that we were employed by the LEA to support and attempt to raise the status of SRE, rather than doing research in a passive way. We tried, therefore, to work supportively with those in schools who were responsible for implementing the new national guidance, with its novel emphasis on relationships. We worked alongside and hoped to facilitate local initiatives: the LEA's employment of a professional external consultant to deliver SRE training days for school PSHE or health coordinators; the DH-funded Young People's Health and Wellbeing project, and, as part of the supportive, rather than preventative arm of the TPS, the Schools Reintegration Officer.

Given specific local concerns, the LEA's Social Inclusion Officer helped design a qualitative study to investigate the processes and pressures surrounding SRE in schools, in the context of changing policies and funding initiatives at national level. We were to identify what was hindering the delivery of good SRE in schools and what factors might help. Rather than evaluate the success of local interventions through studying any changes in the teenage conception rate over time, we were commissioned to investigate the views of the various stakeholders in an inclusive two-year project exploring not only the differing *professional* perspectives (of head-teachers, PSHE coordinators and school nurses) and *pupil* perspectives, but also the views of young people *not in school* (young mothers and pregnant schoolgirls, and long-term non-attenders).

We conducted semi-structured interviews with the teacher responsible for SRE (usually the PSHE coordinator) in each of the schools at least twice over the two years and sometimes we had considerable informal contact. We interviewed the head-teachers, and interviewed or involved in focus groups almost all the borough's school nurses. We gathered qualitative and quantitative data from pupils in transition from Year 8 to Year 9 – the year group usually receiving the 'contraception' and 'abortion' sections of sex education. In all, 164 boys and 161 girls returned questionnaires for our survey of their views and preferences for the delivery of SRE and we also held structured, single-sex discussion groups.

Our in-depth study of the views of those young people not accessing mainstream education is much smaller, and the young men in alternative education or training were much less forthcoming than the young mothers who took part. Arguably the young parents (so called because one young father presented himself for interview) correctly perceived their identification as at risk of social exclusion within the TPS. We believe that issues faced in researching topics associated with the private sphere in a public one actually mirror issues faced in teaching it or in raising its status in school and so sometimes draw on our experiences of the research process to illuminate our object.

We had access to all the secondary schools in the LEA and, given that few private or independent schools existed locally, we had a sense that we were getting a fairly broad-based picture. The locality comprised a small city that had emerged from several towns and still retained something of the socially divergent structure and the feel of an old industrial town. One of the legacies of its traditional, gender-segregated but skilled labour force was a white, working-class culture with a 'local' rather than cosmopolitan flavour. The teachers and other professionals we interviewed emphasised the low aspirations and the undervaluing of education locally, pointing to a disjuncture between the national pro-education emphasis and the local values at play. They saw the area as having little by way of 'culture' – recognisably middle-class culture and 'high culture' amenities – its population having low social and geographical mobility, with a parochial, gender-stereotypical 'family values' culture. Male breadwinner expectations remained, despite high levels of male unemployment for over a generation because of the decline of local industries. These industries had provided female employment down the generations and had led to a culture of 'women coping' with children, families and work. The local labour market now provided flexible, part-time work in the service sector, largely taken by women. Several head-teachers described their struggle with high rates of unauthorised absences and pupils regularly attending school only three or four days per week. They linked the local labour market with what they saw as a lack of parental commitment to education and young people's lack of aspirations for occupational or social mobility.

Arriving from London, although we both grew up in the North of England, we were struck by the area as a white, working-class town. In fact, it has a substantial Asian population, mostly Muslim and geographically very concentrated. Teachers and LEA officers stressed how little the white and Asian communities mixed, except in the three schools with sizeable Asian pupil populations. They highlighted high indices of socio-economic deprivation, the low uptake of higher education and the relatively high teenage pregnancy rate. The project was initiated since the city figured within the top 30 national teenage pregnancy 'hotspots' and considerable local energy was directed to social regeneration, raising educational aspirations and attainment. The LEA's Director of Education also argued about the unfairness of national *per capita* funding for education, since the LEA did not get as much as an equivalent socially deprived inner London borough whose intake might well include some very privileged children. The impression was of a borough struggling valiantly, but rarely hitting the headlines to attract extra funding, and where patterns of gendered educational engagement combined to depress educational achievement overall. The swing in national education policy to a concern with underachieving boys was quickly adopted locally, possibly leaving some girls underachieving for differing reasons.

Of the 17 schools, four were faith schools – three Roman Catholic (RC), one Church of England. The average proportion of pupils receiving free school meals was 22 per cent, a little above the national average (16.5 per cent), with a varied pattern. The four faith schools had few pupils on free school meals (3–13 per cent), whereas the others had more than the national average (22–46 per cent). The faith schools were distinctive through their relative social advantage, their sixth-forms (the other thirteen were all 11–16 schools) and their attainment levels in the schools league tables. The proportion achieving the benchmark five or more grade A*–C GSCEs in 2002 was 32.2 per cent of boys and 43.9 per cent of girls, against the then national figures of 53.4 per cent of boys and 62.4 per cent of girls. This significant 'underachievement' was most marked at the school with the highest percentage of pupils on free school meals (almost three times the national average) and least marked at the faith schools.

In the first year of the project (2000–1) the LEA had 45 pregnant or mothering schoolgirls, the majority in Year 11 (15–16 years old), and in the following year this came down to 31, of whom 16 were in Year 11. In the first year the youngest was a girl in Year 9, in the second there were two in Year 9 and one in Year 8 (12–13 years old).

Several schools had been identified by Ofsted as having difficulties, one having been in 'special measures', another 'serious weaknesses', and two schools became part of an Education Action Zone. Some of the schools were developing new initiatives in response to government policies, with one becoming a beacon school and others achieving specialist status as part of the Excellence in Cities initiative.

We try to present the differing perspectives on SRE in these schools sympathetically, despite looking critically at their implications. People occupying different professional roles in schools might be expected to draw on differing discourses of the aims and importance of SRE. We were not drawing together accounts to either judge their veracity or to triangulate towards a more objective truth. Following discursive work informed by post-structuralism (Parker 1992, 2005; Burman and Parker 1993), we do not require that these accounts 'square with each other' to be valid or real or to help us gain greater proximity to the truth (Rorty 1980). Instead we see them as representing genuinely different perspectives on what sex education is occurring and what obstructs it, from people situated differently and holding varying views of the aims of sex education, or of sex or of schooling. We identify multiple discourses, points of conflict, the assumptions they shore up and their ideological implications (Parker 1992). In our conclusion we bring together the various agendas for sex education and the competing priorities for schooling to illuminate the investments and dynamics surrounding young people's sexuality and learning about sexuality.

Our representation of these divergent perspectives results from the understandings and rapport developed at the time of the study, from our interpretations 'back in the academy' (Burman 1990) and from our retrospective analysis and reflections on the policy context. In acknowledging the researchers' interpretative role of representing others we are not succumbing to a relativist position that allows any interpretation to be equally valid (Burman 1992). Attending to dynamics of power in relation to gender, age, class, professional status, race, ethnicity and sexual orientation does not limit analysis but draws attention to the operation of meanings that carry normative weight and devalue their Others. For instance, bodily as well as sexual norms come to light in attempts to be inclusive.

Pat Smith in the Department of Education at Keele University was significant as the third member of the research team during the data collection and initial dissemination phases (2000–2), and she conducted some of the teacher interviews and group discussions with pupils. She brought the perspective of an ex-teacher involved in initial teacher education on PSHE as part of a social science curriculum, and knowledge of the local community and schools. Pam was employed as the research fellow (*sic*) on the project and was immersed in negotiations in 'the field', collecting most of the data, and Miriam interviewed the head-teachers and the Director of Education. In quotations, we indicate whether the interviewer was PA, PS or MD. In our project discussions we imagined that we each identified with different participants – Pam with the young people, Pat with the teachers and Miriam with the head-teachers – but, in practice, Pam found she identified with each of the participants as establishing rapport, especially over time, entailed viewing the 'problem' from their perspective. Whilst we reported on the research project at the end of the funding (David *et al.* 2002), this book reflects on the study, through themes developed in Pam's PhD thesis and from the broader perspective allowed by a few more years of New Labour government and its more vigorous take on a complex mix of neoliberalism, socially conservative family values and so-called personalised learning.

Organisation of this book

In the next chapter, we discuss how gender and sexuality have been seen within schools, and in education policy for equal opportunities and social inclusion. We look at how neoliberal policy regimes have contributed to these challenging and contradictory developments in the terrain that a decade ago was called 'family values'. We explore value conflicts regarding social justice and individualism within the New Labour project. We analyse New Labour's sex education policies and provide a textual analysis of government guidance on SRE. How schools are expected to tackle young people's sexuality and moral development in the context of rapid social and familial change and a hypersexualised culture is thus set in context.

We then present analyses of empirical material from the original study structured according to the different perspectives. In Chapter 3 we consider teacher perspectives on teaching SRE in the context of policy changes in schools and educational pedagogies and practices around personal, social and health education. Chapter 4 explores the accounts given by boys and girls in school on questionnaires and in single-sex discussions about their preferences for SRE. We situate these within recent social research with young people in and about schools (Mac an Ghaill 1994b; Holland *et al.* 1998; Walkerdine *et al.* 2001; Frosh *et al.* 2002; Kehily 2002) that demonstrate the performative nature of gendered identities and the complexity of school and peer group cultures. We seek neither to romanticise nor to condemn pupil peer group cultures as either more real or feminist than mainstream culture, seeing them as one powerful site of young people's active engagement with discourses of gender as they construct their own and others' gendered identities. We gratefully acknowledge the contribution of undergraduate students Lucy Brosnahan, Kerry Street and Chris Wohler to the analysis of the pupil survey data.

Chapter 5 considers the balance within SRE between health and moral education and views SRE in schools as a site of potential conflict between health and education discourses. We examine the construction of young people within each and the significance of whether sexual health services/education is delivered within or outside of school. The gendered responsibilities of young women in accessing emergency contraception were prominent in public debate at the time, and professional responsibilities towards young people were also, but implicitly, gendered.

Chapter 6 explores the views of young mothers about sex education, their 'early' mothering and their aspirations, situating their mothering in the context of local norms and values, and realistic educational and employment expectations. It was originally intended that both the young men not in school and the young mothers would be presented together. However, we were struck by the overwhelming significance of highly normative gendered expectations of the young people in the community and within their differing performances of self among their peers. For the young mothers, the Government's expectations of education and employment seemed oblivious of the gendered and classed expectations they and their families had of them. For the young men, the hegemonic form of masculinity they seemed obliged to perform constrained even the research process and produced the type of dynamics that researchers report is typical of boys-only sex education sessions, as we discuss in Chapter 7.

Chapter 8 raises the issue of school agendas in the context of shifting government initiatives and priorities for education. We return to the significance of the achievement agenda and the increasing pressure this and the marketisation of education place on schools. Competition between schools – which is further reflected in competition between the league table status 'academic' subjects and the lower-status personal and social education – obstructs the delivery of good SRE. The immense pressure on young people to perform academically distracts from the important issues of their personal, political, emotional and sexual development, and can sometimes backfire. Paralleling the emphasis on their careers, we want to borrow the term to think about young people's sexual development and planning for their future sexual relationships. This contrasts the treatment of young people's employment and sexual careers in policy and in practice. It also helps explore the implications for young men and young women of proposals for young people's sexual citizenship. We imagine some future educational possibilities, on the basis of a feminist project for young mothers' education and for offering young men alternative ways of doing masculinity. We remain critical of the overall culture of education today in which market rationalities are privileged, but we have additional insights into the differential ways these pressures can play out in the gendered, classed and racialised lives of actual young men and young women.

chapter/**two**

Sex, gender and education: Contemporary challenges and contested histories

Sex education as a centralised policy for, and practice in, state schools in England and Wales was formally introduced only 20 years ago, through the Conservative Government's 1986 Education Act. In this chapter we trace the troubled history of sex education and the contested moral values on family and sex underpinning party political debates about equal opportunities and social justice within a global market economy (David 2003a). We focus on both policies and practices, where we define policies as national governmental papers and legislation, and practices as what happens in schools. Our gaze is especially on New Labour Governments from 1997 to 2006, illustrating the value conflicts between equal opportunities, neoliberalism and social justice. Our textual analysis of the key policy document *Sex and Relationship Education Guidance* (DfEE 2000) sets the context for our study of how schools and teachers should deal with problematic, essentially moral questions about sex, sexuality and other health (such as HIV/AIDS, drugs and abortion) matters in personal and social education. Certain personal values are attributed to 'Englishness' in current public policy debate around citizenship, clashing with sex education and fuelling controversy about social values and the schools' role. Questions about how schools can better promote children and young people's self-esteem or self-efficacy, or address issues such as child sexual abuse or bullying are also reverberating in international policy. Here we present an analysis of British sex education within this global debate.

In tracing the post-war history of educational policy as initially part of the social democratic political consensus, we address state secondary schools' reforms around shifting questions of equal opportunities or equality of educational opportunity – from social class, defined in terms of family socio-economic backgrounds of parental privilege or poverty, to debates about diversity, ethnicity, race and sex or gender. We briefly outline the discursive shifts in policy regarding equal opportunities, starting from the demise of the tripartite secondary school system and the hope that comprehensive schools would remove the opposition between academic and 'vocational' education (Ainley 1999). In this 'secondary reorganisation along comprehensive lines', as the 1960s Labour government dubbed it, the concerns were with how pupils of different abilities/merit should be taught and what their pastoral care needs were. The sex/gender of pupils was not usually under scrutiny.

Whilst 'sex' was an implicit organising principle with single-sex and coeducational schools and certain aspects of the curriculum (David 1980), it was not until the 1970s that this became contentious in the British Government's schools policies. The Sex Discrimination Act 1975, linked with the Equal Pay Act 1970, raised principles of school and curriculum organisation around sex (gender), contributing to public debates about how to view gender and sexuality within education. In the 30 years since then, gender equality policies have impacted upon schooling practices. Given the rapidly changing global economy and moves towards neoliberalism, we consider contra- dictions, continuities and contested changes over policies around sex, gender and personal education (David 2003a).

We adopt a post-structuralist feminist perspective (Henriques *et al.* 1984; Weedon 1987; Fraser 1989; Burman 1990; Sawicki 1991) to study these issues. Examining the 'sexual/textual politics' (Moi 1985) is one way feminists have found of highlighting the political nature of language as not merely reflective of the social world but as powerfully productive of its value systems and meanings. We seek to reflect upon our positioning and perspectives from within higher education in part by locating this overview within the developments in feminist approaches to education and social change that we describe.

From sex to gender and education: Gendering the analysis of the curriculum

The ways in which feminist activists and researchers within the social sciences have developed arguments for, and research about, social transformations to reduce gender inequalities have changed as our approaches have embraced more sophisticated understandings through theoretical and methodological approaches (Yates 2004). When we, as feminists, started on this project of social and political transformation to reduce gender inequalities in education we had very little understanding of how strong the resistance to such changes would be and how hard it would be to make policy changes effective (Arnot *et al.* 1999). We now have a greater understanding of the complexities and nuances of social and gender inequalities. Generations of social researchers have begun to publish such reflective accounts (see especially Walkerdine 1990, 1997; Weiner 1994).

Chief amongst the changes have been shifts in the language or discourses of gender and/or sex equality both at the level of public policy and debate, and also within social research practices. In the 1970s public debates focused upon notions of women's position in society and the question of forms of sex or sexual discrimination in areas of public life encompassing economic and social institutions. The focus was on the question of equal opportunities, drawing on a liberal and individualistic social agenda. This drew from other social movements for change and from the extension of social and human rights within the polity and internationally throughout Europe and North America. British movements for social justice and individual rights in relation to social democracy gave rise to movements for women's rights and sexual equality. The women's movement, strongly associated with movements for sexual liberation, developed campaigns and so-called demands for women's rights and equal opportunities with respect to education, employment and pay. Other questions of women's sexuality – free access to abortion and contraception – were also raised and women's family responsibilities were addressed through the campaign for free, state-provided childcare, especially in nurseries. Equal educational opportunities were a strong focus in these campaigns. Indeed the demands were commonly associated not only with women workers and trade unions but also with educational movements and the students' movement (David 2003a).

'Gender' was not a term in the lexicon of social science and educational research until the 1980s. Similarly, notions of feminism as a political movement, and subsequently as an academic research pursuit, were only beginning to take root. Many female education and social researchers began to adopt the term 'feminist' for their political and academic pursuits. Since then the terms 'sex' and 'gender' have taken on significantly different meanings in both public policy and academic analysis, and especially with respect to studies on gender and education or schooling, both nationally and internationally. By the mid-1990s, the term 'gender' had eclipsed the term 'sex' in relation to both educational research and public policies, although notions of sex and sexuality continued to have a place within the lexicon of social and educational research, with specific reference to social norms for bodily prescription and proscription (Oakley 2005). Nevertheless, debate has raged about these terms, especially with respect to connotations of sexuality and/or sexual orientation.

Judith Butler, a North American feminist social philosopher, has had a major impact through her work on what she initially called *Gender Trouble* (Butler 1990). More recently she has written that the terms 'gender' and 'sex' are problematic and yet it is important to keep them distinct for both theory and politics. Her thinking about the term 'gender' has been influenced by the New Gender Politics that emerged in the 1990s, a combination of movements concerned with transgender, transsexuality, and intersex issues and their complex relations to feminist and the new so-called 'queer' theory (Butler 2004). She has argued that it would be a mistake to subscribe to a progressive notion of history in which various frameworks are understood to succeed and supplant one another with notions of 'sexuality' replacing notions of 'gender'. The stories that are constructed about 'gender' and 'sex' continue to be 'told' in simultaneous, overlapping ways since they resonate through the complex ways in which they are taken up by political movements and theoretical practices (Butler 2004). Most importantly, the recognition that gender is socially constructed should not be taken to imply that sex is essential and fixed in the body. Both physical and subjective sex/gender are culturally produced (British Journal of Sociology of Education 2006; Paechter 2006).

From equal opportunities through educational reforms to social inclusion

Tracing the troubled history of educational policy from the Second World War into the twenty-first century has been the central subject of innumerable contested methodological studies and texts within, *inter alia*, educational history (Simon 1992; McCulloch 1998), social policy (Halsey *et al.* 1980; Tomlinson 2001), sociology of education (Banks 1976; Ball 2003), what is now referred to as policy sociology (Ball 1994), and feminist studies (Epstein *et al.* 1998; Arnot *et al.* 1999; Francis and Skelton 2005; Stambach and David 2005). The inclusion of sex or gender has been limited, as has ethnicity and/or race. Only at the turn of the twenty-first century has 'equal opportunities' taken on a more inclusive meaning in policy analysis, covering gender, sexual orientation and dis/abilities, social class, ethnicity, race and religious diversity (Levitas 2005).

The 1944 Education Act set the scene for the expansion of equal educational opportunities (Jones 2003). The principle of equality of educational opportunity for all, crafted as a policy principle during the Second World War, is about social not sex/gender justice, meaning socio-economic dis/advantages or class. Subsequent policy expanded educational opportunities, and incorporated previously private and/or voluntary as well as religious schools into a state system. No attention was paid to gender or sex, although many of those schools, selective academically or vocationally, were single-sex. This legislative framework remained the cornerstone for almost 50 years, although controversy raged over state provision centrally or through LEAs. Gender was not questioned, although single-sex schools (for boys and girls), especially at secondary level, were provided by the Government, nationally or locally, or privately. Throughout, policy-relevant social and educational research concentrated upon either questions of social class or social and economic disadvantage, although parental backgrounds and abilities to access or take advantage of educational provisions inevitably played a part, with views about middle-class privilege versus working-class disadvantage informing policy critique (Ball 2003; Stambach and David 2005).

With the rise of social movements, there were new demands for attention to women's education and equal opportunities, leading to the Sex Discrimination Act 1975 which ensured more equality in the schools curriculum, and limited the practice of creating single-sex schools. Gender equality from legislation introduced 30 years ago has become integral to public policies but not schooling reforms. The legislation on sexual equality originated within a traditional social democratic framework. The Sex Discrimination Act created the Equal Opportunities Commission to be responsible for monitoring the implementation and progress of moves to achieve equal opportunities between men and women, and to deal with sex discrimination and inequality relating to gender including the definition and implementation of good practice in the fair and equal treatment of men and women.

A new ERA of choice and markets?

The Conservative Government of the 1980s began a major economic and social transformation distancing itself from social democracy and highlighting economic liberalism. The Education Reform Act (ERA) 1988 introduced new principles of parental choice to raise educational standards, through specifying the core and compulsory elements of the curriculum, and allied assessment and achievement levels (David 1993). Despite this principle of choice, gender was not seen as a major issue (Arnot *et al.* 1999). The subsequent changing practices at global, national and local levels were within a transformed political system. Introducing market forces into public policy as part of what became known as a new era, through the ERA 1988, was linked in some curiously contradictory way with standardising the school curriculum, through the NC, comprised of 10 subjects, for all pupils regardless of gender. This became an even more contested terrain during the 1990s, and an instance of this concerned local government reforms in the 1990s, and the possibilities of extending anti-discrimination policies to homosexuality. As Epstein and Johnson (1998) have argued, the implication of 'Section 28' (Section 22 of the eventual Local Government Act 1988) for schools became hotly contested.

In putting sex education on the school agenda, the Conservative Government took the decision to allow parents to let their children opt out of such a potentially difficult and dangerous topic. Thus sex education was born in the Education Act 1986, but parents were left holding the baby if they so chose: and this was indeed also the era of parental choice. For the first time government considered that teaching about sex education, in the context of family values, might address broader concerns. However, given that schools remained *in loco parentis* (Shaw 1976) the question was also raised of the extent to which schools might replace parents in teaching about moral or religious issues. The 1993 Education Act made it compulsory for all state-maintained secondary schools to provide sex education, building upon the 1986 Education Act which had given control over sex education policies to school governing bodies in 1986 (David 1986). The 1993 Act required that school governors establish a written policy about sex education. Sex education is not specified by the NC, hence the necessity for each school's statement.

Concerns about what initially was known as 'pastoral care' and the wider social and personal needs of pupils, rather than only their academic needs, were aired more from the 1980s onwards. However, Power (1996: 15) notes claims that the term 'pastoral care' has been in use in secondary schools since the late 1940s. Whilst not widely used initially, she accepts that 'the emergence of pastoral care coincides with the growth of the comprehensive system of secondary schooling' (1996: 17). Her analysis sometimes points to the gendering of schooling practices (such as the mother-like role of form tutors), but she does not examine issues of sexuality or sex education.

New Labour: new values?

In 1997 the New Labour Government committed to 'education, education, education' and, with an overarching social liberal agenda, promised to transform equal opportunities beyond social class and into issues of social inclusion/exclusion, gender and sex education. One of the Government's first initiatives was the setting up of the Social Exclusion Unit, within the Cabinet Office, to consider the broad topics of social and economic disadvantage and social welfare linked to education, including in terms of gender. The first report of the SEU, in 1999, on teenage pregnancy and social inclusion, illustrated how issues of sexuality and adolescence had reached the public policy agenda. It was based upon a review of research evidence from across Europe and North America, and the TPS emerged as a key plank of the Government's new policy for dealing with social exclusion. This was a policy in which young women who were at risk of social exclusion through their sexual behaviour were to be educated to transform their behaviour. A key recommendation from this report was that schools should provide SRE as a way to halt the rise in teenage pregnancy. This report also signalled a major shift from a social welfare to an educational approach to such questions of sex and sexuality which had been debated under previous Conservative administrations but largely in relation to the social welfare of teenage parents (David 1985, 1986, 1989).

New Labour's values are clear in Prime Minister Blair's foreword to the report: 'As a country, we can't afford to continue to ignore this *shameful* record', 'Our failure to tackle this *problem* has cost the teenagers, their children and the country dear', and the role of education is clear in remedying the 'fact' that 'too many teenage mothers – and fathers – simply *fail to understand* the price they, their children and society, will pay' (SEU 1999: 4; emphasis added).

New Labour's values: the third way

Antony Giddens's *The Third Way* (1998) provides the intellectual basis for New Labour's project of combining social democracy and neoliberalism (David 2003a), creating 'a managerialism of the centre-left' (McRobbie 2000: 103). It draws pragmatically on 'what works' to integrate principles of neoliberal economics and communitarian social policies (Franklin 2000; Driver and Martell 2002). Traditional Labour governments had developed social welfare policies to protect from the consequences of free market capitalism. The 'modernised' New Labour Government deconstructs the welfare system (Hall 2003), creates new markets and is responsible only for curbing 'excesses'. Two key principles of 'old style' social democracy are dropped: 'a commitment to social and economic change and a recognition of the state's role in tackling structural inequality' (Franklin 2000: 139). Consensus rather than change becomes the goal, and so dissent must be managed. Individualistic rather than structural solutions become the means:

> By focusing on community and individual agency, where people in families and communities share responsibility with government agencies for social exclusion, there has been a tendency to disregard the significance of wider social and economic forces and the inequalities they produce. Individuals are encouraged to take the opportunities offered them by the Government and if they fail to do so, they become, in effect, responsible for their own inequality. (Franklin 2000: 139)

Social inclusion rather than equality is the vision, but individuals receive entitlements conditional on their meeting individual responsibilities (Levitas 2005). Claims of disadvantage on the basis of class, race or gender are seen as old-fashioned and divisive (Franklin 2000). Conflict is underplayed to create 'a politics without adversaries' (Hall 1998: 10). Instead, the language of pragmatism is used to show that initiatives are based on evidence from policies that 'worked', in a modernist narrative of the new learning from the mistakes of the old.

The sanitising of conflict reflects the 'need for a cohesive and settled society, essential for social order and economic efficiency' where old arguments about inequalities could stir up discontent (Franklin 2000: 138). The Government's concern is to inculcate in individuals the desirable personal qualities to facilitate its political project (Driver and Martell 1999; David 2003a) hence the greater prominence of a discourse of individual psychology (Rose 1989, 1993). This encourages 'a reinterpretation and rearticulation of issues of inequality as matters of individual will, voluntarism and community goal orientation and moral fibre' (McCarthy and Dimitriadis 2000: 174).

The place of women in the New Labour project

Since the 1990s, the British Government has developed special administrative and political responsibilities for women, including an administrative unit for women's equality that was initially located in the prime minister's Cabinet Office. More recently, during the New Labour Government's second term, this unit was renamed the Women and Equality Unit, and responsibility relocated to the Department of Trade and Industry. While there is now a governmental responsibility for women, the post has not always carried ministerial remuneration.

What distinguishes New Labour from Thatcherism is the centrality of women to the project. The prominence of women's inclusion as a theme is because women are key to the policies, the nub of the problem and hence the importance of governing their behaviour. Women and girls find themselves at the forefront of government policy: they are the new, flexible workers required by neoliberal economic policy and also the primary carers in the home (Franklin 2000). Young women are targeted on the basis of their educational performance (McRobbie 2000). Women are propelled into the workforce by the erosion of welfare, but 'the family' has to 'look after its own' or pay others to do so, therefore expanding the need for childcare workers.

New Labour is 'a politics for women without feminism':

> Giddens borrows quite dramatically from the feminist agenda while managing to produce a feminist-free account of modern family life, while Beck acknowledges the changing position of women in society not thanks to feminist demands for equality but as part of the process of individualization. (McRobbie 2000: 105)

Not just central to the economic restructuring of the family, women are also to be mobilised in the project to change cultural expectations about welfare which

> must tap into disparate and as yet only half-formed sensibilities. By fleshing them out ... and then attempting to unify them, this New Labour way of doing government comes to be natural to the point that an alternative is unthinkable (McRobbie 2000: 98)

or as Žižek (1999: ix) put it, to convince us that global capitalism is 'the only game in town'. We are already schooled in the idea that with rights come responsibilities, that state support is not an entitlement of the needy, but conditional on their 'actively seeking work'.

Policy and practice: discursive shifts around sex and gender

The movements around gender politics in Britain have transformed the meanings of sex and gender, and legislation on gender has replaced sex and sexual discrimination. These questions of definition are important. For example, the Gender Recognition Act 2004 uses 'gender' for what is legally changed (sex) in order to match social identity (gender). 'Gender reassignment' is the term now employed for what used to be called 'sex change'. The Equal Opportunities Commission has also developed a gender equality duty which comes into force for public bodies in 2007, drawing upon European legislation and policies through the European Union (EU). Indeed, many of the rights British women now have flow from Europe and British law is influenced by the EU.

The new Equality Act 2006 to develop equality and fairness for all establishes a new body – the Commission for Equality and Human Rights – to provide oversight of essentially individual discrimination in respect of equality and diversity, replacing the individual commissions such as the Equal Opportunities Commission and Commission for Racial Equality and bringing together different practices around gender, race/ethnicity and/or diversity, including religious diversity, disabilities and sexual orientation. This may have particular resonance in future sex education.

The twenty-first century: shifts from girls' towards boys' underachievement

Within education policies a key shift has involved turning invisible issues about gender matters in education into explicit debates and research questions. However, the initial focus on questioning girls' education and schooling (Arnot et al. 1999) has been transformed into major public policy debates about boys' education, underachievement and 'raising boys' achievement in secondary schools' – the title of a recent major educational research publication (Younger and Warrington 2005). Although there is considerable research evidence about the links between social class, economic or social disadvantages and family backgrounds, race and ethnicity and boys' achievements, these do not figure in the public policy debate. Boys have again become the centre of attention, and the question of girls' relative disadvantage across educational provisions and in forms of vocational education and employment has been occluded. The evidence about boys' and girls' achievements in examinations taken at the end of secondary schooling, namely their performance in the General Certificate of Secondary Education (GCSE), is strong. The national benchmark standard of five examination passes at grade A*–C is still not achieved by 50 per cent of the age cohort of 15–16-year-olds, but girls now do relatively better than boys at achieving this benchmark standard, with over 50 per cent of girls achieving this standard compared to a little over 40 per cent of boys. Thus arguments have shifted to how to deal with boys rather than girls, whereas earlier feminist campaigning focused upon girls' educational underachievement (Epstein et al. 1998; Arnot et al. 1999).

In some curiously contradictory way, however, much of the education research and policy debate about forms of secondary schools has again focused on social class dis/advantages or under/achievements, ignoring gender (Stambach and David 2005). The current debates about New Labour's educational reforms, which are heavily contested, have not paid any attention to the potential bearing on either boys' or girls' educational successes. The focus has been on whether the reforms will further advantage middle-class families at the expense of working-class and economically disadvantaged families, including especially black and ethnic minority families. Whilst the Equal Opportunities Commission remained silent, the Commission for Racial Equality has argued that critics of the planned school reforms ignore the educational experiences of black Britons and their desire for community/parental involvement to deliver high standards and personalised education that would address black underachievement. The Commission for Racial Equality may highlight an important absence at certain levels of the debate, but this approach relies on individual remedies such that those 'with the problem' (including disadvantage or discrimination) are responsible for fixing it, whereas we seek something broader and more profound.

These are notions about equality of educational opportunity on individual grounds. Using educational reforms to accomplish either individual or social rights to equal opportunities for education and/or employment has been a particularly vexed issue. Moreover, the question of whose individual rights should be the focus of educational reforms has been highly contested around class, poverty or disadvantage, ethnic, racial and religious diversity, educational and/or academic merit, examination performance and achievements and in relation to difference types and forms of state, public and private schooling. The debate centres upon individual rights as the form of social justice, and therefore represents a retreat from a goal of more radical collective change.

The notions of social inclusion or exclusion, as Levitas (2005) cogently argues, are linked to wider social welfare strategies such as economic redistributive policies, or moral debates about whether particular policies create or sustain an underclass. Ideas of social exclusion as a proxy for social disadvantage, linked to diversity questions such as ethnicity, migrant status, race or religion, have been developed in the European context. Although questions of gender were tangentially linked to definitions of social class through types of family, they were not central, and were only questioned in terms of problematising teenagers' sexual behaviour.

This was also part of a wider programme of transforming the styles of teaching and learning in schools, with moves towards what has been called personalised education or a focus on the individual as a key element in their processes of learning. However, personal and social education has also been mandated as part of the curriculum of schools, together with citizenship education. Recent policy discussions consider extending personalised education into further and higher education,

but again gender barely figures. We turn now to a textual analysis of
New Labour's sex education within these broader policy contexts.

Sex education's sexual/textual politics: The Sex and Relationship Education Guidance

For the first time a national framework in the form of government
'guidelines' on what schools ought to cover is contained in the 2000
SRE Guidance, with the status of 'good practice' and replacing Circular
5/94 (DfEE 2000). It presents three main elements of SRE: 'attitudes
and values', 'personal and social skills' and 'knowledge and understanding' (2000: 5). It stipulates that each school's policy must be
available to parents/carers and must define SRE, describe who is
responsible for it and how it will be provided, monitored and evaluated
and provide information about parents' right to withdraw their child
from these lessons (2000: 7).

The SRE Guidance clearly presumes that all teenage pregnancy is
unplanned, and all unplanned conception is unwanted. Whilst most of
the document refers to 'unplanned pregnancy', it refers twice to
'unwanted pregnancy', perhaps conflating economic with subjective
personal perspectives. Teenage pregnancy and parenthood are constructed as deviant and anti-social through 'teenage parenthood is bad
for parents and children' statements (David 2003b), and young people's
sexuality is constructed as risky, threatening undesirable outcomes for
them, their children and society.

The Introduction states that the Guidance arose from the revised NC
(published in 1999), the new framework for delivering PSHE and the
SEU's (1999) report, and addresses the considerable 'uncertainty about
what sex and relationship education is and how it should be taught'
(DfEE 2000: 3). Whilst we welcome the attention it brings to sex
education, the need to improve sex education pre-dates the TPS, and is
for reasons broader than simply reducing the teenage conception rate.
Reinvigoration carries the risk that SRE is shaped by and, as a
consequence, narrowed to meet this government agenda. Reducing
teenage pregnancy is part of the strategy for combating 'social
exclusion', to meet revised economic and welfare aims with a long
historical legacy (DH 1992) rather than educational goals *per se* (Bullen
et al. 2000).

The SEU (1999) report identified 'ignorance' – that is, lack of
'accurate knowledge about contraception, STIs, what to expect in
relationships and what it means to be a parent' (SEU 1999: 7) – as one
of the three causal explanations for Britain's much lamented teenage

pregnancy rate compared to other western European countries (David 2003b). However, the Learning and Skills Act 2000 actually requires the Secretary of State to issue guidance to schools that they

> must secure that pupils (a) learn the nature of marriage and its importance for family life and the bringing up of children, and (b) are protected from teaching and materials which are inappropriate having regard to the age and the religious and cultural background of the pupils concerned. (Monk 2001: 276)

Producing the SRE Guidance has allowed the Government to fuel the discourse of the 'erosion of family values' with fear of the homosexual 'other' (Monk 2001). Despite a significant shift in the treatment of homosexuality, political conflicts about homosexuality that dominated the recent British history of sex education echo loudly.

Nevertheless, sex education is instrumental to the Government's 2010 teenage pregnancy targets to 'halv[e] the rate of conceptions among under 18s' and to increase the participation of teenage parents in education, training and work to 'reduce their risk of long term social exclusion' (SEU 1999: 8), targets which the Government now admits are unlikely to be met (Armstrong 2006). The most significant change in the 2000 Guidance is from *prohibiting* to *promoting* teachers' provision of contraceptive advice to pupils in group and individual settings, alongside the involvement of health professionals and local health services. This is significant and welcome, but clearly serves the TPS's narrow agenda. The document's production was contested, and we will highlight its discursive connections to the overall New Labour project.

What's in a name? Sex *and Relationship* Education

Changing the title from 'sex education' to 'sex *and relationship* education' (in Northern Ireland it is called 'relationship and sex education') provides a welcome new emphasis on emotions, but using the singular 'relationship' privileges monogamous partnerships or marriage, rather than all relationships including non-sexual ones. References to 'respect, love and care', 'empathy', 'increasing self-esteem', 'managing emotion' and 'removing prejudice' expand SRE beyond the biological 'plumbing' (DfEE 2000: 5). SRE legitimises teaching about family and sexual relationships, which was traditionally regarded as private rather than the state's business (David 1980). Locating SRE within the PSHE and citizenship education curricula represents a shift from the language of morality to political and personal development (Thomson 1994; David 2003a, 2003b). It reflects the ambiguous 'psychologising' of culture and enhanced status of emotions in the public and political sphere (Rose 1989; Parker 2006). This includes the cynical appropriation of discourses of emotion for economic governance, corporate gain or to recapture the 'family values' agenda. As Burman (2006, 2007) argues, this 'feminised' (rather than feminist) appeal to the emotional is not to be celebrated uncritically.

The pupil as a 'moral' subject

The 1986 Education Act, in devolving control of sex education to school governing bodies, imposed the requirement to consult with parents (David 1989) and established 'the requirement that sex education must be taught within a moral framework' (Thomson 1994: 48). The Introduction to the Guidance (DfEE 2000) requires SRE to be firmly rooted in the PSHE framework and to help pupils deal with 'difficult moral and social questions' (2000: 3), 'support young people through their physical, emotional and moral development' (2000: 3), as they learn the 'importance of values and individual conscience and moral considerations' (2000: 5) so that they 'make responsible and well informed decisions about their lives' (2000: 3).

What is new is the educational contribution to individual qualities and emotional experiences, referred to in 'develop the skills and understanding they need to live confident, healthy and independent lives' (2000: 3), 'learn to respect themselves and others' (2000: 3) and 'have the confidence and self-esteem to value themselves and others and respect for individual conscience' (2000: 20). Discourses of self-esteem, confidence and personal identity are part of a 'new, improved' concern for the emotional (Treacher 1989; Richards 1994) and morally unassailable. The elision of psychological with physical health allows reference to 'healthy lives' and public health or health education approaches which are notably more pragmatic about young people's sexual activity than past sex education policy (Thomson 1994; Monk 2000).

Pupils are constructed overtly as people who will face challenges, make decisions, 'take responsibility' in their future lives and must be produced as moral subjects. An increased emphasis on children and young people taking responsibility pervades youth justice and education policy (Corteen 2006; McNamara 2006). This formulation of 'pupils' *future* lives' provides a useful separation of time, and of the moral from the factual, since factual, information-based sex education can proceed on the understanding that decisions about *applying* that information will be morally-based judgement calls made by individuals in the future. It cleverly avoids the *moral 'effects' of sex education* discourse that dominated Conservative debates (Thomson and Blake 2002) and allows for pragmatic sexual health education whilst maintaining the conservative moral high ground.

Gender and the subject

'Young people' and 'pupils' are ungendered subjects, and unsurprisingly 'pupils' tends to be used in discourses of protection – 'Schools should ensure that pupils are protected from teaching and materials which are inappropriate' having regard to pupils' 'age and cultural background' (DfEE 2000: 8) – and 'young people' where their agency or sexual activity is apparent – 'Effective SRE is essential if young people are to make responsible and well informed decisions about their lives' (2000: 1). Young people's feelings of sexual desire are not acknowledged, but there is a more demure reference to 'feeling attraction' (2000: 25).

References to age appropriateness are frequent and serve to affirm the anxiety that pupils hear 'too much too young'. This corroborates a version of the *corruption* discourse that blames sex education for promoting sexual activity: a myth which the SEU (1999) report provides a five-page table of evidence to dispel. A developmental model of the child pupil is evident not just in the overt age-stage discourse (Burman 1994a), but also in repeated references to their maturation: 'the emotional and physical aspects of growing up' and 'the challenges and responsibilities that sexual maturity brings', pupils' 'changing bodies' and 'preparedness for puberty' (DfEE 2000: 25). Gendered bodies are here acknowledged: primary schools need to prepare 'boys and girls' 'for puberty' and, in particular, to ensure girls know about menstruation so that its (increasingly early) onset does not alarm them (2000: 14).

Behind the concern 'that *both boys and girls* know about puberty and how a baby is born' (2000: 9; emphasis added) lies a drive to correct historical bias that is explicit in the instruction to 'Focus on boys and young men as well as girls and young women' (2000: 11). It states that

> Traditionally the focus has been on girls. Boys may have felt that sex education is not relevant to them and are unable or too embarrassed to ask questions about relationships or sex. Boys are also less likely to talk to their parents. For these reasons, programmes should focus on boys as much as girls at primary level as well as secondary. (2000: 11)

This counters the gendered assumption that 'where babies come from' is women's business and contraception is women's responsibility. 'The taking on of responsibility and the consequences of one's actions in relation to sexual activity and parenthood' (2000: 10) theme reflects feminist demands for heterosexual men to take responsibility for contraception and fatherhood and not leave women 'holding the baby'. Reference to parenthood also echoes the Treasury's call for fathers' responsibility for financial support of children irrespective of legal or marital relationships (Boden and Childs 1996; Boden and Corden 1998; Alldred 1999).

Gender is, therefore, evident in that sex education needs to 'engage boys' (DfEE 2000: 11) and teachers are to plan 'activities ... matching their different learning styles'. The Guidance acknowledges all-girl/all-boy classes as important, particularly for pupils 'from cultures where it is only acceptable to speak about the body in single sex groups' (2000: 11). The 'feminisation of schooling' is seen as having resulted in boys being failed by schools which can be interpreted as a backlash against feminism's promotion of girls' educational opportunities (Epstein *et al.* 1998; Arnot *et al.* 1999). However, specifically in relation to SRE, 'engaging boys' can be seen as embodying the feminist challenge to the historical responsibility heterosexual women have carried for child-rearing and contraception (New and David 1985; David 2003a).

Young people's sexuality

The division of the SRE curriculum into three elements allows *values* to be fore-grounded and legitimised ('Attitudes and values'); frames as *skills* individual qualities such as 'developing empathy' and 'managing emotions' (an aspect of emotional articulacy, but a turn of phrase – 'managing' – that suggests keeping emotions in their place) in the second element ('Personal and social skills'); and allows contentious statements to be presented as fact ('Knowledge and understanding'). These are unsurprising but the pragmatic approach to sexual health services is new, in, for example, 'understanding human sexuality, reproduction, sexual health, emotions and relationships' and 'learning about contraception and the range of local and national sexual health advice, contraception and support services'. However, the final two 'Knowledge and understanding' statements are: 'learning the reasons for delaying sexual activity, and the benefits to be gained from such delay, and the avoidance of unplanned pregnancy' (DfEE 2000: 5). Not only is this rather one-sided – what about the reasons to have sex when 'the time' (and relationship) is right? – and rather labouring the point in emphasising that 'benefits' are 'gains', but also these opinion-laden statements are rendered 'fact'.

A more 'sex positive' and less prescriptive approach might invite young people to discuss what *they* see as good or bad sexual experiences (Heckert 2005). Such an alternative could consider, say, 'the role sexual activity can play in relationships and intimacy', which would follow nicely from stated concerns with, and skills to promote, young people's emotional well-being. Even within its own *moral context* discourse, it could have been less prescriptive, saying: 'discuss, within a moral framework, the age at which one might become sexually active'. This would acknowledge the relevance of ethical questions to sexual activity, but would leave open how to 'answer' them, whereas the Government asserts firmly its values as if they represent the consensus.

SRE is framed as about avoiding conception and sexually transmitted infections (STIs), in which the school has an active role to play through 'providing information in which contraception' and 'additional information', individually and in class, on 'where they can obtain confidential advice, counselling and where necessary, treatment' (DfEE 2000: 15).

Throughout, the avoidance of underage, heterosexual, penetrative sex is advocated for legal and health reasons (Corteen 2006). Overall the approach to pupils' sexuality as risky, and to be discouraged or made safe(r), reflects a 'damage limitation' model (Corteen 2006). It lends SRE a legalistic and health-oriented preoccupation with (hetero)sexual health, avoidance of early (hetero)sexual activity, underage/unwanted conceptions, STIs and coitus (Corteen 2006; Epstein and Johnson 1994, 1998; Mac an Ghaill 1994b). The Guidance is not morally neutral about young people's sexuality: it makes more than eight references to the importance of delaying sexual activity, and practical safer sex information is legitimised by reference to pregnancy and infections. The dominance of discussions of sexuality by issues of STIs, abuse, 'unwanted' pregnancy, underage sex, criminal or 'promiscuous' sexual activity are what teachers referred to as 'the usual scare tactics of sex education'. The emphasis on equipping pupils to avoid physical and emotional harm contributes to the negativity around sex and constructs individuals as personally responsible for preventing harm to themselves.

This stance on accessing sexual health information and services is not *for* young people, and is not therefore 'underpinned by an understanding of, or a desire to afford rights to children' (Corteen 2006: 93). A prerequisite of meeting stated aims would be to respect young people as individuals, independent of their parents, and to see SRE as an entitlement. However, it seems that the UN Convention is rarely drawn on to defend the provision of sex education (Corteen 2006). Instead children's right to information or to sexual decision-making autonomy, and the orientation of schools to parents and education's construction of the non-sexual pupil are reconciled through a silence on rights and an emphatic discourse of protection – 'protecting young people from early sex and the consequences of it'. *Protecting children* is used to permit pragmatic sex education. The repeated insistence on 'age-appropriate' measures and construction of pupils through a developmental discourse of maturation retains the notion that SRE could corrupt children and fails to challenge the associated morality. If earlier debates were characterised by a tension between pragmatic health promotion and moralistic positions (Thomson 1993, 1994; Monk 2000) this document provides a 'third way' that plays each off against the others, embedding deeply conservative assumptions about what is responsible and 'respectable'.

Marriage and 'other stable relationships'

The SRE Guidance allowed the Government to reassert positive statements which the House of Lords had succeeded in removing from the Government's original amendments to the statutory requirements, including, for example, references to stable relationships outside of marriage and the role of sex education in encouraging the understanding of difference and to 'preventing or removing prejudice' (Monk 2001). However, whilst 'Section 28' never applied to teachers and has now been repealed (albeit after several unsuccessful attempts), its echo can unfortunately still be heard in this Guidance. The phrase 'protecting pupils from inappropriate teaching materials' (DfEE 2000: 8) is one such allusion to 'Section 28' that allows it to haunt teachers illegitimately (Warwick and Douglas 2001), and draws schools and LEAs into the anxious discourse of 'the inappropriate' – always a matter of opinion, but now apparently rendered fact – because it is now in a document that teachers have to consider. We agree with Monk that it is regrettable that the reference to 'other stable relationships' was removed from the Learning and Skills Act 2000 and that in this and the SRE Guidance 'reference to religious and cultural backgrounds is not balanced by reference to young people's own values' (Monk 2001: 276). Overall the Guidance's statements that tacitly recognise the validity of childbearing outside of marriage are refreshing, even if compromises are apparent in statements such as the second of the five bullet points on 'Attitudes and values' – that pupils must learn 'the value of family life, marriage, and stable and loving relationships for the nurture of children' (DfEE 2000: 5).

The constellation of sentences under 'Relationships' hint at contradictory pulls:

> Within the context of talking about relationships, children should be taught about the nature of marriage and its importance for family life and for bringing up children. The Government recognises that there are strong and mutually supportive relationships outside marriage. Therefore, children should learn the significance of marriage and stable relationships as key building blocks of community and society. Teaching in this area needs to be sensitive so as not to stigmatise children on the basis of their home circumstances. (2000: 11)

The Guidance clearly promotes particular values in its strongly directional statements about 'the benefits of avoiding teenage pregnancy', delaying sexual activity and avoiding underage sex, the 'responsibilities that sexual maturity brings' and the importance of parents 'teaching their children about sex and relationships'. Seeing the British 'record on teenage pregnancies' as 'shameful' (SEU 1999: 4) echoes in the description of the 8000 conceptions to girls under 16 in 1998 as 'clearly totally unacceptable' (DfEE 2000: 15). The values are a New Labour inflected version of 'family values' (Alldred 1999; Fox Harding 2000). They appear as facts linking the health-risks of unprotected sex directly to 'greater dependence, undermining potential achievement in education and in further employment' (DfEE 2000: 15).

The statement about being inclusive of families falls short of the Sex Education Forum's 'values framework' which states: 'we note the diversity of family groups and settings in which children and young people live their lives' (SEF 2003: 4). After a statement about schools having to ensure 'the needs of all pupils are met' and that SRE must be relevant and sensitive to young people 'whatever their developing sexuality' (DfEE 2000: 12) – which makes convenient use of the developmental discourse that locates children's sexuality safely in the future – it states:

> The Secretary of State for Education and Employment is clear that teachers should be able to deal honestly and sensitively with sexual orientation, answer appropriate questions and offer support. There should be no direct promotion of sexual orientation. (2000: 13)

The second of the three paragraphs of the sexual orientation section deals with parents. Noting that sexual orientation is a concern for some parents, it suggests that liaising with them over the school's SRE policy will reassure them about the context for its discussion. The final paragraph deals with bullying. It makes specific reference to homophobic bullying, which 'schools need to be able to deal with' and more general reference to the Social Inclusion: Pupil Support Circular (10/99), underlining the unacceptability of and emotional distress caused by any form of bullying (mentioning racial, appearance or sexual orientation-related specifically).

'Not promoting' 'sexual orientation' can be read as an injunction to avoid the default promotion of heterosexuality too, but this wilful reading will perhaps not inform the SRE that reaches most pupils. The 'accurate information' presented 'for the purpose also of preventing and removing prejudice' (DfEE 2000: 4) is similarly indirect but may be grounds for optimism. It appeals to truth to combat prejudice, and assumes that rationality will triumph over homophobia. By not explicitly placing homosexuality on the curriculum for all pupils, the Guidance fails to meet the needs of young lesbians, gay men or other sexual or gender minorities, let alone guarantee their protection in school. It repeatedly refers to the SRE policy reflecting the values of the local community. What happens when the local community values are violently homophobic? How are head-teachers, who must 'have regard to' these views, to run a school that even adequately protects sexual minority young people or staff? Corteen (2006) found that homophobia in school was used as an excuse for not teaching about homosexuality and lesbianism. One assistant head-teacher said: 'well it [discussing homosexuality in SRE] would have to be a careful introduction as far as the kids are concerned ... we do have quite a high proportion of kids who are homophobic, which is difficult; it's also a parental thing' (Corteen 2006: 82).

The policy discourse of *cultural differences and local values* implies that homophobia among parents or the local community is a cultural value that ought to be respected. This illustrates a tension between a school's accountability to 'parents and the wider community' and its remit to prevent bullying. Like other education policies, the Guidance gives far too much weight to the views of parents/carers as opposed to pupils, and it 'fails to give advice as to how teachers should balance potential expressions of hostility by parents to teaching about homosexuality with the need to promote and protect the welfare of individual pupils' (Monk 2001: 292). Meanwhile young people continue to be put at risk (Ellis and High 2004; Wyss 2004).

The fact that there is explicit reference to classroom discussion about sexual orientation is a welcome relief for practitioners, as is reference to 'preventing and removing prejudice' and the statement that there should be 'no stigmatisation of children based on their home circumstances' in the Introduction. However the weak, indirect defence of 'other stable relationships' leads to concern about failing to meet the needs of lesbian or gay young people in particular (Warwick and Douglas 2001; Jennett 2004; Corteen 2006). At best this may leave pupils 'ill-informed, misinformed and confused' and at worse, 'marginalised, disqualified and discriminated against' (Corteen 2006: 96). Even those whose concern is solely with pastoral responsibilities would recognise this weakness. However, we have additional concerns.

Pastoral relations or social justice?

All pupils should learn about sexual diversity in society and learn to challenge bigotry and prejudice. The section in which 'sexual orientation' is included ('Specific issues which should be addressed when developing a policy') identifies some particular pupil groups under the titles: 'Focus on boys and young men as well as girls and young women', 'Ethnicity' and 'Special education needs and learning difficulties'. These groups are all treated to an approach which, in attempting to identify the specific learning needs of these pupils, marks them out as different, and into which deficit can too easily be read. That sexual orientation is framed in its three paragraphs by individual needs, parental concerns and then anti-bullying is revealing. The *individual needs* discourse – 'It is up to schools to make sure the needs of all pupils are met in their programmes' (DfEE 2000: 12–13) – risks prompting a solely pastoral approach to sexual orientation whereby it is seen as relevant only to those young people who themselves identify as lesbian, gay, bisexual, etc. and whose particular needs are already identified or identifiable. Several limitations are apparent: do teachers necessarily know how their pupils identify? What about pupils who are in the process of questioning their sexual orientation? Does having a gay carer or relative 'count' in this *personally affected by the issue* approach?

The Guidance's statements on bullying are an important but limited intervention. Protection from homophobic bullying cannot be framed within the individual needs discourse without neglecting many bullied young people who would not identify as gay. Homophobic abuse can precede any subjective 'coming out', and occurs irrespective of a pupil's actual sexual orientation since it is often, in fact, about perceived gender non-conformity rather than sexual orientation. Often the targets are boys who are perceived as not conforming to hegemonic masculinity (Haywood and Mac an Ghaill 2003; Wyss 2004), including sometimes simply by engaging with schoolwork (Epstein 1998; Skelton 2001).

Teachers are given a responsive role to 'answer appropriate questions' (DfEE 2000: 13). This gives students responsibility for raising the issue, not necessarily easy, and it allows teachers to avoid answering what they see as inappropriate questions. 'And offer support' follows, clearly indicating a pastoral approach to the pupil who is thereby produced as 'in need' – clearly the 'problem' lies with them. The pastoral approach, whilst necessary for either meeting the needs of or responding to the abuse of individuals, does not help prevent future homophobic bullying. It is responsive and morally passive rather than about social justice. It seeks individual remedies for specific incidents, as opposed to social change and questioning social values throughout the school. How much better if individuals' needs were met *and* there was a commitment to social justice. This would better safeguard individuals' well-being and safety than pupils earning this by their individual identity claims.

The implication of this defence of addressing sexual orientation by reference to a school's anti-bullying policy is that it is only needed by a minority of pupils. The parallel argument would be that anti-racist work in a school is done only to protect those children who might themselves experience racism, to mop up the damage in responsive procedures such as punishments. An alternative, social justice approach seeks to prevent racism and to challenge race privilege amongst those who have it. From this perspective it is even more important that anti-racist work is done in predominantly white schools (Epstein 1993; Gaine 1995). Similarly, comprehensive education on sexual orientation should be an entitlement of all children, and should involve understanding social diversity, challenging stereotypes and prejudice, and recognising the hurt and injustice caused by discrimination. The Guidance's reference to 'sexual orientation' should be taken to mean that it is not only 'homosexuality' that is on the curriculum. Pupils should learn to name heterosexuality, as they should whiteness, to disrupt the silent defaults. Sexual orientation is therefore framed as an educational issue, not only a pastoral one.

This argument has largely been won with regard to race: anti-racist interventions in schools are not seen as *for* the black and ethnic minority children in the school, but for ridding society of racism, and legislation now requires all educational institutions to be proactive in preventing racism. This onus on preventing abuse is paralleled in the DfES Circular on Bullying, where it has already been made clear that head-teachers have a responsibility to prevent homophobic and any other bullying. How odd, then, that this later document steps back and is more passive on this issue of social justice.

Reference to 'preventing and removing prejudice' in the Introduction stands out as the only statement about social values and the school's role in making society safer and more just, rather than just looking out for its own pupils. However, when translated into a bullet point within the 'Personal and social skills' element a page later (DfEE 2000: 5), it has been reduced to an individual issue of personal choice, as if the only agenda is to allow pupils to have a range of sexual identities available: 'learning *to make choices* based on an understanding of difference and with an absence of prejudice' (emphasis added). Even whilst seeking to support individual pupils, approaching sexual orientation as a pastoral issue can sustain a pathologising discourse of 'deviant' sexualities. Meaningful policies should instead construct sexual orientation as an issue of education and justice for all young people (Epstein 1994a).

New Labour's 'family' values: Centralised certainty or devolved diversity?

New Labour's policies on sex education are also ambiguous regarding the new systems of governance – for example, devolving power to school governors means that LEAs have no duties with regard to sex education yet must have regard to the Guidance. Some LEAs deployed Schools Standards money to support SRE and even produced their own local Guidance document. However, the Conservatives' reduction in LEAs' power also suited New Labour, affording more centralised control over education policy and practice. This has been a key feature of their policies since 1997 and yet it permits the rhetorical virtues of both claiming that parental wishes are provided for and that diversity is recognised. Diverse value frameworks can inform schooling, evidenced in the debate over 'faith schools' and their funding by the state. The clear limits for a school's own value framework also allow the Government to avoid some difficulties in responding to parents' diverse views and potential local conflicts.

Another ambiguity about control and autonomy concerns the parental right to withdraw their children from SRE in secondary schools. A school's governing body has to decide how such pupils can 'catch up on another occasion', with the DfES separately providing materials for this. This is unduly complicated, pointing to conflicting government pressures for centralised control over educational provision and yet for individual school and parental control, given the political sensitivity of sex education. Sex education's special status is reaffirmed by this distinctive treatment (Monk 2001).

The third sentence of the document which sets up the need for the Guidance describes good practice: 'There are many excellent examples where schools have established clear sex education policies in consultation with parents, governors and the wider community' (DfEE 2000: 3). This is then addressed in the eighth of the numbered points: 'The role of a school's governing body and head teacher in the determination of a school's policy is crucial. The governing body, in conjunction with parents, will be able to develop policies which reflect the parents' wishes and the community they serve' (2000: 4). Indeed, it constructs a supplementary role for schools to that of parents. A whole section is devoted to 'Working with Parents', stating that: 'Schools should always work in partnership with parents ... parents need to know that the school's sex and relationship education programme will complement and support their role' (2000: 25).

The Introduction stresses the importance of working in partnerships with parents and the wider community, and the next section stipulates that 'Governing bodies and head teachers should consult parents in developing their sex and relationship education policy to ensure that they develop policies which reflect parents' wishes and the culture of the community they serve' (2000: 7). The importance of attending to parents' wishes is mentioned five times before any mention of teachers' or young people's wishes. The status of young people's views is clearly lower. They are 'views', not 'values' or 'culture', and are to be responded to for psychological reasons rather than because they ought to be taken into consideration by right: 'The policy will also need to reflect the views of teachers and pupils. Listening and responding to the views of young people will strengthen their confidence and self-esteem' (2000: 7). It is evident that the 'consumers' of education are the parents and that schools are forced to market themselves to them, not pupils. This is an example of how the institutionalisation of children in schools further 'familializes' them (locates them in the family and subject to their parents' will) (Brannen and O'Brien 1995).

'Teachers and all those contributing to sex and relationship education are expected to work within an agreed values framework as described in the school's policy' (DfEE 2000: 14), and the head-teacher and governing body are responsible for the moral framework within which SRE is delivered, which has to both reflect parents' wishes and the local community, and fit within the national framework. The value-openness and the statement that 'teachers should be able to deal honestly and sensitively with sexual orientation' do not preclude governors of various religious backgrounds wanting to 'honestly' present homosexuality as a sin. This highlights the difficulty (perhaps impossibility) of providing strong guidance yet allowing different value frameworks to be acceptable. A conflict exists between the Guidance's commitment to value plurality and the need to protect young people, particularly young men, from homophobia. The same tension between centralised and localised values in SRE occurs in relation to schools' value frameworks: these are devolved to individual schools and yet are also subject to inspection by Ofsted and the involvement of other external agencies such as for the National Healthy Schools Standard.

This tension 'between parental rights and governors and head teachers' discretion and, on the other hand, uniform standards and central regulation is a recurrent theme across many areas of education' (Monk 2001: 280).

For New Labour local control over this aspect of curriculum is at first paradoxical, standing out as it does in comparison with all the other subjects in the statutory NC. The Guidance is powerful in that governors must now have regard to it and the Government lent it more weight by requiring the inclusion of SRE in Ofsted inspections as well as promoting it through the Healthy School Standards. This reinforces the message that granting leeway in ethos does not mean that schools can afford to neglect it. Local devolution requiring schools to produce their own policy and, significant in pre-empting complaints, ensure it is communicated to parents, allows the Government to avoid dissatisfied parents. In fact, such parents can be told that they could become more involved in setting the values framework from the outset.

There is ambivalence about whether education involves promoting certain values or can be the delivery of information within different value frameworks. Prescriptive aspects of the Guidance contrast with its claims to value plurality (Halstead and Reiss 2003), and illustrate New Labour's 'cultural turn' (Driver and Martell 1999; Jones 2003). The rhetorical function of references to the values frameworks for SRE implies that the rest of the curriculum is value-free, and that the rest of the Guidance's content is merely factual material to be delivered through the values lens that the school (in consultation with parents and local community) provides. A claim to value-neutrality is a failure to acknowledge, perhaps even recognise one's own perspective, usually because it is culturally hegemonic.

Policy in practice (national and local)

In practice, half the PSHE coordinators in our study had not yet heard about the Guidance when we first interviewed them early in 2001. Others had heard of it but not managed to read it. All were positive about the new title, but it was striking how difficult they felt 'getting hold of' the document was. The LEA had put it on their intranet for schools, but neither electronic resources nor paper copies sent reached them. The problem was one of information overload, as one teacher indicated by gesturing at a 6 inch pile of papers on her desk – all the policies she should have read before the year's teaching began. Over the course of the project, through the LEA-run training days to support PSHE coordinators in (re)writing their school sex education policy, the

Guidance became more familiar. Initially it had appeared as rather threatening, making demands on an overwhelming workload, and raising issues that teachers would have to 'get their head round'. It took the LEA's *requirement* that someone from each school attended this training course to 'buy' them this time, and even then three or four of the city's 17 schools could not spare the staff to attend.

In terms of local policy, most of our 17 schools failed to provide us with their school sex education statement. The difficulty we experienced in obtaining the document in some schools was considerable and told of the anxiety circulating around sex education. Whilst school offices were busy places and staff under pressure to complete administrative tasks and also deal with issues at the office 'window', this did not fully account for the difficulties. Often it simply proved impossible to 'find' the policy while we waited; sometimes we were promised copies that never arrived. Our project's association with the LEA perhaps worked against us at this point, making administrative staff (and/or management) nervous about admitting the non-existence of documents or exposing outdated ones. We wondered whether parents would be met with the same response or would have the time to persist.

Some PSHE coordinators were unsure of whether a school SRE policy existed, and many knew they had not yet 'got around to it', but hoped an old one existed. In a study of three schools whose SRE policy and practice was examined in depth (Corteen 2006), none of the teachers knew of the existence of the school's SRE policy. The school nurse and even the assistant head-teacher claimed that the programme for the two-day SRE block was all there was by way of documentation, but a youth worker passed a copy to the researcher because she had checked the policy before delivering her session. Corteen (2006) also found that policies were not regularly reviewed or updated. In our case, one of the 'services' on offer to schools through the Young People's Health and Well-Being Project was support in rewriting their policy. The project worker had tremendous expertise and enthusiasm and reported great success in working with schools where the PSHE coordinator welcomed her involvement. However, other more needy schools which could have had her work time for free did not take up the offer. Ultimately, we concluded that anxiety about the topic and about the school's lack of confidence or of previous attention to it compounded workload pressures: for instance, things put 'on the back burner' whilst schools underwent Ofsted inspections were never addressed.

What this reflection on school policies reveals is how little used these documents were. Oriented to an external audience, rather than as an organising document for those delivering SRE, they were perhaps only occasionally consulted and then most likely in relation to problems arising. This reminds us of how government policies about schooling are oriented to parents as the consumers of education. One head-teacher in Corteen's study illustrated the external public relation role of school policies when he explained the 'Section 28'-like reference to teachers not presenting homosexuality as 'the norm'. He knew 'Section 28' had never applied to schools, but said the statement was 'written for parents', clearly expecting them to be conservative, and that he 'hoped' the practice 'would be different ... more progressive' (Corteen 2006: 82–3).

The LEA's role in promoting and implementing the national Guidance was crucial: the training courses, the individual support from the Health and Well-Being project and our project worked together to address what tired teachers felt was 'yet another' initiative. So suffused in anxiety was sex education – something also demon-strated by the teachers described in Epstein *et al.* (2003) – that curious institutional responses sometimes resulted. Mysterious 'misfilings' of policy documents, which one might expect could simply be reprinted, could result in their being lost forever. Processes by which anxiety was managed included splitting, such that the external audience of parents were imagined to be critical and conservative, in contrast to the progressive, supportive people in school, and blocking, such that our research enquiries were met with replies positioning us as the LEA's policing agents.

This review and textual analysis demonstrates that although there have been major changes in the official and public rhetoric about sex, gender and education, the transformations in educational policies are deeply embedded within other forms of social and economic transformation and continue to construct young people in particular ways rather than viewing sexuality as an integral part of personhood throughout childhood (Thomson and Blake 2002) and in relation to their gender and sexuality (Epstein and Johnson 1994, 1998). What are the practical implications for delivering sex education in secondary schools of dominant policy priorities and anxieties surrounding sex education from the perspectives of PSHE coordinators themselves? It is to this issue that we now turn.

chapter / **three**

Views from the staffroom: Teachers' perspectives on sex education

Personal growth, emotional development and subjects such as PSHE and SRE are not valued like the NC subjects since they do not count in the league tables. However, there is a contradictory process at work of valorising *the personal* and yet simultaneously devaluing the pupil as an embodied and gendered individual. Pupils are not usually seen as gendered social beings, despite recent moves towards more personalised learning. Gender is present in the discourse of teenage pregnancy but absent in education policies, although girls now routinely do better than boys in school examinations. The notion of *the personal* or personalisation is increasingly prominent in education policy rhetoric but, like the discourse of individualisation, it is about essentially disembodied individuals rather than social and physical beings. Yet aspects of personal and social development, regarding citizenship, health or sex education, are brought onto schools' agendas with little consideration of the links between emotional development or happiness and educational success – even 'the personal' seems stripped of the emotional. British adversarial politics and conflicts around SRE policy add to these contradictions (Lewis and Knijn 2002). The Government increasingly uses education policy to tackle social welfare, economic and social disadvantage or poverty (Bullen *et al.* 2000; Driver and Martell 1999, 2002). Educational or academic achievement is also loaded with responsibility for employment 'success' and individual economic self-sufficiency. The intense pressure this puts on individual young people and on schools to improve their performance means that the 'achievement agenda' reigns supreme in schools. It is an unassailable agenda and it leads to the widening of the gap between academic and personal welfare goals (O'Flynn and Epstein 2005).

In this chapter we look at teachers' perspectives through the lens of those usually responsible for SRE, the PSHE coordinators. We look first at the delivery of sex education, and then at the relations between personal, social, sex and academic education. The teachers we spoke to questioned the wisdom of splitting 'the social' from 'the academic' in thinking about individual pupils. Using their accounts, we illustrate how pupils' social and emotional well-being and gendered development are treated.

The issue of *status* is our central theme as all the teachers felt that the status of SRE and PSHE was so low, relative to NC subjects, that it competed with and continually lost out to them in the battle for time and attention. We hoped to help raise the status of SRE in our study's 17 secondary schools (Alldred *et al.* 2003). Here we review the obstacles that we faced and consider how they reflect teachers' experiences, and contrast this with recommended pedagogic styles for delivering SRE. We also describe the strategies that were successful in raising the status of SRE and discuss the relationship between the achievement agenda and SRE to explore the strategic development of combined personal *and* academic agendas.

The PSHE coordinators all felt that the low status of PSHE in general was most significant in limiting SRE and, despite their own professional opinions, SRE's low status limited its timetabling and pedagogy. Its low priority on head-teachers' agendas sits uneasily next to the particular constellation of anxiety regarding SRE amongst the teachers, their need for specialist training and the potential value of SRE to pupils and of PSHE to relationships in schools. This particular constellation of the low status yet controversial nature of SRE produces a peculiar set of difficulties for PSHE coordinators. They must deal with their own and others' uncertainties and embarrassment, the considerable anxiety of form tutors and head-teachers, and the potential concern or involvement of parents. Unsurprisingly, these are sometimes dealt with through denial or delegation in schools.

Whilst highly committed and often adopting government rationales for SRE, PSHE coordinators were torn by competing priorities and dismayed by their perception that PSHE was losing ground, and that SRE was upstaged by other themes within PSHE. We explore how their arguments about the status of PSHE challenge the dominant value hierarchies between subjects. We examine the discourse of NC subject competition to challenge the perceived opposition between personal/ social and academic education.

How does this discourse of *competition with NC subjects* come to be so pervasive when practitioners overwhelmingly reject this opposition and the narrow emphasis on achievement? The intense pressures on educators in the current policy context reveal tensions between national and local teacher discourses over core issues and priorities. Since we supported schools in raising the status of SRE, we identify the links between good practice in SRE and broader benefits to the pupils, school and community.

We see the disappearing tail of child-centred or holistic education as it is eaten up by the monster of academic success. It may be necessary to remind advocates of the achievement agenda of the importance of self-esteem and personal well-being to academic success. Presenting an academic achievement rationale for PSHE or SRE can raise its status, and this might, in turn, help contain, rather than fuel, the anxiety around young people's sexuality and its discussion in school. It may therefore be an effective strategy in the present context of performative pressures on schools and particular government priorities. Nevertheless, we criticise the instrumental deployment of SRE for league table success.

'The poisoned chalice': Views from PSHE coordinators

The teachers responsible for SRE in all of the city's secondary schools participated in our study. Most held the position of PSHE coordinator, but some used its older name, personal and social education (PSE), and two were health coordinators. In two schools, the key SRE contact was not the official PSHE coordinator but the more junior person delegated responsibility where the head of pastoral care had overall responsibility. It was the head of religious education (RE) in two of the RC schools, whilst in the other two faith schools (one Church of England and one RC) responsibility was taken by a member of the RE team and of the history department respectively. The latter's enthusiasm for political history led to appointment as citizenship education (CE) coordinator, and since PSHE coordination was rolled into the post, he reluctantly had responsibility for SRE.

Being the PSHE coordinator was a 'feminised' role: more than twice as many women held the post as men, in line with the pattern for non-academic responsibilities in schools, but with signs that this was changing. The men were typically senior, head of pastoral care or other members of the senior management team (SMT), and sole post-holders. Where men had recently taken the post, they had been invited in a deliberately gendered move by the LEA to 'reach boys' with SRE, and they sometimes shared the post with a woman teacher. Where the coordinator was a woman, she tended to be highly motivated and confident about SRE. One, however, was too absorbed by responsibility for improving health and nutrition across the school to focus on SRE.

For the older, senior post-holders SRE was low on their active priorities. Most had been given half, one or two points on the management scale for the responsibility. They were given between no and four non-contact periods for this post, including writing curriculum, producing materials and resources for the year group, liaising with any external speakers, supporting other teachers delivering material and auditing provision.

SRE's low status and high stress impacted on the continuity of post-holders. During our two years' involvement, high turnover was characteristic: three new coordinators replaced staff who left schools; three had temporary cover through sickness, injury or maternity leave; and two were assigned other responsibilities. The coordinators were generally dissatisfied with how the post was recognised through management points. Inevitably, better-rewarded staff tended to remain in post longer. Given this, it is dismaying that the national system for allocating 'management points' has been changed so that 'teaching and responsibility points' are only for attainment-related success and not pastoral care, confirming the national policy preoccupation with attainment. Our PSHE coordinators desperately wanted recognition for their work, further devalued nationally.

'*A poisoned chalice*' was the teachers' view of the role, given the pressures faced – socially, politically and resource-wise. Despite their frustrations, many had managed to improve provision by the end of the study and had plans for the future. The uncertain implications of statutory CE (from September 2002) caused more staff turnover, disruption and the involvement of more men – illustrating the construction of the political as masculine versus the personal as feminine. PSHE remained politically lightweight and feminised compared with the academic, especially the more masculine-associated subjects (Paechter 2000).

The pedagogy and practice of SRE

The PSHE coordinators were eager to develop SRE, but school ethos and national context provided immense difficulties. PSHE and SRE in particular were unwelcome topics for form tutors since most teachers had not received any training in delivering PSHE. Indeed, only two PSHE coordinators had training for it. This lack of training in SRE among even coordinators reflected and reinforced its low status amongst staff in general, who were often uncomfortable with the content and pedagogical style. PSHE was cross-curricular to some degree in all the schools, and auditing provision was a huge and seemingly insurmountable task for coordinators.

Initially SRE was delivered in three different ways. Most schools were delivering SRE *within PSHE,* involving form tutors delivering PSHE to their classes either in one 50-minute weekly lesson or in a rolling programme whereby at the start of term PSHE was scheduled for lesson 1 of the weekly timetable, in week 2 for lesson 2, shifting timetable slots throughout the term. This complicated system of an 'extra' class confirmed that PSHE was not important enough to warrant a slot of its own. Delivery in a weekly lesson was preferable, but often this was not in a regular dedicated time slot; for instance, where it was merely an extended registration session and so in competition with administrative and general matters. The time that form tutors had for registration *and* PSHE – 15–20 minutes – was completely unrealistic and meant little consideration of appropriate pedagogies for sensitive topics.

The second approach, in each of the four faith schools, was to cover the SRE topics of pregnancy, birth and relationships in the Family Life programme *within RE.* At two schools the teachers were confident that their Family Life programme was being delivered to a very high standard and had been ahead of the Government in its emphasis on the relationship context for sex. The other two made little specific provision, relying on a cross-curricular approach, since they had no SRE expertise and little confidence. A new staff member joining one school was keen to update the Family Life programme.

A *timetable collapse* model for the delivery of PSHE, with either full or half days dedicated to different topics, including SRE, was the third approach. One school allotted two full days in the timetable per term; and in both, each year group focused on a different topic per day, such as SRE, safety issues, health education, European studies, careers or drugs education. Form tutors stayed with their forms for the block, although their input was supplemented by external speakers. Another school was extending this after having found it an effective way to run a multicultural awareness day. Staff coordinating it said it was highly successful and had many benefits: allowing specific and varied pedagogies, and the involvement of sexual health experts alongside teachers. The opportunity for staff to be thoroughly prepared and to develop a specialist interest (such that pupils moved to different tutors of their year group for different sessions of the day) and to make efficient 'use' of outside experts in one visit all made this the most popular option. In this context, SRE was the high-status equivalent to NC subjects. Other schools' PSHE coordinators were interested in the success of this mode of delivery and its involvement of school nurses.

Factors influencing the status accorded SRE: Resources and pressures

We found that two interlocking factors hindered raising the status of SRE – *resources* (which also reflect status) and *pressures* (including values and different professional roles) – and that these operated at school, PSHE and SRE teaching levels. The status of SRE was so low as to be barely recognised at school level. Head-teachers saw their main concern as raising achievement and improving their school's performance, with overriding concerns about Ofsted inspections, bids for specialist school status, building projects or developing their learning support units. These left little room for PSHE or SRE on SMT or heads' agendas. Budgetary pressures on schools were mentioned frequently by both head-teachers and PSHE coordinators, and finding adequate staffing to cover for high rates of teacher illness and stress increased pressures. This compromised the rationale for delivery of PSHE by form tutors within an established teacher–pupil relationship as it was therefore sometimes delivered by 'supply teachers'.

Subject status was a key issue for coordinators: SRE not being examined or assessed made its *low status* more acute, but its potential to contribute to improvements in school behaviour, discipline and achievement is evident. Even where PSHE was recognised as valuable, as one PSHE coordinator said:

> Everybody says it's really important, but you're under pressure to try and fit everything [else] in. The worry of course with PSHE is that, at the end of the day, it's non-statutory, so can be squeezed.

The PSHE coordinator post was frequently delegated to a relatively junior woman teacher, which was unusual for a whole-school, cross-curricular or development role. They reported little recognition of the breadth of or degree of responsibility inherent in the post and identified how delegating PSHE served to shield head-teachers and their SMTs, allowing the compartmentalisation of 'tricky' matters such as SRE.

Coordinators found that, given limited official recognition, their designated non-contact time was easily filled by covering for absent staff or their pastoral responsibilities. It was hard to prepare materials, hold meetings to update the SRE policy or deal with practical matters such as involving speakers, let alone to read and develop the curriculum. As a non-examined subject, there was no associated departmental structure for PSHE, and no process for promotion. Difficulties in auditing and monitoring the quality of PSHE were more acute than for other subjects, because of the sensitive subject matter, discursive pedagogy and the topic's developmental, social, emotional and attitudinal nature:

It's very difficult to manage a subject where there's no allotted time for it. That has to be the major problem. Take the audit: two problems – provision and quality. [Regarding] provision we've managed to plug a few gaps, but for an audit, how can you point to things that are as vague and wishy-washy as the PSHE framework document, when like, well a citizenship example is awareness of cultural or national identity, I mean it's the overall aim of history really, but hard to point to lessons and outcomes, and even harder for PSHE. Regarding quality, you end up having to make department heads responsible for monitoring quality, which is a lot more to fall on their shoulders and means you don't really know yourself.

In terms of *resources*, PSHE suffered from general school funding pressures, exacerbated by its low status. The small PSHE budget was expected to cover all expenses: teaching materials (books, packs, learning games, demonstration kits and equipment), visitors' expenses and photocopying. The most popular PSHE events, plays by visiting theatre companies, were not affordable without compromises such as gathering the whole year group together, which tended to undermine its participatory aims. Pressure on the school timetable was intense, with PE or art being cut for NC subjects. It was anticipated that CE would be squeezed into PSHE, possibly also with RE. Some PSHE coordinators felt that CE could raise the status of PSHE, whilst others felt this would compromise the personal aspects of PSHE.

PSHE often conflicted directly with a teacher's 'official' (NC) subject and pressure to improve grades therein. Some described regrettably 'stealing' time to prepare PSHE from a class doing well and were happy to give up PSHE coordination:

I've a big enough job trying to boost the uptake and grades in my subject, without worrying about PSHE.
It's frustrating because it's so low on everybody's agenda.

For those teachers at 'successful' schools, PSHE had even lower status, and committed teachers were frustrated that important issues were neglected until problems arose:

It isn't seen as an issue at a school like this, with a highly selective, very privileged intake, so it means that there has to be a problem, an incident, before it gets any attention.

This concurs with Carrie Paechter's (2000) findings about the subordination of non-academic subjects, such as those associated with the body (PE, sex education) or manual crafts in elite schools. The lack of training for teaching PSHE and SRE reinforced its low status amongst staff and pupils and was reflected in pedagogic difficulties presented by discursive, value-based material, and for skills-based learning outcomes such as regarding communication. Discursive pedagogies were at odds with the usual pedagogy of some teachers and potentially damaging to their existing rapport with pupils.

Within the PSHE programme, SRE might be one of five topics, competing with drugs education, careers, health and hygiene, safety or media education, and for school nurses SRE competed with whole-school health priorities, such as statutory immunisations. Nurses' training in sexual health education was not acknowledged by teachers, perhaps reflecting their lack of knowledge about nurses' expertise. PSHE coordinators reported considerable professional anxiety about the nature of SRE. The material in – or believed to be in – the SRE curriculum was the focus of anxiety for other staff and for SMTs, governors or parents. PSHE coordinators provided support for staff and pupils, and they were sought out for personal support. Their responsibilities needed better recognition and reward to retain experienced teachers. Training, greater teaching release and a career structure could demonstrate that PSHE or SRE was a legitimate and valued specialism. The 'poisoned chalice' threatened highly committed staff with 'burnout', and the pressure on teachers to raise standards in their 'real' subjects undermined them.

Furthermore, national discourses of outrage or concern about young people's sexual activity led to anxiety at all levels in school, for parents and governors, and were felt acutely by coordinators, form tutors and also the young men and women in the classroom. Like Buston et al.'s (2001) findings in Scottish schools, the words 'difficult' and 'un-comfortable' and their derivatives featured heavily in coordinators' reports of how other teachers found materials. They themselves were usually confident discussing sex and relationships, but they recognised the reasons others were not (Buston et al. 2001, 2002b; Kehily 2002). Many teachers, form tutors and coordinators felt that SRE should be the parents' responsibility. They reluctantly accepted the need to make up for a parental deficit but were anxious about criticism of their personal values. The resentment or anxiety coordinators faced from the other staff about teaching SRE was most unpleasant. One very successful PSHE coordinator said:

> No, I wouldn't do it again. It's a lot of hard work, very little appreciation from anybody else. And because there's a lot of staff who don't feel comfortable teaching it, you're the one who gets it in the neck at the end of the day because they're angry about it. Where staff or pupils aren't happy about it, or are threatened by it, it can come out in aggression.

Similarly, their reports of teachers' views contained frequent mentions of the pressures around SRE:

We don't get enough training. Some staff would argue as well that Year 9 pupils are too young and some of them aren't ready for sex education. And fair enough, there's probably three or four that are very young Year 9s, but there's some who need it in Years 7 and 8. Some staff argue it's not their job, it's the parents' job. And there's a whole range of reasons ... You should get the whole staff group in and they'll tell you just why they shouldn't have to teach it! It's not a popular subject! People do it reluctantly, even the staff that don't feel uncomfortable with it ... with the training and planning the way it is ... they feel underprepared for it. Being underprepared for it is horrible: I think the biggest fear as a teacher in a situation like that is being asked a question that you just don't know how to answer.

Many teachers felt uncertain about professional values and boundaries, constraints from school rules, LEA or national policy and therefore operated with extreme caution, but hoped that their own child's questions would be answered more openly. Many saw SRE as a necessary compensation for parental neglect of a difficult topic, and as a response to a hypersexualised culture in which the commodification of sexuality intensified pressures on young people to be 'sexy', attractive and sexually available. All the PSHE coordinators and nurses we spoke to thought the contraceptive lesson given to students in Year 9 should be moved down a year, but reported that not all staff agreed.

The *older* generation of staff tended to feel more uncomfortable with the subject matter than the younger. However, key factors reported in teachers' degree of comfort with SRE included their own openness as parents, their personalities and the nature of their subject disciplines. Examples given corresponded with age and gender conventions – younger women teachers were more open and approachable about social or emotional issues, while for some male teachers the relationship with their pupils did not necessarily embrace intimate or personal matters comfortably. 'You're a form teacher and you don't just want to go in and suddenly talk about sex', said one.

Many described feeling 'caught' between conservative school governors, whose reactions could block entire programmes, and their own professional judgement about teaching SRE. This was echoed in the recognition by the SEF (2004: 4) that

Some governors will not understand the significance of SRE or may be suspicious of its content. It is important to secure their commitment and involvement. One strategy might be to ask representatives from the school council to talk about why an SRE policy is important and what they think is needed. Alternatively, a survey of children and young people's views on SRE could be circulated and comments invited.

Teachers' awareness that pupils' parents or carers could withdraw them solely from SRE undermined their sense of legitimacy about delivering it. Indeed this statutory provision seems remarkable given the increasingly centralised and mandated NC. In practice, very few parents take up this option – only 0.04 per cent of children are actually withdrawn (Ofsted 2002). The SEF (2004: 4) tried to reassure teachers about it:

> This [withdrawal] is not necessarily a sign that schools are doing a bad job. Some parents/carers believe that it is their responsibility to educate their child about sex and relationships. In this situation it is important that the SRE programme is not significantly compromised to meet the wishes of a tiny minority.

Such parents can be offered a DfES leaflet that details organisations that can help them in discussing these matters with their child (DfES 2001).

The anxiety shown in teachers' comments sometimes resulted in retreat from SRE altogether or from the attitudes and values and the personal and social skills strands (leaving the knowledge and understanding strand). This allowed them to present SRE as closer to biology and 'factual information'. This 'don't scare the horses' approach might have governors, parents, or particular faith communities in mind, or simply be related to the general climate of anxiety around sex education. However, the discourse of *knowledge and information* is important for ensuring that teachers' concerns not to offend religious groups do not result in limited SRE provision. The SEF also found that teachers and other sex educators sometimes shy away from including religious perspectives on marriage, contraception or homosexuality in case they frighten or exclude some young people. However, they point out that differences of view exist even among those with a shared religious tradition:

> a lesson on contraception may include a variety of religious views including the Catholic belief that forbids contraception. Young people ... need to know that they are legally able to access confidential contraception services and advice even if they are under sixteen. (SEF 2004: 5)

What the discourse of *information* allows is the clear distinction between knowing about and deciding personally what to do about contraception, for instance. By implication, it constructs the pupil as a moral agent, whom lessons merely inform rather than 'corrupt'. Values and learning need not be seen as oppositional. We would argue that education always involves the transmission of values even when considered fact-based. Of importance to reassuring anxious teachers is the SEF (2004: 5) advice that 'a range of faith and secular perspectives can be discussed within the process of learning. Views and opinions can be explored, rather than prescribed as fixed.'

Pedagogic approaches to SRE and PSHE: Embodiment versus 'the cerebral'

Discussing sex or emotions felt like a breach of the cerebral sphere of school to some coordinators and as disrupting some teachers' attempts to contain or control sexualised behaviour and comments. Even those who were not uncomfortable with the material could resent the resulting changed relationship or did not feel confident using a discursive pedagogy. A common, gendered illustration was that discussing 'loving relationships' or 'having children' with 'Mr "write this down from the board" Science' differed from discussing it with 'Ms "let's talk about your feelings about this character" English'. Promoting emotional literacy was not always seen as the teachers' role and competing pulls on teachers were evident: they were increasingly expected to be subject specialists raising grades, and counsellors, behaviour managers and key professionals in promoting pupils' social and emotional well-being, increasingly linked to social, welfare and health services for pupils and families.

Even those who fully supported the SRE agenda for schools resented having no time to prepare a class, especially where the material was important or controversial and hence more anxiety provoking. Illicitly taking time from other areas was a skill many coordinators resented having had to develop. They could not do all they were meant to in the time available, and were uncomfortable and dissatisfied with the job. Ensuring quality and the stress of supporting reluctant staff were key concerns:

> Where staff don't have any choice, it's very difficult to monitor what goes on behind closed doors once staff have been sent off, 'that's it you've got to do it' – if they're really uncomfortable about it, they don't do it.

Worksheet-dominated classes were not seen as meeting the aims of PSHE or ensuring pupils actually learned even the material on them. At one school, while the coordinator had eased the time pressure by not having her own PSHE class, she had thereby lost the chance to develop her own pedagogy, which she felt would help her support other staff.

Pedagogical practices: Timetable collapse or team teaching?

Rather than delivery by a form tutor, the two preferred modes of delivery of SRE were timetable collapse or team teaching. To reduce problems of monitoring quality, over the course of our study one school (with the support of the Young People's Health and Wellbeing project) introduced team teaching. Staff chose one of five PSHE topics and worked with a team leader to deliver it across the school, where previously form tutors had taught these on a rolling programme. This change was introduced to raise the perceived importance of PSHE and to allow staff to teach the same material repeatedly rather than covering every topic. It was very successful, raised staff expertise, and brought improvements in training, preparation and confidence. Many other PSHE coordinators hoped to win the support of their SMT for this way of teaching, but were despondent about the likelihood of extra staffing since appointing trained PSHE teachers could not compete with recruiting NC subject teachers.

SRE was not taught by specialists in timetable collapse models, but more external input *was* possible, as pupils moved between sessions with the sexual health expert, youth worker and their form tutor. Having a whole day (or two) raised its status, as SRE was evidently important enough to override the usual timetable, and quality improved with the greater preparation required of form tutors:

> A lot of staff do it really well, don't get me wrong, but those who aren't keen can easily entertain a class for 50 minutes a week but not necessarily get the message across for that particular week. But if they've got a day or two full days to plan for, they know they can't get away with that, it needs planning properly. They have got to get the pupils involved and make the activities interesting. It also needs more input from staff if they've got to plan for a longer period of time.

SRE competed with other topics for the six days annually and there were risks too – pupil absenteeism or a lack of readiness for particular material could significantly impact the SRE curriculum for a pupil's whole year. In addition, the chance for progressive learning in a 'spiral curriculum' was compromised by the intensity of concentration in one day, but, where successful, it made for a memorable lesson. Outside speakers preferred this since they could concentrate efforts in a single day, rather than coming in for a different form each week. Team teaching benefits from staff with specialist training and commitment to teaching SRE, and maintaining their pre-existing teacher–pupil relationships. Only one school used team teaching, although others aspired to it. One school reduced the timetable collapse blocks to half-day sessions.

Several coordinators had resisted taking on coordinating CE, although there were mixed views about whether it competed with or complemented PSHE. One PSHE coordinator had successfully argued for doubling PSHE time; one for timetable collapse; and another had successfully bid, against weighty topics such as health and careers, for an extra day on SRE for Year 9 students. Others campaigned for more resources by linking PSHE to improving grades and behaviour. Some embraced CE to make PSHE more heavyweight. Another introduced team teaching for PSHE specialisms.

Some had drawn on support of the Healthy Schools Standards SRE strand, and the Young People's Health and Wellbeing project to develop SRE policy and curriculum. Some involved nurses because they were not paid for by schools, and some were very enthusiastic about nurse drop-in sessions that could provide a professional one-to-one service for pupils, linked to local health services. These allayed fears amongst PSHE coordinators that they could not meet pupils' sexual health needs. This use of school nurses was popular perhaps because, unlike their involvement in the classroom, it retained clearly distinct professional roles for nurses and teachers.

Good practice for SRE: A secure home

At the top of PSHE coordinators' wish-list was either to recruit a specially trained PSHE teacher or establish a PSHE *department* to raise its status – an ideal none achieved over the two years, yet which would meet the Government's requirement for SRE embedded within the PSHE framework. As a coordinator from one of the faith schools put it:

> I wish the Government would have the balls to make it [PSHE] statutory and say 'Right this has to be timetabled' or get rid of it completely, having modified the National Curriculum to mean that certain subjects, like biology, include some reflection. ... It just doesn't work, this half-way house, especially in a school like this ... Very few schools have PSHE trained staff, there aren't many of them around, and many schools don't have the money to pay them.

They wanted the Government or LEA to *raise the status* of PSHE amongst head-teachers and SMTs, thus influencing form tutors and pupils, and they wanted the LEA to provide training for coordinators and form tutors, a specified minimum teaching release across the LEA and parity of management points. They at least needed a minimum level of resources for PSHE in each school, for (re)producing materials and resources and/or a library of approved materials and equipment, which many suggested the LEA could hold. In addition, they wanted the LEA to buy in services for SRE from youth, nursing or voluntary sector organisations across the city and events that individual schools could not afford. The SEF (2004: 5) made a similar plea:

> SRE needs to be developed in line with best available evidence as to what works. It should form part of an overall PSHE and Citizenship programme that aims to improve children and young people's self-esteem and support their emotional development.

These aims highlight the importance of giving teachers the chance to develop their personal and social skills before applying them in pedagogical situations: the SEF's (2004: 5) statement applies to both teachers and pupils: 'We need personal and social skills to put knowledge into action and we need to practise using them.'

These aims and ideals also reflect current practices and expectations around gender, in particular that female teachers preferred 'feminine' subjects, and more discursive forms of teaching and, equally, gendered forms of learning were assumed, with girls' pedagogic preferences being for discussion-based learning and subjects rather than information-based topics or didactic pedagogies. The SEF (2005) recommends as effective learning methods for SRE: debates, discussions and forms of enquiry including reflective practices to develop sensitivities. It does not, however, address the question of gendered learning styles. Yet this is important for understanding attainment patterns, classroom dynamics and individual learning styles, and without it sets self-fulfilling expectations which can ultimately limit girls to feminine and boys to masculine norms.

Factors hindering improvements in SRE and PSHE

The Government's *achievement agenda* was the critical barrier to the successful implementation of good practice in SRE and PSHE, as we now argue. The PSHE coordinators criticised the pressure on pupils as increasing the need for personal support. They even felt that PSHE and SRE could complement the achievement agenda in pedagogies of learning and teaching, supporting pupils in their emotional development and learning communication skills.

A second barrier is education policy *initiative overload* (a term coined by the late Ted Wragg). The head-teachers interviewed were preoccupied with new initiatives such as Excellence in Cities, specialist college status and Education Action Zones, as well as with league tables. Teachers also felt these added to their time pressures, through their involvement with drafting bids, such as for sports college status. These all contributed to resource pressures and intensified competition between schools. Powell describes teachers' feeling when the topic of a forthcoming training day is announced as the NABI (not another bloody initiative) syndrome, which applies to the whole gamut of new programmes, projects, initiatives, interventions and funding streams. This NABI syndrome is common in schools in England, Wales and Northern Ireland given education reforms stretching back to the ERA 1988 and 'where daily life is characterized by new initiatives and curriculum change' (Powell 1997: 94).

Whilst the Government's attention to SRE is welcomed because of anticipated resource allocation, it inevitably brings new regulatory mechanisms such as quality audit and performance indicators. Head-teachers were exhausted by cycles of bidding and lamented the lack of stability, continuity and cumulative learning, and the short-term thinking that such funding produces. Thus 'interest' was seen as fickle, populist and paying only 'lip-service' to issues. Where teachers felt confident in their 'sex education' provision before 2000, they could be forgiven for greeting 'SRE' with scepticism. Their concerns were more broadly with students' well-being but they welcomed delegating bodily health to health professionals.

Thirdly, the PSHE coordinators identified the *culture of anxiety around sex* in contemporary society – particularly sex education in schools – as extremely unhelpful. The British adversarial politics (Lewis and Knijn 2002) around SRE provoked anxiety for all parties. Good practice was hindered by the denial of or intense interest in young people's sexuality. Moreover, anxieties around sexual harassment and abuse, which could reinforce the need for 'no nonsense' SRE, actually hindered good practice where they rested on uninformed opinions, misleading and alarming tabloid media headlines.

Indeed, whilst SRE and PSHE could contribute to raising pupils' academic and educational achievements by addressing rather than occluding their emergent sexual and social identities, government policies had not addressed this. The two agendas – SRE and achievement – were ostensibly in conflict, exacerbating anxieties of head-teachers, teachers, PSHE coordinators, governors, parents and the pupils themselves. Different pedagogies for SRE and PSHE did nothing to allay anxieties. Providing opportunities for young people to learn about and reflect upon their emerging social and sexual identities is not incompatible with but integral to academic success.

Competing agendas: Academic achievement versus personal and social education

Since the NC was established by the ERA 1988, concern about 'soft' non-NC subjects or 'cross-curricular themes' has been expressed, exacerbated in the 1990s with the introduction of performance league tables. Could cross-curricular themes hold 'parity of esteem' with examined subjects when schools had to show their worth in league tables of examination grades alone (David *et al.* 1994; Gewirtz *et al.* 1995)? Lawton (1996: 36) recognised this 'fundamental problem':

> Critics were told at the time that all would be well eventually, because 'cross-curricular elements' would fill in all the gaps such as social and political understanding, economic awareness, health education, etc. By 1994 this had been shown to be a completely empty promise. Those schools which declared that the national curriculum was not the whole curriculum were thwarted in their desire for breadth because the timetable was already overcrowded.

Whilst the National Curriculum Council produced interesting documents on cross-curricular themes, education ministers after Kenneth Baker either ignored them or refused to countenance anything not expressed in terms of subjects (Graham and Tytler 1993). Consequently, those schools who wanted to operationalise their view that the NC did not represent the whole curriculum struggled to introduce material for the cross-curricular themes because of the time requirements of ten foundation subjects. Sir Ron Dearing was officially asked to address the question of pressures of NC subjects (The National Curriculum and its assessment: final report, 1994), but there was little debate about cross-curricular themes and the fundamental problems of the NC were simply ignored (Lawton 1996).

If 'citizenship and health' were to be the vehicles of cross-curricular themes, the ambiguities about their status in school had to be clarified. Citizenship as a topic had no status in schools until September 2002, when it became compulsory at Key Stages 3 and 4 but without a necessary timetable slot of its own. Health education remains an issue promoted in *ad hoc* initiatives and schemes such as the National Healthy Schools Programme which schools may *choose* to sign up to, but the school's role in health education remains contested as the field of sex education itself illustrates (Thomson 1984; Monk 1998).

Teachers were explicit about tensions between PSHE coordination and subject specialisms and sometimes opted out of or quietly neglected the lower-status work. Teachers find themselves pulled both ways: expected to enhance their pastoral role in response to the widespread perception that pupils' social and emotional needs are greater than they were a generation ago, and expected to further develop their subject specialism and improve their technical competency to raise grades. SMTs claimed to recognise the importance of PSHE, and staff reluctantly accepted the competing demands for management attention, staff time or financial resources:

> [PSHE is] an important part of the curriculum, but I think you've got to be perfectly honest and say that in this day and age, it's all about meeting targets and getting results and getting them through GCSE etc., and PSE is very low down the list of important subjects. I mean, it's obvious and I'd be a fool to think it was any other way.

One coordinator's suggestions for PSHE topics on staff training days had

> fallen on deaf ears because obviously [the head-teacher's] got exams to do, got everything else to see to . . . she's very committed to raising the standards of the school.

This discourse of competition between academic and lower-status subjects, such as PSHE and other cross-curricular themes, was the dominant narrative of the relationship between academic success and PSHE. The balance between these pulls depended on how the discourse of competing agendas was used by management or PSHE coordinators, which we explore in the next section.

The dual pressure on schools and pupils we have described to improve academic performance at GCSE level and yet attend to pupils' greater social, psychological and welfare needs reflects the intensification of a long-standing tension between pastoral and academic agendas in schools. Our study demonstrated the pressure on the education system as a whole to meet broadened goals on both agendas. The increased psychologisation of our cultural understanding of the individual and heightened prominence and apparent acceptance of discourses of the emotions in public life (but see Burman 2006; Parker 2006) frame these debates. Yet the seemingly increasingly powerful discourse of the emotional is up against a fearsome opponent in the educational achievement agenda.

Conflicting pressures and motives: 'That's not why I came into teaching'

What is at stake here is the role of teachers in young people's lives and of the school in society. The policy agenda indicates a shift from a previously more autonomous and holistic model of teachers' work to a performativity- and accountability-driven model emphasising the need to raise pupils' attainment in predefined ways (Sultana 1994, cited in McNess *et al.* 2003). In terms of pedagogy, 'a performance-oriented, transmission model of learning has been given preference over a socio-cultural model which recognised and included the emotional and social aspects necessary for a more learner-centred approach' (McNess *et al.* 2003: 246). The impact on teachers, McNess *et al.* (2003: 245) conclude, is that their work is

> seen as increasingly dependent upon an externally imposed apparatus of behavioural objectives, assessment and accountability, leading to a proliferation of paperwork and administrative tasks, chronic work overload and the loss of opportunities for creative work and for developing caring relationships with pupils.

We add that the model of pupils constructed in the contemporary 'performative' pedagogy undoes the work of Plowden (1967) and returns us to a limited, partial, *cognitive* subject, whose learning can again be taken out of context of his or her social, emotional, physically embodied and culturally situated existence.

McNess *et al.* (2003) draw together evidence to consider whether the current British policy priority of school 'effectiveness' compromises the affective dimension of pupils' learning, arguing that teachers reported a 'growing tension between the requirements of government and the needs of their pupils' (2003: 243). The demand to improve their own and their pupils' 'performance' and to manage effectively in the interests of accountability ignored teachers' commitment to the affective aspects of teaching and learning, which have been identified as key to teachers' professional 'satisfaction' (Nias 1989, cited in McNess *et al.* 2003), yet under threat (Hoyle and John 1995, cited in McNess *et al.* 2003) where external pressures run counter to the 'holistic and humanistic' values of many teachers (Jeffrey and Woods 1996, cited in McNess *et al.* 2003). Others warn of the 'growing disenchantment with an over-emphasis on IQ and on cognitive skills' and an education increasingly defined in solely academic terms (Sharp 2000: 8).

Teachers in our study also drew in contradictory ways on discourses of the importance of academic or social success, including in their own lives. Their commitment to young people's personal and social education contradicted their preference for their own child's teacher to prepare maths instead of PSHE, for instance. This reflects their own view of or confidence in the parental role in personal/social matters relative to the teacher's. We explored what exactly the 'highly committed' valued: many gave versions of 'the personal development of the pupils in my class' or 'their general well-being', and one said 'how they're coping with the big scary world'. One illustrated that this priority meant needing to be flexible about the PSHE curriculum, so that 'if a child comes in who's been bullied or who's worried about something' or a news event that is relevant to discuss, form tutors should discuss that in the (fortnightly) session. The events in the USA of 11 September 2001 were given as an example of something that had legitimately usurped the planned topic, but she reported telling tutors that practising for assembly or collecting in notes were not legitimate uses of scant PSHE time. They also described how form teachers' resistance to delivering SRE was not out of a lack of support for PSHE or SRE in principle, but about their confidence and competence: 'It's not my job, I'm not trained to do this' was a common remark. This reluctance was such that one coordinator could see benefits in more time for PSHE than the fortnightly hour, but knew it would not go down well with staff who 'would not respond constructively'. Staff were happier for someone else to come in to deliver both sensitive or highly technical topics.

Contradictory accounts

The term *discourse* avoids implying that the ideas expressed in interviews directly reflect individuals' consistent world-views or map neatly onto certain professional roles. Instead the accounts produced draw on cultural repertoires of meaning that are differentially available to people according to their social positioning (Davies and Harré 1990), and work in particular context-related ways, including within the research itself (Burman 1992; Alldred and Gillies 2002). The specific context of being interviewed about SRE in school by a LEA-funded researcher is significant, in addition to the personal dynamics of rapport established (Miller and Bell 2002), which were friendly and positive with all the coordinators, increasingly so as the project developed.

Many coordinators embraced the school's responsibility for SRE since it was 'such an important issue' whilst at the same time arguing that responsibility for educating young people about sex lies with parents. They sometimes reflected on the irony that their views as the parents of young people did not tally completely with their views 'as teachers'. Their contradictory subject positions meant that they sometimes supported government policy on teenage pregnancy or the achievement agenda, and yet at other times presented cogent critiques. Our interview method allowed PSHE coordinators to adopt a position of some distance from what other teachers felt about delivering sex education and gave them flexibility regarding the positions they occupied. For instance, the anxiety around sex education in school was highly prominent within their reports of *others'* views, which also tended to draw from more popular discourses of young people's sexuality, but not in their accounts of their own views of SRE. Their accounts of form tutors' resistance to their SRE programme were both critical and sympathetic, sharing common anxieties and yet at other times being champions of containment, control or policy objectives.

As trust grew, teachers' initial apparent support of the Government (suggested by their orthodox accounts of why the school should deliver SRE to the TPS targets) often became more critical of what they saw as overintervention and populist responses to moral panics around young people's sexuality or sexual orientation. They sometimes drew on different, even contradictory discourses within the course of an interview, either self-consciously or not. We understand such contra-dictory statements as indicating the multiplicity of cultural thinking on a topic, and as offering insights into the complex ways education policy discourses actually operate 'on the ground'.

Status-enhancing strategies: 'contributing to the school ethos'?

The opposition between the achievement agenda and cross-curricular themes can be undone if PSHE is presented as contributing to the achievement agenda. The discourses of social and emotional well-being that present a critique of the achievement agenda's narrowness can be employed to remedy its limitations. One successful use of this rhetorical strategy was that sport (another cross-curricular theme) would contribute to a school's success attainment-wise. In developing a bid for sports college status, one PSHE coordinator, a senior member of the PE department, used PSHE to justify the bid. She explained she was

> trying to get all staff to realise the benefits if the kids are better motivated and do more in PE and have better facilities, it should have a knock-on effect in every other subject ... in French they'll be talking about what sports the French are good at etc.

In particular this was identified as potentially helpful in stimulating boys' achievement:

> the school's very good at sports, but we have great problems with the boys not performing as well as girls academically.

The bid was successful and a year later she was school sport coordinator for PE at Key Stages 1 and 2 to link the feeder primary schools with the sports college, as well as PSHE coordinator, and was combining CE coordination into the post without an extra management point. She had one point but no teaching release for the PSHE coordinator responsibility. By this time, the link drawn between sports and achievement differed slightly. League-table grades, she argued, self-conscious of the task of persuasion, would be improved largely as a result of improved *behaviour* in school:

> The way it's being sold is hopefully the behaviour of the pupils will be improved, because we have better facilities, because the idea is you challenge the less academic pupils towards PE and perhaps it'll have a knock-on effect, they may behave better for you, er, there are more opportunities for pupils ...

Participation in prestigious sports events would give the teachers more leverage of the 'If you don't work in geography why should we let you play football for us?' variety, introducing 'a bit of give and take'. The official version of the sports college was about improving pupils' self-esteem, morale and identification with the school. Informally, perhaps in practice in the classrooms, it provided teachers with a bargaining chip. The initiative would improve the school's standing in attainment tables because all pupils would be expected to take an additional GCSE in PE, which would be compulsory. Improving school ethos was a positive way of reducing bad behaviour:

> Ethos, that's the crux of it, the head has always pushed that the ethos of the school will improve, will change slightly cos we all appreciate that if the kids are involved in something and challenged in something else they won't have that behavioural issue, but we all know that there are those kids who aren't interested in sport and never will be, and will still be badly behaved, but we're hoping we can shift the experience [of school] for them ...

It has been possible to gain substantial additional funding for a non-academic area of the curriculum by arguing that it would promote academic success. The status of sport in the school was raised by becoming a sports college, but also, in the minds of staff not part of the sports agenda, by its association with funding to improve attainment. The status of other cross-curricular themes was enhanced too, either by being attached to promoting a positive school ethos, or by association with this one teacher who simultaneously held prominent sport, PSHE and CE posts.

Resisting competition: PSHE's contribution to the achievement agenda

The government logic that sees improving educational aspirations and engagement as a way of reducing social exclusion (Bullen *et al.* 2000) can be enhanced by the argument that better emotional well-being leads to better learning. This was used by some of our PSHE coordinators. Whilst effective in the current climate, using this rhetorical strategy compromises the integrity of the discourse of personal and social education as valuable in its own right.

One successful LEA project to develop emotional literacy, running since 1998, was launched when the Chief Inspector for Southampton Education Service and educational psychologist, Peter Sharp, 'came to agree that emotional literacy should be an equal priority with literacy and numeracy for all children' (Sharp 2000: 8). The hypothesis was that:

> if teachers, pupils, parents, officers and others feel positively about themselves then they will learn more effectively. Put more succinctly:
>
> Improving Emotional Literacy = Improving Standards
> Feel Good = Learn Good

However, government policy here is equivocal, according to James Park of Antidote: Campaign for Emotional Literacy. In spite of the recognition in the 2000 National Curriculum Guidance 'of the significance of emotional processes on learning, government policy as a whole does not appear to acknowledge this' (Park 2000: 11). He views thinking and feeling as engaged in a continuous dance:

> Young people, it seems, need to be able to access, manage and deploy their emotional powers if they are to think clearly, critically and creatively. The more they can enhance their 'emotional literacy', the more powerful will be their rationality. The quality of their feeling shapes the depth and meaningfulness of their thinking. (2000: 12)

Park believes that gliding between thinking and feeling brings energy to the task of learning, and drawing on emotional capacities can develop cognitive 'muscles' to equip pupils to 'respond to changing situations, learn from mistakes, embrace new challenges and handle complexity' (2000: 13). He links the management of emotional states to the ability to avoid being threatened by difference and to discriminate more subtly between people, concepts or things. Greater understanding of the minds of others allows recognition of complexity and ambivalence – preparing for engagement in other forms of complexity in science, for instance. Responding to the diversity of other people's experiences and views helps us learn how to move between states that allow for different types of thinking – for example, being open to new information, closed and task-focused, or free-floating and playfully creative (Park 2000). He admits, however, that there is still too little empirical evidence of the link between the emotional culture of our schools and their standards of attainment for sceptics to be convinced.

An alternative strategy is to draw on the discourse of the whole person, where educating the whole person means embracing the personal and the social, along with the academic, and arguing that they are inseparable. Related appeals to the holistic subject link with child-centred pedagogies, fashionable in the 1970s. Recognising the role of affect is linked with a critique of splitting pupils' cognitive from their emotional lives (Burman 1992, 1994a) and renews appeal about the psychological subject. The complicated task lies in analysing the emotional and embodied aspects of the subject and yet critiquing the liberal humanist individual.

Linking SRE to the achievement agenda

The legitimacy and status of PSHE could be improved, in the present educational climate, by adopting a discourse of PSHE as a subject or discipline, with its own pedagogy and requiring specific training after initial training of teachers. The alternative is to emphasise PSHE's difference from other subjects and its legitimacy in cross-cutting NC subjects. This latter is like the 1988 promise of cross-curricular themes as a core part of the school and NC, 'just organised differently'. This was thwarted by the intensifying market forces that require schools to compete by performance in NC subjects. Piggybacking on the new status of citizenship education offers a powerful strategy. It may, however, compromise the nature of PSHE, and SRE may be reduced to the 'hard', testable version (reproductive science, perhaps) akin to the 'public' approach to politics that is taken in CE (Ofsted 2006). Finally, by the end of our study only one coordinator reported success in raising the status of SRE by emphasising its potential contribution to the achievement agenda, despite this strategy being applauded both in the interviews and by other LEAs.

chapter four

Sexy bodies in the classroom: Pupils' values and views about sex education

We turn now to the perspectives of young people in schools. We collected material from 13–14-year-olds in the classrooms of 16 schools in response to the Government's requirement that school policies 'reflect the views of teachers *and pupils*' (DfEE 2000: 7; emphasis added). Pupils in Year 8 are yet to start the Key Stage 4 PSHE curriculum but are thought by both PSHE coordinators and school nurses to be in need of earlier SRE. When two schools postponed our visits because of teacher sickness and shortage, we studied classes at the start of Year 9. Involving all pupils in a class at each school, we hoped to gain insight into how young people from diverse family and social backgrounds view sex education. Teachers had described this age cohort of adolescents as particularly variable in terms of sexual maturity and social skills. We did indeed find this, but we were particularly interested in other dimensions of difference among them. What views would young men and young women express in the context of their peers about an issue steeped in discourses of masculinity, femininity, sexuality, family values and relationships and 'the private'? What 'value context' would this suggest national SRE policy played into in these schools and peer groups?

As we saw in Chapter 3, schools emphasise the NC subjects at the expense of non-examinable subjects, with league tables the rationale and motivation for developing curricula. Regardless of whether or not a subject is examinable and gender is a lesson topic, schools and classroom practices are heavily implicated in the gendering of pupils' bodies and identities. The practices of schooling powerfully inscribe meanings to pupils (Walkerdine 1984; Burman 1994a). Researchers (Epstein *et al.* 1998; Skelton 2001; Reay 2001a; Renold 2005) analyse the pedagogic and peer processes of assigning and performing gender in the classroom, and their simultaneous constructions of race, class, sexual and academic identities.

Gendered identities are increasingly drawn on to understand the academic identities of pupils in primary and secondary schools. The particular gender- and class-differentiated experiences, expectations and identities that pupils bring to the classroom are especially significant for sex education (Hey 1997; Holland *et al.* 1998; Thomson 2000). In sex education research, gender dynamics and young people's gender and sexual identities are key to understanding the success of sex education. Mac an Ghaill (1994b), Lenderyou and Ray (1997), Measor (2004) and Buston and Wight (2006) discuss the difficulties of engaging boys actively and constructively in SRE given the pressures they feel to perform 'acceptable' masculinities in school (Frosh *et al.* 2002), and with differing concerns about peer group perceptions, Lees (1986, 1993), Measor *et al.* (2000) and Buston *et al.* (2002a) argue that the social setting is significant for girls' confident and comfortable engagement in SRE. It is not surprising that dominant cultural discourses of gender enter the sex education classroom. Research findings on young people's heterosexuality highlight conventional discourses of femininity and masculinity being powerful in sexual experiences. Young women's negotiation of safer or any other sexual practices has to be located 'within structurally unequal social relationships' despite their expectations of egalitarian relationships (Holland *et al.* 1998: 6).

We have explored teachers' difficulties in discussing sexuality in the classroom and prioritising SRE or PSHE. Both staff and pupils are under pressure from the achievement agenda that privileges and exacerbates the mind/body split in schools. Despite a relatively new concern with health, this agenda makes SRE difficult and it takes place in unpromising circumstances with untrained teachers who are largely ill-equipped to deal with the diverse needs of young people. How young men and women express their needs and desires about sex, sexual relationships or sex education is not easy to study in schools because of the cerebral emphasis of academic subjects (Paechter 2006). Research suggests that this is particularly difficult for boys who feel impelled to establish their heterosexual credentials. The disengagement of some, particularly working-class, boys from schoolwork may be explained by the mind/body split in school subjects.

We had 325 pupils (164 boys and 161 girls) take part in single-sex focus group discussions in class, and fill in questionnaires under our instruction. These were all the pupils present on the particular days we visited one of the Year 8/9 classes at each of 16 secondary schools. One of the RC schools decided its pupils would not participate in the research. Sixty-three pupils (19%) were at faith schools, but 11 per cent of the overall set defined themselves as Muslim and 17 per cent as Christian. One of the secular schools also had a sizeable Muslim minority, but there were very few other ethnic minority, such as African Caribbean, pupils at the schools.

Our previous research (Edwards and Alldred 1999) shows that young people provide differing accounts of personal issues when interviewed at school or at home. First we wanted to get young people's perspectives on sex education from their everyday school settings. The young people here are 'in role' as pupils, and this is how we will refer to them in this chapter. This distinguishes them from the young people interviewed in non-school settings who were sometimes a year or two older, but, more importantly, were not enmeshed in school communities.

Our key finding is of clear differences between boys and girls in their preferences for school-based sex education, not only in what they want but how they express it and the reasons they give. Their 'views' are significantly nuanced by context, including type of school and focus group dynamics. Accounts elicited within groups are of interest because of what these suggest is valued or permissible within the peer group, which discourses reign and which are subordinated (Burman 1994b), the reason why Chambers *et al.* (2004) also used group discussions to explore young people's peer group sexual cultures. Whilst individuals completed their own questionnaires, this was in their classroom context and in the presence of their peers. The distinctness of the accounts from pupils in faith schools suggests either the influence of these schools, or of the parents choosing them, over and above pupil gender differences. Most importantly, these different accounts are deeply embedded in social and locally nuanced discourses of what men's and women's lives are or should be, in a broader cultural context of increasing commercial pressures around sexual practice and desirability, and entwined with discourses about childhood and the 'pupil as child'. We start by describing the current pressured contexts for their accounts at either faith schools or at secular schools, with a remit to consult local communities.

Values, schools and consulting 'the community'

DfEE (2000) stipulates that the school's SRE policy be developed in consultation with parents, governors and the wider community and reflecting the values of the community it serves. The Sex Education Forum (2004: 4) tries to reassure that 'Consultation with parents about the content and organisation of SRE is likely to build their confidence and avoid some of the common misunderstandings', but reminds that 'People cannot always agree' and whilst 'misunderstanding is potentially destructive, ... disagreement is not a sign of failure'. The revised NC sets limits on the values that can be written into the policy as it has an explicit values statement including 'respect for self, others, society and the environment' and 'the core values of justice, responsibility, care, love, commitment, marriage, protection and preservation'. The values framework that each school should agree with its parents/carers, children, teachers and local community should be in line with this (SEF 2004: 2).

Blake and Katrak (2002) in the SRE, Faith and Values Project found that misunderstandings about SRE are common among parents and carers; but so too are misunderstandings about faith groups' perspectives on sexuality and misplaced assumptions about their opposition to SRE. However, there is clearly the potential for differences and tensions within and between the views of parents and teachers, young people and their parents. Appeals to 'consulting the community' are a weak strategy given the problems faced regarding sex education, gender equity or anti-homophobia in faith schools or in schools with vocal faith groups among parents or governors. In 'consulting communities' cultural norms and established power inequalities within faith communities can mean that women and young people do not have much voice in them, and when representatives are needed for beyond the community, the 'community leaders' are usually men (Blakey et al. 2006). In addition, 'race anxiety' and the concern not to offend religious minorities can lead to mainstream service providers taking a 'hands off' approach to sensitive topics in the belief that the community will 'take care of its own'. This can be deeply problematic over issues such as domestic violence (Burman et al. 2004) or sexual minorities, including lesbian, gay, bisexual or trans- or ambiguously gendered young people (Keogh et al. 2004; Ali 2006).

The Children Act 1989 established children's rights and requires that children are consulted on issues affecting them and, where practicable, their preferences taken into account. But it cannot apply to SRE and so the discourse of *children's needs* may help the lobby for comprehensive rather than restrictive sex education. As the SEF (2004: 3) says:

> By keeping the expressed needs of children and young people central to the development of SRE, it is possible to find a way forward. Parents and faith leaders can develop greater confidence in school-based SRE if we work to examine assumptions and beliefs about SRE and ensure that communication is effective. The process can also be aided by developing an explicit values framework for SRE, and by including a range of religious and faith perspectives in classroom practice.

The SEF and DfES emphasise the entitlement of children and young people from all faiths and cultures to SRE that can support them on their journey through childhood to adolescence and adulthood. The SEF (2004: 1) quotes one young woman, aged 15:

I have a faith and I trust my parents to talk to me about values. At school what I need in sex education is to understand about sex and relationships, and understand what different people think.

As we saw in Chapter 2, listening to pupils' views is stipulated by the Guidance, but their views are seriously undermined by their status relative to parents. Pupils are, of course, part of the community and key stakeholders in the school community. Schools can draw on reports of the views of young people in general, rather than specifically consult their own (although Ofsted likes to see some evidence of this too).

The Sex Education Forum and National Children's Bureau consulted with young people to develop a video resource for use with parents and governors in developing SRE policy and practice. They emphasise that consulting with children and young people can be through: the school council, classroom surveys, SRE monitoring and assessing, the web, a questionnaire at a health day, or older pupils reviewing provision for younger pupils. The discourses of children's rights on consultation and consumer satisfaction surveys echo here, but parental voices, including those of religious minorities in secular schools, are likely to be louder. The SRE guidance gives schools little help in weighting or working with direct discrepancies between expressed views.

The discourse of *information* offers a way out of the potential problem of meeting parental wishes of different faiths whilst developing practices that are both 'culturally appropriate and inclusive of all children' (DfEE 2000). The SEF (2004: 1) states:

Children and young people need opportunities to understand the law and health issues in relation to sex, sexuality and sexual health. So, for example, if religious doctrine forbids sex before marriage or the use of contraception, young people need to know and understand the legal and health implications of these behaviours as well as different religious perspectives.

Multiplicity is the answer to our question in Chapter 2 about how the aims for SRE are to be met alongside the promise of value plurality. However, boys and girls express their views and desires in different ways, and many feel that the school is not the best place for talking about these issues, illustrating how deeply engrained particular views about school, sex and the body are.

Sex on the school curriculum

As Paechter (2006: 129) argues: 'Boys and girls are seen as having different interests and abilities, different temperaments and different learning styles, different patterns of emotional development, and thus different needs in the classroom'. Self-consciousness about 'gender', that is, its socially constructed nature, does not offer teachers and pupils a way out of the production of sexed bodies and gendered subjectivities in schools. Bodies may be sexed – assigned a category male or female – but they are not necessarily sexual. Sex can be an attribution from outside in the disciplining practices of 'Boys line up here', 'Girls, tidy the pencils', but the body is passive, subjectivity in the classroom is seldom embodied.

Sex education discourse in schools (its language and practices) is how norms, values and identities about gender and about the individual's relation to their body are produced. Placing sex on the curriculum breaches at least two boundaries. Suggesting that the body might occupy the focus of the class's attention is threatening to this established order in which children's bodies are 'sidelined, if not erased, for the purposes of education' (Paechter 2006: 122), since bodies are to be subdued, contained, controlled and kept out of the way of the main, important business of improving the mind (Foucault 1977). Putting sex on the curriculum also threatens the assumption that children are not sexual beings (Jackson 1982; Corteen and Scraton 1997; Jenks 2005). Constructing the child as sexually unawakened leads to schools treating pupils as sexually neutral (Epstein and Johnson 1998). To the rescue: a developmental model of the child, which tries to hold in tension a non-sexual present with a (potentially) sexual future for the child. Couple this with a risk analysis that highlights early sexual experiences and we see the key features of sex education over the last decade. The erotic has been sanitised from contemporary sex education (Wilson 2003; Isherwood 2004; Ingham 2005) and as Thomson and Blake (2002: 187) state: 'The focus, then, has been on young people as they become sexually active as opposed to a view that sexuality is an integral part of personhood throughout childhood'.

Negativity about sex is embedded in SRE policy to inhibit young people's sexual expression through teachers' 'scare tactics' focusing on danger and the risk of HIV or unplanned conception. Sex taught in a negative way, devoid of reference to pleasure, fails to connect to young people's lusty interest in it. Two alternative risks are that out of a respect for the 'awesome', 'magical' or powerful nature of sex, it is routinely left outside of the curriculum, or that it is trivialised and domesticated, reducing erotic encounters to merely physical interchange for which only factual knowledge is needed (Wilson 2003). In the latter we see the treatment of the body as an object, as in education about healthy eating, for instance. The body may be an unruly object but it can be known and therefore 'mastered'. Sexuality, similarly, can be safely contained, and this move effectively distances the learner from their experience of, in favour of their knowledge of, the sexual body. Little surprise, then, that girls report physical pleasure and the clitoris as totally absent from both school and home-based discussions of sexuality (Holland *et al.* 1998) and that we are shocked by, for instance, the suggestion (e.g. Isherwood 2004) that masturbation be encouraged as part of building self-esteem and self-understanding.

Setting ground-rules for discussion provides pupils and staff with clarity about boundaries and etiquette. Distancing techniques, such as vignettes to discuss scenarios in the third person or using a post-box for raising issues anonymously, help to manage the anxiety and excitement elicited. Not all teachers are comfortable with the material, the pedagogic style required or the dynamic usually entailed in delivering sex education. Another common suggestion for making the sex education classroom more manageable is single-sex teaching. A generation ago, girls were 'told about' menstruation separately from boys, by a woman teacher, nurse or 'lady' visitor representing a sanitary towel manufacturer.

Some theorists of masculinity, such as Seidler (1995), see sexuality as particularly threatening to men because they have learned to be suspicious of the spontaneity and surrender involved. They regain control of it only by rendering it a performance, devoid of intimacy and the potential for vulnerability. Sex education might raise specific issues for boys, even before its breach of the 'public' sphere by private issues is considered.

General discussion about boys and girls and how they should be taught in schools builds upon cultural norms within families and communities about the appropriate time to talk about sex and sexual relationships and to whom. Not only do schools find dealing with sex on the curriculum difficult, as we have seen, but families from particular communities also have difficulties. We found significant differences in views of sex education not only between boys and girls but also by type of school, reaching beyond individual religious affiliation. This finding about school ethos is not surprising since New Labour governments have encouraged schools to develop their own ethos.

Some faiths, such as committed Christians and some Muslim communities, hold strong views about the appropriateness of 'public' discussion of sexual relationships or activity, especially in coeducational groups. The SRE Guidance states that: 'Single sex groups may be particularly important for pupils who come from cultures where it is only acceptable to speak about the body in single gender groups' (2000: 11), generally understood to refer to Islamic cultures.

Faith schools and pupils of faith

About a third of British state schools are faith-based, and since New Labour policy has allowed faith primary and secondary schools to become voluntary-aided, this has encouraged demand. Since 1998 more than seven Muslim, 30 Jewish orthodox and reform, a primary and a secondary Sikh, a Greek Orthodox primary, a Seventh Day Adventist secondary and an evangelical city technology college have become state-aided. The overwhelming majority of voluntary-aided schools remain Christian, with more than twice as many Church of England as RC primary schools, but more RC secondary schools. Ofsted and the DfES testify to good academic results, but critics argue that the selection of pupils is the reason for their success in the academic league tables. Faith schools have a legacy from the relationship of Church and state in the nineteenth century (David 1980). Church of England head-teachers claim that church schools exist to serve their local community and do not necessarily serve middle-class families. A government report into interracial violence in Oldham in 2000 found growing concern that faith schools increase polarisation and lack of trust between different faith communities, particularly where local children are educated separately according to religion. There is a clear and unresolved tension between forms of multiculturalism and faith-based voluntary schools serving not only their own faith, but any faith or none for a minority and the school's role in promoting social cohesion.

Another concern about faith schools is gender equality. All schools will have a duty to promote gender equity from April 2007, and how will faith schools square that with their beliefs about women's roles in the family? Will the academic curriculum become the preserve of the boys in faith schools, since Islamic, RC, Jewish and evangelical Christian elders argue that girls should be educated according to women's family roles? There are specific concerns about sex education, since RC schools teach abstinence rather than safer sex, because, as one nun who until recently taught sex education put it, 'you have sex once for each child'. Few schools have nuns teaching today, but they do invite Life or other anti-abortion charities into school to talk to pupils as part of sex education. The religious and secular principles about sexual morality are deeply held, leading to numerous conflicts over gender equality, heterosexuality and children's right to information to protect their health.

Faith-based schools are popular with parents of all faiths and none since they are seen as embodying 'middle-class' values of discipline, order and family commitment over and above high ranking in league tables (Pyke 2003). It is the family values and caring ethos that appeal to Muslim or Christian parents – although these qualities are not only found in church schools. In our LEA there were only RC, Church of

England or secular schools to choose from, and most children go to their nearest. However, all four faith school head-teachers told us that their parents valued their caring ethos and family values whether they were Christian or Muslim. We decided to explore pupil views about sex education by comparing pupils in faith and secular schools, noting the complication that one secular school had a sizeable Asian minority, most of whom were Muslim.

Family cultural and religious background, whether Christian or Muslim, is not necessarily an indicator of faith. For Muslim children, their sense of ethnic Otherness in this majority white city made them more aware of their Asian ethnicity and Muslim heritage. Some pupils in the secular schools were unsure about what to write for 'Religion, if any', with one asking if he was Christian because he was white. Conflating religion and ethnicity occurred for some pupils since the white children's lack of familiarity with naming their ethnicity hindered their thinking, while the Asian children were accustomed to accounting for their 'difference'. A Christian history confers a default religion from which it is imagined others differ. Alongside gender, we compare faith and secular school pupils' views, and there is one key issue that differentiates Asian and white pupils' views.

Of the three faith schools that participated, two were Church of England, one of which was 'high church' and very similar to the RC school where one teacher interviewed was against sex before marriage and felt it was not the business of the school to promote contraception. However, there was a socially liberal attitude towards sexual orientation and concern was voiced for pupils who might be lesbian or gay. One of the faith schools extended a Christian ethic of care to young lesbian and gay pupils when prompted, but another seemed to believe that, like teenage pregnancy, this did not apply to their pupils. However, it is hard to know whether the teachers interviewed accurately characterised the school ethos.

There is diversity in how Muslims view Islam, and what is considered correct and morally acceptable, as for Christians. Reformist and feminist Muslim scholars have challenged the idea that Islam requires men and women to live in accordance with prescribed gender roles or impedes women from being sexuality autonomous. However, progressive Muslim scholarship may not be available to young Muslims exploring their sexualities. Most Muslims (and indeed non-Muslims) *believe* that Islam prohibits any same-sex sexual activity and that homosexuality is irreconcilable with being Muslim (Ali 2006). It is all too easy for schools and sex educators to leave this alone and let minorities 'look after their own'. In practice this might leave young people who are questioning their sexuality vulnerable. Instead specific and sensitive support should be available to all young people according to their individual needs (DfEE 2000). We turn now to what the various pupils told us about their preferences for sex education.

Pupils' views and values

We explored pupils' views on three main questions:

- whether teaching young people about sex and relationships should be the role of schools or parents;
- who is preferred for the delivery of SRE in school and what skills or qualities are most important; and
- whether single-sex or mixed classes are preferred for SRE.

In the single-sex groups, discussion of each question was unprompted, but on the questionnaire, for each question, they could distinguish between the different topics:

- sex;
- relationships;
- contraception;
- if and when to start a family;
- pregnancy and birth;
- values and beliefs;
- feelings and emotions;
- teenage pregnancy;
- health and illness; and
- sexual health.

Questions about school and home responsibilities were framed as *talking about* sex and relationships, but our questions about SRE in schools concerned *learning about* sex. This distinction between receiving information/'education' and discussing or confiding personal experiences is sometimes lost in young people's responses, because of the strength of feeling about the importance of *confidentiality*. Confidentiality was their paramount concern. This meant that they often resisted talking about these issues to teachers. The move from 'learning' to 'telling' about intimate matters has a clear gendered dimension. Chambers *et al.* (2004) found that boys' discussion groups tended to use the term 'talking about sex' rather than 'asking for advice' and noted that the association of advice with ignorance or vulnerability may make it gender-charged. In our study, this distinction overlaps with home and school over their role in discussions of sex and relationships. In general, we support a similar interpretation that boys are sometimes uncomfortable with being needful of information or advice in groups of their male peers.

All the pupils were overwhelmingly in favour of SRE in schools, especially around *sex* and *sexual health*, as opposed to *relationships*. That SRE was as important as exam subjects was the most frequently expressed view. The desire for knowledge was underpinned, recognising how important sexual health information is for keeping themselves well. This tallies with previous findings about school sex education that the school is the most significant source of information about sex for young people (Wellings *et al.* 2001). Girls tended to see SRE as more important than academic work compared to boys, as Figure 1 shows. For instance, more boys than girls saw SRE as 'less important than exam subjects' and more girls than boys rated it 'more important than exam subjects'. In the focus groups, several of the girls agreed it was probably the 'most important stuff you learn'.

These reflect the historical presumption that sex education relates to girls' concerns with pregnancy and babies, and the association of boys with academic subjects or the hegemonic masculine tenet that boys don't want or need to talk about such matters. Slightly more boys than girls saw SRE as 'important, but private, so not for school to cover', and both boys *and* girls at faith schools were especially likely to see SRE as just 'as important' as exam subjects but as 'private'. This reflects the liberal notion that 'private' concerns are a domestic matter, distinct from the historically male public sphere.

Occasionally comments about 'family matters' being none of the school's business were made. This constructs young people's sexual development as a family matter, as indeed does the parental right to

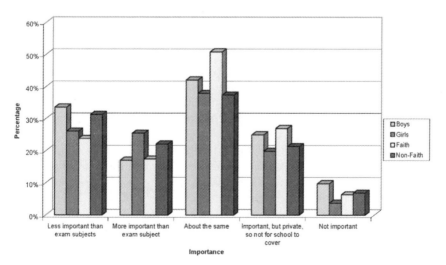

Figure 4.1 How important do you think sex education is?

withdraw pupils from SRE. This illustrates what Brannen and O'Brien (1995) call the 'familializing' of children: placing issues such as their sexuality firmly within the family can be problematic for some, notably lesbian, gay or bisexual young people. However, the overwhelming majority of boys and girls, in their separate discussions and their questionnaire responses, saw an important role for schools.

In the course of discussion with their classmates, even those few who believed it ought to be the parents' role to talk to young people about *sex* admitted that for some pupils schools had to play this role because parents did not or could not. This was especially true for boys and regarding matters of *values, relationships* and *family* as opposed to *sex, sexual health, STIs* and *contraception*. Sometimes there was a distinction between gaining *information* from school and discussing *feelings* and *values* at home.

PA: Do you think you should learn about sex and relationships in lessons?

Boy 1: Yeah, because if you don't and your parents don't talk about it, you're going to get in trouble

Boy 2: Yeh my auntie doesn't

Boy 3: A lot of parents don't

Boy 4: My dad talks about relationships

PA: Does he? And do you feel able to talk to him about sex as well?

Boy 4: Yeh, [giggling]

PA: Do you think they're quite glad the school talks to you about sex?

Boys: Yeh, saves them doing it

Boy: It's in case you ask embarrassing questions

Boy: They probably feel awkward

In 'it saves them doing it', SRE is framed as a substitute for talking with parents, where parental and sometimes their own embarrassment was the issue. Mostly, parents were constructed as lacking the capacity to discuss personal matters with their children, but this could be a gloss on young people's own embarrassment.

Mothers and school friends were usually the preferred person to talk with, although boys occasionally referred to their fathers as their ideal (see Figure 2 for preferences for talking about *sex*). A preference for school friends or family, rather than school, emerged for talking about *sex, relationships* or if they felt *pressured to have sex*. School friends were the people most pupils, especially girls, wanted to talk to about these issues. Pupils at faith schools though showed more of a leaning towards parents than to school friends even for these issues, particularly the girls and especially for talking about *sex* or *pressure to have sex*.

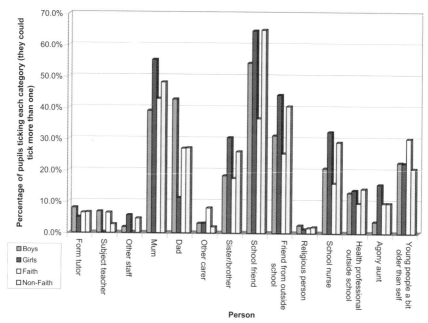

Figure 4.2 Who do you want to talk to about sex?

For talking about *relationships*, though, girls preferred their friends by far to their mums, although mums were the second most popular preference. Boys did not mention friends as often as did girls, again chiming with accounts of friendship amongst young women (Hey 1997). Boys did mention fathers more than the girls. The school nurse was next most popular among both, but form tutors and other teachers were much lower down the list. Interestingly, pupils at faith schools mentioned mums more than friends for relationship discussions, preferring therefore to keep discussion of *sex* and *relationships* in the family, matching the 'family-oriented' description faith school head-teachers gave of their pupils. Muslim boys in discussion groups in Louise Archer's (2003) study constructed parental roles through the gender-differentiated breadwinning male versus domesticated female roles, which carried over into their own relationships with their emotional and nurturing mothers and 'strict', 'hardworking' fathers. There may be an association with faith or faith schooling and a privatised sense of *mothers'* role particularly in discussing intimate matters with their children. This was hard to confirm because it was such a general finding across our data. There was also a much more common preference among boys than girls for dads for talking to about *sex* or *pressure to have sex* (as opposed to mums or friends), suggesting a specifically sexual (rather than emotional) terrain for (ideal) father–son discussions.

School nurses were most commonly identified for talking about *sex*, as opposed to *relationships*, in line with expectations of medical sources of sex education. For girls, the nurse was also significant in relation to *pressure to have sex* though. Other external health professionals were mostly significant as people to talk to about *sex* or *pressure to have sex*, but form tutors were slightly more popular than external professionals for talking about *relationships*, especially for faith school pupils. The pedagogic rationale for form tutors conducting SRE because they know pupils best did gain some support from pupils to the extent that they indicated they would be reasonably comfortable talking about *relationships* and having value-based discussions. However, for discussing sexual issues they far preferred the school nurse or external professionals because this was seen as lessening embarrassment and protecting confidentiality.

The significance of peers – either friends (especially friends *out of school*), older siblings or cousins – echoed the findings of Holland *et al.* (1998). The single-sex discussions confirmed that 'talking about' relationships, meaning sharing feelings and concerns, was particularly the role of peers. Boys especially referred to older brothers or male cousins, and girls mentioned friends, sisters and their mums more than the boys did.

PA: What could you talk to your parents about?
Boy: They never take it that seriously really
PA: So, mates? School mates?
Boy: Mates out of school are best

Sex education – a school or family matter?

Girls and boys differentiated *sex*, which they expected to learn about in lessons, from *relationships* and *feelings*, which they were reluctant to discuss in class. Boys asserted this in their responses and discussions and did so more often than the girls.

Boy 1: You're asking about things we should learn in lessons? We should know about things like condoms and how to put 'em on
Boy 2: And how to have safe sex and things like that
PS: But you don't want to talk about your feelings, emotions?
Boy 1: Not to teachers in school, no. To mates and family
Boy 2: If you had a bigger brother, I haven't mine is younger, but if you did have, someone like that.

Sometimes boys prioritised social aspects of the relationship with their preferred confidante over that person's actual knowledge-base:

PA: Is it better if it's from your form tutor?
Boy: No, somebody else, like a friend or somebody older from the school
Boy: A cousin or something
PA: And do you think the information they have is always right?
Boy: Probably not always, but most of the time
PA: So you might take it with a pinch of salt?
Boys (chorus): Yeah

The reasons why most mentioned their peers were to do with 'being understood' by someone who's 'been through it' and 'knows what it's like these days'. By implication the age and social differences between themselves and teachers created a gulf that could make such discussions either difficult or less relevant than with peers. The RIPPLE study concluded that pupils felt more able to talk openly in peer- rather than teacher-led SRE (Strange *et al.* 2002b), and Kidger (2004) found young people attributed authenticity to peer educators' accounts which meant they engaged more intensely and more personally. Peer education is more developed in SRE than any other subject for this reason, but there have also been suggestions that it is of particular benefit to the peer educators themselves (Strange *et al.* 2002a) and that greater clarity and agreement over aims and learning outcomes might sometimes be needed (Kidger 2004).

Girls preferred school nurses and, secondly, outside experts. Boys no more preferred nurses than form tutors, curiously. The preference for outside experts, interestingly, was even stronger for pupils at faith schools, although they were notably more keen to talk to form tutors and RE teachers about *feelings*. They seemed comfortable sharing emotionally intimate discussions, and saw these as related to their values education, but preferred not to share discussions about *sex* with their teachers. Unsurprisingly, RE teachers were not significant preferences for pupils at secular schools where they are not necessarily linked to the school's pastoral system.

The most popular response to the overall questions about who should teach or provide SRE lessons was 'People who are trained to provide sex education' for all but two of the topics: that is, for *sex, relationships, contraception, when to start a family, teenage pregnancy, pregnancy and birth, feelings and emotions*, and *sexual health*. However, the RE teacher, particularly at faith schools, was thought most appropriate for learning about *values and beliefs* (although *when to start a family* might also have been considered value-based). Predictably, the school nurse was thought most appropriate for learning about *health and illness* and *contraception*, especially by girls, but also by pupils at faith schools, probably reflecting pupils' awareness of their teachers' views of contraception.

Overall, form tutors were not a popular choice for SRE, although more popular than subject teachers. *Relationships, when to start a family, teenage pregnancy, values and beliefs,* and *feelings and emotions* were the topics on which form tutors might play a role (in third or fourth place preference), as opposed to *sex, contraception, pregnancy and birth,* and *sexual health,* for which school nurses, sex educators or sexual health experts were preferred. This shows clear recognition of the specialism of sexual health experts relative to teachers. It suggests that training for teachers on SRE might focus on helping them gain confidence in value-based and relationship-related discussions and pedagogy, rather than improving their knowledge of, say, contraception.

When asked why they wanted people other than teachers to provide SRE, they described their embarrassment at discussing sexual and personal matters with teachers they already knew. It seemed that new or specific teachers would not necessarily be a problem, because it was about the potential to disrupt existing relationships. The following illustrates the common themes of embarrassment, and of the privacy of feelings, in relation to teachers, and the preference for 'someone you don't know'.

PA: Who do you want to learn it from?
Girls: (chorus) Somebody we don't know
Girl: The school nurse or somebody that comes in
PA: So you all agree? What are the reasons for having somebody you don't know?
Girl: So when you tell them something, they don't know you
Girl: You don't get embarrassed like in front of teachers
Girl: Well, you'd be embarrassed the next day with a teacher
Girl: We don't want them to know all about us
PA: Is it about privacy?
Girl: Yeah. It's like your own feelings … it was our form tutor!
PA: Who would you rather?
Girl: The school nurse
Girl: In PE, this nurse came in telling us about your periods and stuff
PA: And was that OK?
Girl: Yeah [several voices at once]

Privacy was a very common theme in the boys' groups, but the following also reveals the significance of social setting as opposed to simply who is teaching.

PA: Would you rather be talking to your form teacher or somebody you don't know about sex?
Boy 1: Someone you don't know [several at once]

PA: Why's that then?

Boy 1: Cos if you're embarrassed about something you can tell them and you won't see them again

Boy 2: It's embarrassing if it's a tutor cos you see them every day

Boy 3: Cos they might ask you 'Are you okay now?' in front of the whole class, and then you've got to explain to your mates

Boy 2: You wouldn't tell *them* about your relationship

Boy 4: You don't want to talk to a teacher about your girlfriend or anything. No.

Boys commonly related such discomfort to the fact that a prior relationship with a form teacher would be disrupted, its usual boundaries breached. Pupils wanted privacy for their feelings, their discussion of actual relationships and for asking questions. The intimacy and potential vulnerability of discussions linked with their relationships with girlfriends, for instance, was something they were keen to resist with teachers. In the extract above, Boy 3 envisages a one-to-one interaction with a teacher and, in common with his classmates, assumes that 'talking to' involves making personal disclosures. The prior relationship that stands to be affected is his relationship with his peers.

Buston and Wight (2004) found that teachers new to pupils were among those eliciting high participation levels in SRE and conclude that teachers' active concern to create a safe environment is probably more important than simply how well they know pupils. We agree with them that the involvement of specialist staff (from inside or outside of school) should not be discounted because they do not know the pupils well. Indeed, it might be that particular issues such as sexual orientation can be discussed more confidently by and more comfortably with external professions, ideally in a whole-school equalities framework, but teachers must be, and be seen to be, working in partnership with such visitors (Douglas *et al.* 2001).

Girls' groups commonly constructed certain women teachers as 'nice' and who 'wouldn't tell', but for the most part restricted the role of teachers to their subject. Distrust of teachers came up among boys and girls, and in almost every small group there were comments about how anything one gave away about oneself would be 'all around the staffroom the next morning'. Girls in particular feared the judgements they felt teachers would make about their sexual morality as a result of any questions they asked, so that a request for information about contraception, for instance, would be taken to imply they were sexually active. It was clear that being seen as 'at it' was esteem-damaging for girls. They accused 'the boys' of making this same attribution, and shouting out and hooting with delight at supposed disclosures of personal information. This same process of personalising a question, assuming it reflected a current need for the information, functioned differently for boys because of the different value assigned their (hetero)sexual activity. The same personalisation 'error' is made by boys in response to any other boy's reference to homosexuality which is taken to implicate, with those negative connotations, the speaker's sexual orientation, as Nayak and Kehily (1997) show.

Kehily (2002) and Measor et al. (2000) have observed in sex education classrooms that asking questions (so long as they are not seen as 'stupid' questions) was more likely to boost boys' status among the peer group. Being seen as 'at it' or 'up for it' and any indications of heterosexual activity or interest were welcomed, and indeed sometimes this impression was deliberately cultivated. We observed this vividly in our class sessions to feed back research findings, which reproduced some of the reported dynamics of sex education teaching. In their questionnaire responses, we note that for the boys there was no corollary of the girls' concern about their reputation in the staffroom. In spite of girls' feisty, sometimes aggressive, defence of their sexuality, this old sexual double standard still coded sexual activity as reputation-damaging for girls, but not for boys (Lafrance 1991; Lees 1993). Although, as Cowie and Lees (1987) argue, girls are damned if they do, and damned if they don't. The girls' awareness of this limited what they felt able to ask in class, and provided reasons for who they preferred to deliver sex education. This confirms work by Holland et al. (1998) and later by Measor et al. (2000): girls indeed scrutinised their own performance through the eyes of a 'male-in-the-head'.

Sex is status-enhancing for young men, so long as it is strictly within heterosexual boundaries (Mac an Ghaill 1994b; Nayak and Kehily 1997). Indeed, boys who do not show motivation towards heterosexual gratification or brag about it risk derogatory labels as unattractive or gay (Moore and Rosenthal 1993, cited in Nayak and Kehily 1997). Heterosexuality functions as a strong norm within schools, the presumed centre around which other sexualities are enacted and marked as deviant (Epstein and Johnson 1994; Epstein et al. 2003).

Breach of confidentiality was not a concern in relation to school nurses or experts coming into school. Trust and confidentiality were occasionally mentioned in relation to friends: some pupils said this was why they preferred talking about personal issues with friends outside of school, but many girls said that school friends were generally good at respecting their confidentiality. Sometimes girls distinguished *learning about* from *talking about*, but often it was assumed these went hand in hand, so that the problems with teachers were related to what you ended up telling them. For others, the very fact of a subject teacher 'trying' to speak to you about sex or relationships would be highly embarrassing or 'cringey'.

We asked: 'What's most important to you about who teaches about sex and relationships?' and offered the following options:

- 'What information and training they have'.
- 'Whether they're good at talking about this sort of issue'.
- 'Whether they can talk about their own experiences'.
- 'That they're not embarrassed'.
- Whether they will listen to your experiences'.

Being *good at talking about this sort of issue* emerged as the most important consideration for pupils, *information and training* was rated second, followed by being *listened to* and not being *embarrassed* (see Figure 3). Being *good at talking about this sort of issue* was by far the most important factor for girls, and for pupils at faith schools. This highlights the significance of the social dynamics of SRE lessons, as did comments about SRE being uncomfortable with older, male or science teachers, and underlines the importance of appropriate pedagogies. In line with boys' stated preference for 'People trained to provide Sex Ed', they identified the *information and training* a person has as very important, as well as being *good at talking about this sort of issue*. Pupils at faith schools seemed to value more highly than other pupils whether speakers could *talk about their own experiences* as well.

Hilton's (2003) study of the views of slightly older boys similarly identified the importance of teachers' ability to talk about 'this kind of stuff'. This included adopting a relaxed style of pedagogy, being non-

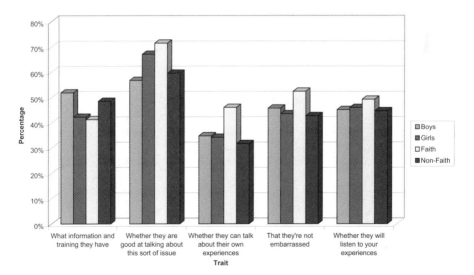

Figure 4.3 What's most important about who teaches SRE?

judgemental, but also highlighted the importance to the boys of teacher's ability to control the classroom. Similar characteristics were observed in successful SRE classes by Buston *et al*. (2002a), who note that while a strong sense of humour and making SRE fun could make pupils more likely to participate, this was not sufficient: willingness to discipline the class, prohibiting comments about individual pupils and hence engendering trust, was the most important thing.

Single-sex classes for sexy bodies?

Given the gendered thread through all the answers, it is no surprise that single-sex classes were generally more popular than mixed classes (31% compared with 23%), but a surprising number of pupils (26%) said they didn't mind (see Figure 4). However, boys' and girls' views differed as to whether they wanted single-sex or mixed groups – in the predictable direction:

PA: Should lessons about sex and relationships be taught to boys and girls separately?
Girl: Yeh, cos they take the mick out of us.
PA: So what would be good about being in girls only?
Girl 2: You'd feel like you could ask more questions.

Girls preferred single-sex to mixed groups (37% against 19%), and boys slightly preferred mixed groups (27% against 21%). Preference for

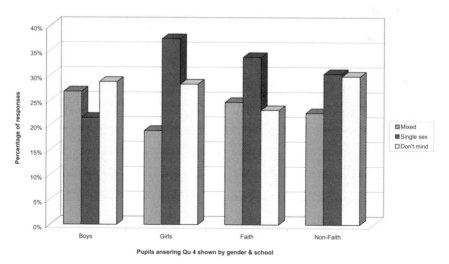

Figure 4.4 Would you prefer mixed or single-sex classes?

single-sex classes was a little stronger among pupils at faith schools. Pupils wanted single-sex groups for learning about *sex, contraception, pregnancy and birth, teenage pregnancy* and *health and illness*, but were happy with mixed classes for *values and beliefs, relationships,* and *feelings and emotions.*

In the discussion groups, girls criticised boys' use of sexual innuendo during SRE classes, echoing comments by teachers and nurses about the difficult and sexualising dynamics of mixed classes. The potential of boys and girls to learn from and about each other was lost, particularly for boys to learn from listening to girls' questions and comments. Besides not wanting to ask questions in front of the boys 'because of embarrassment' or 'because they make judgements about you' (as we discussed earlier), another reason girls often gave for girl-only lessons was that boys 'don't take it seriously' and are too busy using every opportunity to make sexual remarks.

One meaning of 'not taking it seriously' was that boys' disruptive behaviour undermined the importance of SRE as a whole: 'they just laugh and make silly comments', 'they tease and take the mick'. Another version of this argument named specific issues that the boys 'just can't handle, but we want to discuss'. The example of homosexuality was given by a girl who said she thought it was important: 'because there's more people going the other way these days' but 'the boys just take it as a joke'. Hegemonic schoolboy masculinities often require boys to invest in homophobia (Mac an Ghaill 1994b). Nayak and Kehily (1997) describe how young men struggle to talk about homosexuality in anything other than an abusive or jocular way, and how homophobia functions as a chance for male exhibitionists to perform and have confirmed their heterosexual masculinity. While young men's uses of homophobia are neither monolithic or unambiguous, the way pupils' cultures 'organize themselves collectively around issues such as homosexuality is intermeshed with gender dynamics' (1997: 150).

Overall it was clear that the girls wanted single-sex classes, but for discussion of *relationships* they were more divided, some preferring to stay separate from the boys, but others identifying mixed classes for discussing love, values, and having children. The boys, however, wanted mixed lessons, and mixed sessions did not inhibit them as it might the girls:

PA: So having girls there won't stop you asking questions?
Boys: No
PA: Do you mind if it's a man or a woman teaching you?
Boys: No [several at once]

Despite this common type of remark, their comments and behaviour

suggested they were immensely self-conscious in class and that asking
questions was 'loaded' for them too, albeit in different ways. They did
not appear to 'feel free' to ask whatever they wished to know because
'embarrassment' was an even bigger focus of boys' groups than girls'.
They did not want to risk revealing themselves as sexually
inexperienced by asking a question, and, as mentioned earlier, did
not want to disclose personal information. Postures that implied they
were interested in sex and, better still, sexually experienced were
important, but so too was guarding their privacy. *Control* over what
was revealed about themselves (by themselves, their classmates or
teachers) was of the utmost importance.

Although a few boys preferred a male teacher, many didn't mind, in
contrast to the girls:

PA: Is it better to have a woman [teacher]?
Girl 1: Yeh much better if it's a woman teacher
PA: Yeah? Why's that?
Girl 1: Because it happens to them as well
Girl 2: They'd be more confident
Girl 3: Can ask more private stuff to a woman

It became clear that the preference for single-sex SRE classes was
because the social dynamic was simplified, and in particular, the
immediately heterosexual dynamic was removed. Whilst heterosexualising assumptions still occur in single-sex classes, the girls would not have
to deal directly with harassment from boys. However, the homoerotic
taboo might be so strong that it might be even harder to 'come out' in an
all-boy group than a mixed class. A single-sex environment reduces the
number of audiences the boys perceived themselves as 'playing to' (the
girls, their (male) mates, the teacher) and, for the girls, removed the
irritation and disruption of some boys' behaviour. One boy made a
notable remark about valuing mixed sessions for the chance to learn
from girls which illustrates that not all the boys invested in the mixed
classroom for its opportunity for macho displays of heterosexuality or
for heterosexual titillation. However, hegemonic masculinities among
this peer group seemed to require heterosexualising and objectifying
girls/women at every opportunity, at least in the setting created by these
boys-only groups for discussing SRE.

The Asian girls, all of whom were Muslim, preferred single-sex
classes for all topics and cared more about this than whether they were
taught by teachers they knew or professionals they did not know, so
long as they were women. These girls' overall preference was to have
the immediately heterosexual context removed, and to operate within a
wholly single-sex environment for SRE. The Asian boys, almost all of
whom were Muslim, also favoured single-sex lessons and preferred a

male teacher, but had mixed views about familiar/unknown teachers. We got the distinct impression that some of the white boys would prefer SRE without the heterosexual dynamic, and without the intense peer group dynamics that arise among boys in single-sex environments, but this was probably not easy to say directly since they were discussing this in boys-only groups. Even these groups rewarded the macho posturing of some who clearly wanted other boys as an audience for their behaviour. The girls showed more trust in other girls, but were wary of getting a 'reputation' and being judged harshly by teachers or the boys.

Learning about sexy bodies in the classroom

The overall support among Year 8 pupils for school-based SRE, implying the appropriateness of developing the curriculum for this year group; the perceived benefits of external professionals; and the preference of girls and some, including Muslim, boys for single-sex lessons are our foremost findings. Girls' preference for single-sex sex education is reported elsewhere (Measor *et al.* 1996; Strange *et al.* 2003; Measor 2004), and we found it extended across both faith and secular schools, and to the gender of staff. Concerns about classroom dynamics regarding teachers and pupils suggested that simplifying the social situation would be preferable, reducing the number of different 'audiences' that girls and boys, each in different ways, felt were judging them. The boys were self-conscious about how they were perceived by other boys and by teachers primarily, whereas the girls were concerned about judgements that teachers or the boys might make about them. Given this, single-sex classes for at least parts of SRE might benefit male as well as female pupils, and in all sessions firm ground-rules can help create a non-judgemental atmosphere and reduce inappropriate remarks.

The school nurse was trusted for that most highly valued quality, confidentiality. Girls identified her as a source of sexual health information more frequently than boys, and importantly also as a source of support regarding *pressure to have sex*. In the next chapter we explore the role of school nurses relative to teachers. Teachers were not popular for explicitly sexual (or medical) topics, for which external sexual health professionals were preferred, nor for emotional or value-related issues that pupils preferred to locate at home or, most importantly, out of school. All schools might meet resistance regarding values and relationship discussions because pupils construct them as 'none of the school's business', and friends and peers are instead identified for discussion of relationships, and faith school pupils identify family members. Pupils at faith schools were more welcoming of value-based discussions with teachers than other pupils, but they were keen that sexual matters were covered by external visitors.

The reluctance of male pupils in particular to discuss *relationships* in class brings them into conflict with the government agenda for SRE to include teaching particular values regarding relationships. For young men, the idea of broaching personal matters on school turf perhaps provoked fears relating to their emotional vulnerability. The anxiety caused by breaching social boundaries elicits from some boys 'the mixture of fear, fascination, comedy and masculine display' that Nayak and Kehily (1997: 147) and others have shown to be regular features of classrooms. Young men perform their heterosexual masculinities through sex talk (Wood 1984), homophobias and embodied elements such as posture, gait, gesture and even volume of speech – talking loudly seems to help consolidate those masculinities to which sexual prowess is important (Nayak and Kehily 1997). Remaining *in control* in the face of threatening topics is all important and so, for instance, 'the homosexual threat' is Othered or physically isolated like a contagious disease. Uncritical attention to the body is not simply to be celebrated. We return to boys' self-convincing performances of masculinity in Chapter 7.

The sanitisation of what is meant by sexuality from the formal curriculum, the superior status of educating the mind, the notion of the child-pupil and our understandable anxieties about the potential for abuse limit what is understood by sex education. Even in today's brave new SRE, schools do little to educate the body, except for attempts to get canteens to put into practice what pupils are taught in lessons about a healthy diet. The sexual body is nowhere educated. Learning might involve naming body parts and sexual health risks, but the body and its pleasures are cleanly 'out of sight'– the superior mind is master to the body with its mistrusted, licentious ways.

It is this that allows explicit sexual talk to disrupt classroom norms and middle-class sensibilities, and in this sense they can be resistive of the school regime. It can 'be a scream', enliven and entertain (so long as the butt of the joke is someone else). However, we do not wish to romanticise young people's use of the sexual to resist school culture, when it involves enacting homophobic, heterosexist, misogynistic or otherwise oppressive meanings. As Epstein and Johnson (1994: 223) argue, pupils' sexual culture is not necessarily transformative and 'may police boundaries even more effectively than government decrees or school rules'. Sex may be deployed in dominant or subversive ways (Kehily and Nayak 1996) and to abuse other pupils or teachers (Nayak and Kehily 1997). As Skeggs (1991) and others have argued, young men's resistance can be problematic for young women.

Another consequence of this sanitisation of sexuality from schooling is the construction of the pupil as ideally non-sexual, which means that where sexuality is apparent, it may shock momentarily, as in boys' intrusive sexual remarks, but may be defined as bad behaviour or pathology and viewed as essentially problematic and deviant even when it is not offensive. We see this in relation to those pupils whose sexuality is visible – school-aged mothers – in their rhetorical exclusion from the category of child in public discourse, from the 'pupil' within educational discourse, and often, in practice, their exclusion from schools themselves, as we find in Chapter 6. At present, therefore, sexuality is contradictory in schools, reflecting the ambivalence about sexuality evident in mainstream British culture: on the one hand, the *normalised absence* of sexuality from official education discourses, and on the other, its pathologised presence (Phoenix 1987). What this means in practice is that pupils' sexuality is either denied or ignored or perhaps interpreted as something else. If this is not possible – for instance, the pregnant belly cannot be interpreted other than as evidence of sexual activity – one of the pathologising interpretations that 'rescues' the non-sexual girl-child is perhaps an overwillingness to interpret her sexual activity as non-consensual.

Education for the sphere of life in which sex and relationships occur might be far more than we currently take it to be. It might actually be a more practical education than we can currently imagine without anxiety clouding our thoughts. Recognising the sexuality, and perhaps sex lives, of pupils might be the basis of an honest, pragmatic, supportive sexualities education. It could be more than information about sexuality as a physical phenomenon (sex, STIs, etc.), and more than the government-approved morality of sex, instead providing practical examples and role models rather than letting erotic literature or pornographic videos be the only sexually explicit material most young people see (Wilson 2003). How much more helpful if young men and women are helped to decide what they and others understand as 'good manners' in a particular social (sexual) context. Pupils cannot discuss their experiences with teachers unless they have a problem. Our abandonment of young people to struggle individually in isolation with this important area of life, after only meagre education in even the broadest interpretation of the Guidance, appears irresponsible once we have put aside our view of sexuality as essentially shameful, indecent and therefore taboo (Wilson 2003). We might employ a concept of young people's 'sexual careers' that parallels the approach taken to preparation for their work lives. This approach might offer much of use in devising a helpful sexualities education which would also include historical evidence to demonstrate the political nature of the current gender/sexuality regime. Such radical agendas could not be pursued in our research sessions, alas. Instead we focused on features of SRE delivery that could be expected to fall within the PSHE coordinator's sphere of influence and that pupils could probably imagine done differently, but we allow ourselves to think more creatively in the final chapter.

Paechter's (2006) analysis of the Cartesian legacy highlights the need for a radical reconception of the gendered body, in which sex and gender are not separated in a dualistic way but are both seen as socioculturally *and* physically produced, and in which embodiment is a fundamental part of identity, so that individuals are seen as 'fully and always embodied' (2006: 132). This, she believes, should help undermine the dualisms of male/female, sex/gender and mind/body.

A more embodied approach to sexualities education would better acknowledge the role of desire and the physicality of sex, and would show precisely why overly rational approaches that sideline the body are of little use to young people in lusty moments. 'Outing' the body is no more guaranteed to be progressive than its sudden eruption into the classroom as a result of a boy's (hetero)sexualising harassment of a girl, and like this, can reinforce existing power relations. However, whilst the body remains so relegated in the sphere of education, how are young people to gain from sex education the knowledge, skills and attitudes to be able to pleasure and honour their own and anyone else's bodies?

chapter five

Healthy bodies in healthy schools: Joined-up policy and the health/education divide

We now address SRE from a health perspective. Does this necessarily reduce the agenda to one specifically around sexual health? Is there a contradiction between the policy reframing it as 'sex and *relationship*' education and stipulating that, in practice, health professionals ought to be more involved in its delivery? We add the school nurses into the picture and explore their professional perspective on SRE in schools, discussing how they delivered SRE in our study schools, their views of and values regarding SRE and the TPS. We then offer a broader analysis of the values underpinning health professionals' work and the difficulties of work on health in schools. By making explicit the assumptions underpinning the health discourse, the taken-for-granted features of education discourse can be seen and the implications for sex and relationships thrown into sharp relief. Two distinct discourses of SRE pedagogy emerge: 'educating' or 'informing' young people (not boys and girls), differentiated by the role accorded embodiment. 'Informing' conceptualises SRE as a rational matter of safeguarding the body's health, and 'educating' implies a moral, cerebral approach that engenders the young person to self-govern in particular ways. Some of the obstacles to good SRE begin to make sense: SRE becomes a site of potential conflict between health and education. Given their different framing of young people and of the role of professionals, we end by considering the significance of a new health education initiative and its potential to move beyond the 'turf war' symbolised by this 'culture clash'.

The work of school nurses is currently receiving a boost, as at time of writing new guidance has been published jointly by the DH and DfES (2006), giving grounds for optimism as an instance of the 'joined-up government' New Labour promised. The broader cultural context for SRE initiatives still has some dinosaurs to contend with, however, and even if they represent minority views according to polls of parents, they are sometimes presented as a broad constituency: 'right-minded' people concerned to 'protect children' and defend 'the family'.

Policy context: education policy or health policy?

Thomson (1994) has shown how sex education was framed to deliver health outcomes through education from the 1960s, describing the tension between social authoritarianism and public health pragmatism in the development of sex education in the UK:

> Where medical discourses dominate, the aims of sex education are defined in terms of limiting unplanned pregnancy and the spread of STDs. Where moral discourses hold ascendancy, the role of sex education is formulated in terms of the legitimacy of adolescent sexual activity and concerns over the sexual exploitation of women and children. (Thomson 1994: 41)

Since the nineteenth century there have been varying constellations of family morality versus medically based discourses of pregnancy and childbirth (David 1980; Thomson 1994). By the 1960s progressive educational pedagogies and holistic approaches such as in PSHE gained ascendancy, meaning that, even though the aims of sex education were still framed by public health imperatives, the development of self-esteem and contraceptive awareness was seen as the basis of sexual responsibility which 'inevitably perpetuated a gendered, information based, and reproductively oriented approach' (Thomson 1994: 44). By the 1980s the influence of feminist anti-sexism work in education and youth work, challenging stereotypes of gender, sexuality and race, produced a critical approach to sex education which included the questioning of gender roles, sexual identity, control and consent in sexual relationships. A growing consensus between education, health and voluntary agencies developed which was not represented in government, media or public opinion (Thomson 1994).

Describing a 1976 debate in the House of Lords about the government funding that the FPA used to receive to provide teacher training on sex education as marking the end of what had been a consensus between education, health and voluntary agencies, Thomson writes that independent interest groups taking both traditionalist and progressive stances exploited the absence of a clearly defined rationale and code of conduct for sex education and the 'ideological differences' between government departments. The Department of Health was left to defend the FPA single-handed, without the support of the

Department of Education: 'Tensions between these two government departments have played an increasingly important part in the politics of sex education in recent years' (1994: 45).

During the 1980s Thatcherism employed a health discourse and one of 'moralism' instrumentally (David 1989), for instance, meeting moral traditionalists' demands on teaching about homosexuality but not on abortion or under-16s contraception (Durham 1991). In fact,

> where medical, health or scientific research was involved, the Thatcher government was likely to hearken to the advice of its civil servants, the [British Medical Association] or scientific bodies. But on other, more populist issues, where it believed expertise was a guise for sexual liberalism and where there was a chance to lambaste the Labour Party, then the government took up some of the hopes of the moral majority. (1991: 140)

The discourse of public health and 'promoting healthy schools' has become prominent on New Labour's agenda, together with targets, initiatives and policy statements. The National Healthy Schools programme, launched jointly by the DH and DfEE in 1999, aims to promote the health and well-being of those in schools and to ensure that schools are safe places for children to learn. Several of its strands are relevant to PSHE (SRE, safety, and emotional health and well-being) and through support provided by LEA 'Healthy Schools' teams some of the PSHE agenda may gain higher prominence in schools. However, PSHE is not all health-related and includes careers advice, work-based learning and financial awareness as well as drugs education (Ofsted 2005), and some teams feel that their remit exceeds what their staffing enables. This addition of health objectives to the curriculum could help raise the status of PSHE in schools. Employing the discourse of health certainly makes the aims and language of PSHE more concrete-sounding and objective and less value-laden and intangible than emotional literacy or self-esteem, aims of hitherto low-status PSHE. Health outcomes may be more easily demonstrated than emotional or psychological outcomes, meeting the audit culture's requirement for performance indicators. Less cynically, this joint work can be seen as a truly collaborative enterprise resisting the artificial separation of mind from body.

Listening to children and young people's views is now recognised as good practice across services, but the discourse of the consumer of health services was established earlier than in education. Children were only later identified as consumers by corporate marketeers, and assumptions of their economic dependency kept their potential worth low: schools represented the last bastion of authoritarian paternalism of the 'do as I say because I know what's best for you' variety. Exactly how schools and educational projects today hear what children and young people say requires close scrutiny (Burman 1991; Alldred 1998; David *et al.* 2000). Tensions exist between parents and pupils as consumers of education – with SRE at the forefront of the pupil–parent power interface. The construction of morality and values as a family matter makes SRE parents' business, whilst the construction of sex as personal locates it back with young people themselves. Some recent research concludes that achieving 'healthy schools' is hampered by not listening to and incorporating insights from children's experiential accounts (Duckett *et al.* 2007).

Cultural context: The 'birth control school scandal'

Provision for a massive increase in school nurses to help reach 'the Government's aim of having at least one, full-time, year round, qualified school nurse working with every cluster of primary schools and their linked secondary school by 2010' was announced by the DH and DfES in March 2006. Schools Minister Andrew Adonis described this as the Government expanding the work of school nurses and giving 'greater priority to school nursing as part of the Government's drive to improve the health of children and young people'. The Chancellor's 2006 Budget reduced VAT on condoms and other contraceptives to make access easier (HM Treasury 2006).

The *Daily Mail*'s headline was 'A birth control nurse for *all* schools' (24 March 2006), but further coverage vented tabloid outrage about the infringement of parental 'rights': 'School birth control outrage' (p. 2) and 'The pill handed out like smarties' (p. 26). Its 'More girls to get contraceptives without their parents knowing' illustrates the 'secret abortions' discourse which constructs it as a parent's right to know about and have some control over their child's sexual health.

However, nurses are defended as best placed to assess need, prescribe appropriate medication and provide specialist contraceptive advice, and clearly their medical status is significant here. The resource pack for school nurses issued simultaneously reflected the access and confidentiality concerns that we highlight here:

> nurses should 'provide and promote confidential drop-ins' for students at school or community venues and even text or email pupils who cannot attend sessions face-to-face. They must be 'aware of confidentiality issues' which give under-16s the right to contraceptive services without parental consent [and] 'Ensure the school policy on confidentiality is clear, meets the best interests of

young people and is workable by staff'. (*Daily Mail*, 24 March 2006)

This new policy reveals the ambiguous status of parents: over-represented in DfES policy yet not visible in sexual health services sited in schools. This is further illustrated in the *Mail*'s coverage of a recent 'controversy' about a school helping a 14-year-old girl get an abortion without her mother's knowledge: 'Mother-of-five Sue Axton, who recently lost her High Court battle to overturn Government policy which allows girls under 16 to terminate a pregnancy without their parents' knowledge' (13 March 2006). Axton is quoted saying: 'This is undermining the role of parents. I believe this will encourage children to have under-age sex'. The *Mail* claims that 'thousands of 13-year-old girls have been handed the morning-after pill by health service staff without their parents' permission' and finds an academic to contest the evidence of the teenage pregnancy report (SEU 1999) that such schemes cut the teenage pregnancy rate. Whilst the 'mother-of-five' points to potentially worrying gender dynamics which 'put even more pressure on girls as boys can say "It doesn't matter, you can get the morning-after pill"', the Government itself is described as 'relentlessly pressuring young people to be sexually active' by Jack Scarisbrick, chairman of the anti-abortion charity, Life! This formulation of young people's vulnerability to corrupting sexual pressure from 'outside' constructs young people themselves as without sexual desire or agency. The popularity of this corruption discourse in the *Mail* is shown by its use in another article that day to describe both a 14-year-old boy convicted of rape (as mesmerised by violent pornography) and his victims (as robbed of their innocence).

Whilst attracting the nickname the *Daily 'Hate' Mail* for its right-wing vitriol, the corporate desire to sell newspapers by sensationalism scuppers any coherent ideological position. Standard kneejerk reactions to school sex education are employed, such as the 'even little children' discourse: 'I do believe it's beyond the pale if this is extended to primary schools', Axton is quoted as saying. There was, in fact, nothing new to report about school nurses' roles, just their increasing number, yet this was enough for 'obscenity', 'pupils' and 'girls' to be mobilised for headlines – an opportunity not to be missed by those selling tabloids. A readers' poll (25 March 2006) reported that 69 per cent of voters agreed the 'school nurse birth control scheme was outrageous' (actually worded 'obscene' on the poll) and 31 per cent that it was 'responsible'; however, this poll allowed repeat votes, as in fact was required in order to see the results.

This media coverage illustrates the polarised and gendered debate in the UK. In the same week, the liberal/centre left newspaper *The Guardian* covered supportively the trip by three head-teachers to study The Netherlands' delivery of SRE to much younger children than in Britain. The resources promised since our interviews (to help nurses provide 'contraceptive advice to pupils and emergency contraception and pregnancy testing to young women') are a welcome response to the constraints reported by the nurses in our study.

Sexual health experts?

We interviewed 15 school nurses – all women – serving the 17 secondary schools in our study. Nine were interviewed individually, and some of these also participated in the two focus groups of five and six nurses in their area teams. Most had responsibility for a secondary and four primary schools, creating a caseload of about 2000 children each. School nurses saw themselves playing a key role in SRE in schools, one clearly distinguished from teachers, and they spoke with notable unity about their professional perspective, specific training and competence on sexual health and in delivering sexual health education to young people. They saw themselves as *sexual health experts*. Unlike teachers, SRE was their central focus; they had complete confidence in their knowledge of sexual health matters; and they emphasised their specific training on this issue. Their role as health professionals was to give information both on an individual basis and to whole classes. As health educators, *sexual* health education was increasingly their primary concern (as opposed to hygiene, alcohol or drugs education). All the recently trained school nurses had taken a core unit on delivering SRE to young people in group settings. One had taken an SRE option on the school nurse qualifying course earlier, and the only two who had not originally done so, were now undertaking it. The culture of continued professional development was striking, and three were completing degrees. They all felt ideally qualified for, and had clear ownership of and expected to deliver core elements of SRE. However, they felt their professional expertise should be better recognised and more fully used: only one was satisfied with the role she was currently playing.

Their actual roles in schools varied, as did the integration of their whole-class sessions into the SRE curriculum. Most nurses provided two services: health 'drop-in' sessions (without an appointment) during one lunch-hour per week, and a few SRE sessions – mostly providing an hour's class teaching for Year 7 on puberty, and an hour for Year 9 on contraception and, in those schools where Year 9 had a second session, an hour on STIs and abortion. Most nurses reported that the information they provided was tailored specifically to the needs of Year 9 pupils, but many agreed with the PSHE coordinators that it could profitably be moved down a year. Only a couple were involved in curriculum development.

The 'drop-in' clinic was popular with pupils, especially where it had been running on the same day for a while. Its success relied on the pupils knowing the school nurse. The whole-class sessions acted as an introduction so that the pupils were aware of, recognised and trusted her. Girls made far more use of this than boys, as might be expected, and presented with different issues. Drop-ins were a source of information about sexual health, and pupils called in with questions following whole-class sessions. As a proportion of drop-ins, however, the amount of time spent on sexual health was small compared with general medical questions, small injuries, school- (especially exam-) and family-related stress. What sexual health consultancy occurred was with girls, and boys typically brought playground or sports injuries.

All the nurses embraced whole-class teaching fully and all but one felt confident in their skills, communication style and their use of hands-on materials. Most said that pupils appreciated and rapidly adjusted to their 'no-nonsense', forthright approach, and their ability to handle crude language – making sessions constructive and engaging directly with young people's current understandings. The distinction between nurses' and teachers' roles in school produced a different pedagogic style and rapport:

> They can ask me absolutely anything and I won't be fazed by it. I'm not going to send them out of the classroom. They can't do that with the teachers: at the end of the day that's a power relationship. The teacher has the power, they don't, whereas I think in my class the power is far more evenly distributed.

This nurse may underestimate her institutionally sanctioned power as an adult and a health professional and indeed, the power vested in her by the school, albeit temporarily for the duration of the class, but like others she shows an awareness of the importance of rapport and confidence in the pedagogic relationship. Most aimed to set a relatively informal tone by introducing themselves by their first name and by using humour wherever possible. They modified their 'language' when teachers were present and generally preferred it when teachers were absent. They suspended the school's usual language embargos, although those in RC schools in particular noted and respected that schools reserved the right to monitor the content of sessions.

Pedagogies for the boys?

Interactive pedagogic techniques were used to promote active learning, *engage the boys* and to minimise embarrassment so that they could work with quite large, *mixed* form groups on sensitive topics. For instance, they used distancing techniques such as relationship case studies or vignettes as the basis of class discussions, helping young people discuss issues without getting too personal or disclosing anything they might regret. To minimise embarrassment they used a 'question box' so that issues could be raised anonymously. They set up competitions between table groups to see which group could complete the 'condom test' quickest, and reported that these and other game-style activities worked well in providing enough of a focus on activity to prevent embarrassment or showing off distracting from the session's content. Alternatively these can be seen as catering to (most) boys' learning styles and enjoyment of competition and activity. All the nurses stressed the importance of minimising embarrassment and the value of particular pedagogical techniques to do so. They had clearly considered whether distinct teaching styles and activities were required for delivering SRE to boys and to girls.

Where it worked well, the school nurse's specific role and expertise was properly recognised and her contribution was integrated into overall provision, and the school was not wary about her contribution to SRE, recognising pupils' right to a confidential service. The drop-in sessions were seen as an important element of school provision and a place for pupils to direct the 'tricky' questions that teachers were not comfortable with or able to answer, not as merely a way for pupils to 'get out' of lessons (where it was not at lunchtime). Pupils' trust in the service was helped by continuity of staffing, whole-class contact with the nurse, and permanent and private (and privately accessed) office space. Effective work in schools usually relied on close cooperation with a sympathetic teacher, usually the PSHE coordinator, who valued the nurse's expertise, and at its best, nurses were involved in curriculum development. Three nurses had great relationships with teaching staff, were appreciated for their manner and described as 'wonderful' and 'very at ease with the kids'.

However, most of the nurses felt frustrated that their training for delivering SRE was not being put to better use by their school, with the lack of awareness of their specific training contributing to their underuse. They worried that health information would be left to teachers who might be uncomfortable or ignorant of up-to-date information, compounding public ignorance on sexual health matters. They also wanted their expertise in planning and delivery of SRE to be used. However, they were also aware of the perceived status differential between themselves and the teachers in school.

Not 'the nit nurse'?

Whilst all the school nurses saw themselves as sexual health experts trained to deliver sexual health education to young people individually and in group settings, they did not feel that they were recognised as such in schools. Instead their overwhelming perception was that their status in school was damaged by their traditional role as 'the nit nurse', a name that indicates the changing concerns about the health of the nation's children. They were committed to their own professional development, and those without training in classroom delivery were undertaking it. They spurned the 'nit nurse' label that they felt saddled with by both staff and pupils. They felt their expertise was underrecognised at all levels of the education system, with pupils seeing them as much lower status than teachers, and devoid of teachers' professional status. This was reflected in changes made to their work without discussion, and schools' expectation that they could make use of them however they saw fit. Whilst they acknowledged that they worked in an education system, with its own priorities, they pointed to where they could have made valuable contributions had they been consulted. The legacy of the nit nurse was that their work was seen as marginal to the 'real' work of school. Their association with the body, in an educational setting concerned with the mind, rendered their work low status (Paechter 1996). A consequence of the mind/body split is that nurses' potential contribution to young people's knowledge and understanding of their gendered and sexual bodies and health was underappreciated.

The increased national prominence of SRE meant schools were revising their provision, but nurses were not having the specialist input they sought. Their organisation into cross-school teams meant that they were developing their expertise beyond their particular school, comparing schools and swapping good practice among them. In addition, their team approach meant that, despite their tight schedules, they could cover, for instance, a whole year group in one timetable slot if necessary, or in the case of one nurse who did not yet feel confident working with a double class of boys, a more experienced colleague led the testicular cancer session to model good practice. With their huge case-loads and health responsibilities – immunisation, routine health checks ('school medicals'), nutrition and helping schools improve the health of pupils – it was remarkable that SRE was such a priority. We detected a new priority in the school nursing service that schools were unaware of that addressed concerns about sexual bodies and emergent sexual identities, and particularly gendered needs and learning styles.

The critical factor in achieving a good programme of SRE was the relationship between the individual nurse and PSHE coordinator or, in faith schools, the head of RE, and the overall attitude of the SMT to delivering health agendas, with some SMTs expecting outdated 'scare tactics' to be employed. All the nurses were enthusiastic about 'Clinic-in-a-Box' (CIB) and hoped young people's sexual health clinics would reduce barriers to young women (and men) accessing sexual health services. Those at faith schools recognised that the SMT and governors would not welcome such a service in school, but this seemed less about staff's values than about avoiding panicking parents.

Clinic-in-a-Box: Local sexual health services for 'young people'

The Clinic-in-a-Box initiative was set up in 2000 with funding from Health Action Zones, the Single Regeneration Budget and Sure Start, responding to the drive to reduce teenage pregnancy and STI rates. Since young men were not accessing mainstream services, this was an attempt to take services to where they 'hang out'. The 'box' contains a range of contraceptive supplies (particularly condoms and emergency contraception), pregnancy tests and sexual health information. CIB projects are run by health staff in non-traditional settings: often in youth clubs or schools. Two schools started to provide lunchtime drop-in CIB sessions where health education classes already in the curriculum introduced the staff and service so that pupils could visit for individual consultations.

One CIB had been established very successfully in an area of generally low health service use, located in a converted house close to a school and run as a project targeting young people at risk of exclusion. It was staffed by a family planning doctor and two nurses. Young people sought contraceptive services, sexual health advice and termination counselling. Barna *et al.* (2002) studied this CIB, admiringly reporting its staff's flexibility, range of information and support through drop-in sessions, focused group-work and health education teaching resources. Youth workers supported young people in accessing the service, and staff developed relationships with pupils in youth work settings where discussions performed an educational role.

Young people described CIB as feeling private, confidential and comfortable. One boy said: 'at mainstream clinics you have to wait with loads of adults who might know who you are' and another that 'talking about stuff not just picking up condoms' was important, as was the fact that the staff 'don't make you feel awkward. You can ask them anything and they tell you the truth and you know what you say will not go any further' (Barna *et al.* 2002). Trusting the confidential health practitioner relationship, and the practitioner as a source of factual information, echo points made by the Year 8 and 9 pupils about preferences for SRE delivery. Even the relationship context seemed more consistent: 'I would rather come here to sort out my problems than go to someone at school. At least you see the same person who gets to know you better' said one young person. Whilst funded as part of the Teenage Pregnancy Strategy, the CIB initiative was welcomed as part of the general need to develop specific health services for young people.

The health authority continued to run CIB services as they grew into general health services, specialising in sexual health advice and contraceptive supplies for young people. The number of CIBs has expanded since our research: four of the 17 secondary schools now host CIB sessions, as do local youth clubs, the college, the football club, a couple of community centres, projects for young offenders, the 'Youth Inclusion project' and a day-centre project for young mums. Generally they run for an hour a week at lunch time or 7–8 p.m. providing a free and confidential service, 'even' for under-16s. The Government's 'RU thinking about it?' website (www.ruthinking.co.uk) demonstrates an awareness of young people's concerns that inhibit their trust in services:

> *Will your doctor tell your parents you're having sex?* Doctors and nurses follow a professional code of practice which makes sure that even if you are under 16 you have the same right to confidentiality as adults. This means they should not pass on any information about your visit unless they think you are in serious danger and even then they should discuss the issue with you first.

It also seeks to engage young men and women separately with a 'for girls' and a 'for lads' page. The latter includes 'Sex: a girl's point of view' and the 'Pantman' game where STIs chase the player and condoms are 'the best protection' but will only last a limited time.

Local cultures of sex and gender

Young people's participation in drop-in or CIB sessions with school nurses reflected the usual gendered patterns of medical service use: more girls attended overall and usually with a friend. The one specifically male sexual health issue raised was usually after the boys' session on testicular cancer, when a few boys would seek reassurance about their testicles. Solely on this issue did the nurses feel that the lack of male nurses hampered SRE effectiveness for boys. Many nurses advocated coeducational information-giving sessions followed by single-sex sessions for pupils to ask questions and check under-standings. They all said they expected to work with boys as much as girls, and knew no teams that included a male school nurse. They described how the dynamics this created in the classroom might contribute to boys' apparent need to 'play up' or 'play to the crowd' in SRE sessions. Notions of playfulness can function to excuse boys' disruptive, sexualising or potentially harassing behaviour within child-centred pedagogy (Walkerdine 1981).

Despite being one-to-one, drop-in sessions were primarily requested for information-giving rather than medical consultation. It was not the case that nurses' roles differed in the classroom from the 'drop-in' service. Sometimes girls wanted contraceptive information before they had scheduled class sessions, or appointments were for those where class material had become 'relevant'. The nurses had a clear sense of how sexually active young people were and recognised peer group pressure around this, and so embraced dispelling myths within their SRE:

> Most of the children aren't doing it [intercourse], but are made to feel it's not normal if they're not.

They recognised the traditional sexual and gender culture of the city and its 'static' population. They located women's empowerment in the context of conventional gender relations and the bearing these had on attitudes to unplanned pregnancy, safer sex and fertility decisions. Those working in faith schools felt they were viewed with suspicion by staff and their work limited to biological facts so that teachers kept hold of the Family Life programme. Several felt self-conscious talking to pupils about contraception and abortion, but were clear that their professional codes meant that schools had nothing to fear – they did not *advocate* abortion or condone underage sex, but simply *provided medical and legal information*, which young people had a right to know. Their information-giving remit was important in defending their work here.

From a health perspective, providing information about avoiding unplanned pregnancy is morally neutral: the information itself is not moral in content. However, the way it is presented can be, as when framed by moral obligations for children or young people. This defence of sex education avoids moralistic claims that young people are encouraged to engage in underage sex by SRE (a claim which the SEU's 1999 report debunked). However, this risks reifying an understanding of medical facts as free from bias, as somehow not 'social', and distinguishes between informing and educating. If the nurses' approach to SRE was about informing young people to make their own decisions, the teachers' was one of educating pupils on social and moral issues, inculcating social values, such as the undesirability of teenage pregnancy (DfEE 2000). This is the nub of the difference between health and education discourses, and the implications for professionals' construction of the identities of young men and women in schools are quite profound.

Nurses' views of the Teenage Pregnancy Strategy

Many nurses agreed with the teenage pregnancy agenda, although most said that this had been their approach before – another instance of their work being underrecognised. They welcomed the national emphasis and hoped that funding would follow. Some nurses explicitly sought to reduce unplanned conception rates, but most emphasised the broader role of sexual health education in providing information but accepting young people's own culturally situated and gendered decisions about sex and pregnancy. It is clear in their accounts that their primary client is female, although this is only usually implicit:

> What I'm interested in is: at the point they got pregnant, had they got all the information that they needed? Could they have prevented it had they wanted to? Whatever choice they make, as long as it's an informed choice and they make it because it's what they want to make, I've no problem with it. ... I don't just pick out the pregnancy bits. I think it's equally important that they know how to protect themselves from sexually transmitted diseases. They get a lot of mixed messages and I want them to know there is somebody there that they can talk to, who won't tell their parents and who will point them in the right direction. That it is confidential.

They saw providing information as empowering, which draws on a liberal model of education:

> I want them to be able to say to their boyfriend who says 'I'm not using a condom because they don't work, they split', 'If you use them properly they are very reliable'. I want them to be equipped with that information. I am there to give them the information, and they act on the information.

But they rejected a service evaluation by conception or teenage pregnancy rates:

> I don't consider I've failed if a girl gets pregnant as long as she's got pregnant because she knew where advice was and chose not to access it.

There were scandalised media reports about the imminent deregulation of emergency contraception during our study, meaning that the 'morning after pill' – as it is still known, despite health professionals' efforts to publicise its effectiveness up to 72 hours after unprotected intercourse – became available over the counter from pharmacies. It could be bought for £20, although with some questioning by the pharmacist (about whether it's been taken before). The nurses were highly supportive of this, although some were worried that the cost would prove prohibitive to many local girls. This widened availability in terms of where and at what times it was available, but, they stressed, considerable health education work was needed for young women to understand its availability. Educating – in the sense of delivering information – was embraced within their health practitioner role.

In practice, emergency contraception did not become freely available. Individual pharmacists are at liberty to decide whether or not to dispense it, and even if they do, facing potentially judgemental questioning, publicly, over the counter, would be enough to put off some women, young or not. At least three local pharmacies were run by Irish or Asian pharmacists who refused to sell it, in which case asking and being refused could feel shameful and stigmatising. A study of 18 community pharmacists and six general practitioners (GPs) just before deregulation found that the majority had overwhelmingly negative views, in contrast with those of their professional bodies (Barrett and Harper 2000). Their opposition to deregulation resulted from vividly articulated assumptions about female sexuality – that women are sexually irresponsible, chaotic and devious, ideas which have a long and tenacious history – and Barrett and Harper (2000) concluded that the values of individual pharmacists, particularly their attitudes to women's sexuality, would undermine the provision of emergency contraception. Local cultures of gendered attributions of shame must, in practice, limit access.

School nurses as informants?

As we have shown above, the nurses saw themselves as providing up-to-date, accessible, medical information, empowering pupils to make informed decisions, about which nurses were not judgemental. Regardless of whether they were conducting whole-class sessions or individual consultations, young people were their *clients*: the service was young person (and mainly female-) rather than school-centred. The principle of 'the child's best interests' and the primacy of their client's needs guided their work: pupils, as 'young people', were entitled to access services. This principle contrasts starkly with the educational view of pupils: schools are not oriented towards young people as consumers of the service, but to their parents (Tomlinson 2001). Pupils are not stakeholders in dominant education discourse. A young person's right to sexual health information at school is juxtaposed to parents' rights to withdraw their children from SRE. School nurses recognised this contradiction with teachers' orientation to parents but criticised teachers' muddled thinking about meeting young people's needs. Teachers are simultaneously serving pupils, parents, the SMT and governors. SRE Guidance (DfEE 2000) makes clear that it is the responsibility of the head-teacher to be guided by the views of the governors in consultation with parents.

This relatively new constellation of constructions of young people in consumerist, rights and empowerment discourses tallies with the personal responsibility aspect of wider sociopolitical ideas about 'the project of the self' (Rose 1989) and about changing forms of subjectivity in the context of social policy moves towards risk and choice (Beck and Beck-Gernsheim 1995). The neoliberal subject is fashioned through policies and practices regarding learning, schooling and families (Clegg and David 2006).

Client or community-centred confidentiality?

As health professionals, the nurses were clear they provided a confidential service for individual girls and boys and that where there were child protection concerns, confidentiality would not be breached without explaining their responsibilities to the young person. This clarity about responsibilities seemed to prevent the immense anxiety that child protection elicited in teachers. Confidentiality was consistently raised as the key to young people's decision to use services or trust teachers and was important for pupils using the 'drop-in' clinic. Nurses' clarity about confidentiality contrasted with teachers' uncertainty about their legal and professional responsibilities. Teachers experienced conflicting loyalties to pupils, parents and school – with the balance of power in favour of school and parents. This 'muddled thinking', nurses argued, led teachers to making disclosures about pupils' concerns to the head of pastoral care, SMT or administrative staff in the office.

Instances were mentioned of teachers asking nurses for information, advice about confidentiality or support for decisions about sharing confidential information with other teachers, and examples were given of school staff not fully respecting the confidentiality of the drop-in clinic – for instance, asking a pupil why they wanted an appointment or even insisting that the nurse tell them what was discussed in a consultation. One assistant head-teacher (with pastoral responsibilities) clearly expected a nurse to report to him about a pupil consultation, two deputy heads asked nurses to breach client confidentiality, and one nurse described her refusal as marking the end of her positive relationship with a school's SMT. Whilst a deputy head appointed child protection officer ought to be informed of serious concerns, the nurses recounted expected or actual breaches of confidentiality below this threshold that did not respect the nurses' professional judgement and responsibility for this decision. Schools could be very uncomfortable about pupils accessing services without parental knowledge: one head-teacher had telephoned a parent to disclose their child's appointment with the nurse. School administrators were sometimes involved in making appointments for pupils with nurses, passing information to the SMT or parents, and nurses sometimes did not trust that care was always taken to protect pupils' privacy.

The low status accorded the nurse or health matters generally becomes an issue if teachers question pupils wanting to be excused lessons to speak to the nurse because they see it as not a priority or an excuse to miss classes. The nurses believed this contravened the young people's right to privacy and to access health services and demonstrated teachers' lack of respect for young people. This reflects contrasting notions of professionalism: nurses versus teachers, health versus education. Nurses felt they owed confidentiality and a professional, individual consultation service to pupils, whilst schools felt that they were accountable primarily to parents. The nurses' understanding was of a private, client relationship whilst teachers were keen to avoid upsetting parents and 'the community'.

The SRE Guidance (DfEE 2000) stipulates that health professionals are bound by their professional codes of conduct to maintain confidentiality in individual consultations, but while in classrooms are subject to the school's confidentiality policy. Whilst a school's confidentiality policy explains that 'teachers cannot offer or guarantee unconditional confidentiality' (DfEE 2000: 30), 'teachers are not legally bound to inform parents or the head-teacher of any disclosure unless the head-teacher has specifically requested them to do so' (2000: 33). The nurses were irritated by teachers' misperception of or lack of clarity about the school's policy or its implementation. Teachers were expected to 'follow a set procedure if a child under the age of 16 is having, or contemplating having, sex', whereas health professionals can 'exercise their own professional judgement as to whether a young person has the maturity to consent to medical treatment including contraceptive treatment' (2000: 33).

Resource and other pressures

The nurses' delivery of SRE was constrained by resources and by competing professional agendas. Lack of teacher expertise in SRE was deplored for allowing the perpetuation of myths, such as that most under-16s were sexually active. Nurses resented a weekly PSHE timetable structure which meant they repeated a session to Year 9 classes over, say, eight weeks and yet they preferred this, for pedagogic reasons, to addressing all the Year 9 girls in the school hall. As we have already argued, the most significant competing agenda was the achievement agenda, and in schools that particularly emphasised NC subjects there was greater timetable inflexibility and devaluing of SRE. Overall the nurses seemed more concerned with appropriate pedagogic tools for SRE than did teachers. One described as 'typical' only finding out at the last minute that she was addressing a whole year group (rather than a class) about contraception, meaning that her planned session's materials and pedagogy were inappropriate, and many mentioned finding classes had not been adequately prepared for a session nor allowed appropriate follow-up time for questions.

Another constraint was the breadth of their remit and caseload, and term-time contracts. Having only a weekly lunchtime drop-in session sometimes was not enough to see all the waiting pupils without going into class-time; and they worried that a single weekly time-slot could be 'too late' for girls needing emergency contraception, illustrating their consciousness of gendered needs. Teacher referral was the main means of advertising the drop-in, and some were reluctant to advertise more vigorously, given the potentially increased use. The nurses were overstretched and many worked overtime to get the job done. Post-qualifying training put extra (though legitimate) pressure on their time, so it was regrettable that schools did not make the most use of staff funded, after all, from the authority's health budget.

Territorial issues

The setting for SRE was a key, if implicit theme in the nurses' accounts of obstacles and tensions. School setting determined the moral context – for instance, one nurse received a message from the head of an RC school to 'remember that this is a Catholic school and don't talk about abortion'. Whilst the nurses were sensitive to the values of faith schools, their professional role also embodies a set of values articulated as 'truth', the right to information, and a respect for clients' own values. The schools' expectation that their values overrode the nurse's reflected their sense that health was of lower status, or perhaps that this was education territory. Nurses were left in no doubt as to whose turf they were on and they were reminded of teachers' 'ownership' of the space by the treatment of their equipment or posters. Even where there was a designated medical room, some felt 'permitted' to operate a different (medical, young person-as-client) approach in those specified times-slots, but not by right. One described being 'allowed' to sit in a 'cupboard' to run her drop-in, and lamented the message this gave young people about the importance of the issues they were discussing.

The school nurses all felt that recent LEA work on PSHE planning had begun to influence schools, and several had started to enjoy a bigger role in relation to nutrition and hygiene through the Healthy Schools Standard. Whether sexual health services were located physically inside the school grounds or not was significant, and when CIBs were located in schools similar dynamics played out between the school and the service. Before CIBs, one successful initiative involved a sexual health bus, parking at school gates but beyond the school's territory – a symbolic gesture not wasted on the young people themselves. The two discourses could map in complex ways across sites: pupils and sex educators are clear about wanting SRE to encompass more than the medical model of sex, so they are hesitant about health professionals, but these professionals clearly saw SRE as more than simply sexual health. The health authority had produced an entire resource pack on sex and *relationship* education, and nurses were ready and willing to cover more than the biology of sex.

These different theoretical approaches to SRE also gave rise to practical tensions between the health and education parts of SRE, as well as regarding who delivered them. A lack of information on each side about each specific contribution added to the generalised anxiety around SRE in schools. One issue of contention was the health authority's materials for school SRE, which teachers felt was an intrusion onto their turf, although content-wise it represented nothing particularly controversial. Consultation could have saved ego damage, built trust and prevented each side from reinventing the wheel. That the local Healthy Schools coordinator was an ex-teacher rather than a health professional was read by some as an attempt by educators to retain ideological control. Conversely, it was noted that the DH's multi-faith forum to involve faith communities in reducing teenage pregnancy and supporting young mothers was without regard to education.

Engendering good practice in SRE delivery?

Barna *et al.*'s (2002) study reported that young people said they wanted sexual health services that were confidential, informal, designed for their exclusive use, had friendly staff who treated them with respect, did not require queuing in a stigmatised place and were fitted around school commitments. They also wanted staff continuity to develop trusting relationships. A key finding from its survey of nearly 300 community health or primary care trusts was that the increased use of short-term, output-driven funding packages meant skewing services to specific targets, such as reducing teenage pregnancy, 'which do not necessarily address the service needs of young people nor encourage their participation in design or delivery' (2002: 4).

Its recommendations included the need for dedicated and accessible services for young people, across a range of access routes, including community, clinic, school or college, and town-centre based services, with informal, discreet titles and a welcoming ambience. There was an urgent need to share good practice regarding services, including in young people's involvement in design and evaluation; and in 'multi-agency partnership working, where roles and responsibilities are clear and the skills of non-medical staff, such as youth workers or teachers, are used effectively' (2002: 5). It went on: 'It should be recognised and accepted that young people's health problems often require solutions which are non-medical in nature and in this context the skills of other professionals should be equally valued' (2002: 5). The need for long-term funding was seen as particularly important to establish clear roles among professionals and given that word-of-mouth is how young people usually learn of such services. Innovative services, aside from CIB in school, community and youth projects, included mobile outreach projects, one-stop shops, and young people's sessions at family planning and genito-urinary clinics. The report's recommendations echo the views of young people in our study regarding the importance of confidentiality and privacy, rapport with staff, non-judgemental attitudes and clarity about roles in sexual health education provision.

Many of the local strategies linking service provision to SRE were innovative, involving training or supporting other professionals, particularly youth workers. These helped to destigmatise sexual health services. One-stop shops, for example, are attractive because they allow anonymity about which service a young person is accessing. Half of those providing dedicated services were doing so in partnership with non-medical agencies such as schools, colleges and youth work organisations. The difficulty of partnerships within the health sector, for instance between family planning and school nurses, reflected the fragmented nature of today's health service.

Health versus education perspectives on SRE: A culture clash?

Framing SRE as a health rather than an education matter clearly has particular implications, rendering it concerned with fact, not morality, as if the two can truly be separated (Epstein and Johnson 1998). The two discourses provide notably different pedagogies for SRE that embody alternative constructions of young people (to differing gendered effects) and of the role of health versus education professionals in relation to teenage pregnancy. The health discourse views pupils as 'young people', whereas in the education discourse they remain 'pupils', constructed therefore as non-sexually active, as ideally non-sexual, with their sexuality framed reassuringly by futurity (Jenks 2005). Sexuality in the present is therefore problematic and framed as a child protection issue, about abusive or undesirable sexual activity – say, between underage pupils or between a girl and her older boyfriend (see Waites 2005). The connotations of innocence and passivity within the notion of the child have gendered effects, constructing female pupils as at risk of corruption by sexual predators, and sexually knowing girls as damaged goods (Kitzinger 1988). The sexuality of boy pupils is occluded to the extent that gendered access to power might be underacknowledged, and apparent sexuality evidence of precociousness rather than damage. By contrast, calling pupils 'young people' is a radical gesture in schools as it opens up ways of seeing them as active agents in decision-making and as potentially sexually active.

The health (information) discourse can obscure the complex processes involved in using information by presuming an oversimplified model of the subject who unfailingly employs self-control and rationality; that is, receiving information about safer sex and applying such knowledge logically in their own straightforward best interest. This forgets the 'body' or constructs it as a libidinous, 'risky', wilful 'child' to be kept under control by the sensible, disciplined 'adult' mind. It can forget the significance of sexual desire and its embodiment in lusty young people's bodies. Assumptions of rationality take sexual decision-making out of context – of desire and of complex social dynamics, views and relationships within which, in practice, it is embedded. It sustains an oversimplified and unrealistic 'subject', whose gendered and sexual body and emotions are subordinate to the mind's reason. This has damaging political implications for all those constructed as more closely associated with the body because they are the modern/neoliberal subject's Others (Alldred and Gillies 2002).

The language of *information* may, however, be helpful for sex educators drawing on a language of scientific knowledge and of entitlement to counter the popular yet discredited view that sex education promotes sexual activity among young people. Different parties will employ the discourse of information to differing effects and are invested in particular understandings of the boundaries of 'information'. For instance, for those striving to convince parents or governors of faith of the need for SRE in order to meet young people's need for honest information with which to protect themselves, such as the nurses in RC schools, this boundary might be that they merely tell young people 'facts' about contraception, while the priest, other religious leader or head of RE teaches about its morality.

Yet distinctions between education as moral and health as factual are too rigid a separation. It was clearly not the case in the Thatcherite 1980s (Durham 1991), and nor is it today. Indeed, the discourse of health is today powerful through the moral imperatives it creates as individual responsibilities. It also functions to secure the moral claim that young people are entitled to knowledge that helps them protect their health or to health care services (Article 24 of the UNCRC). Within the discourse of responsibility to maintain a healthy body is a threshold about when a mind is healthy enough or mature enough to make decisions. Judging whether someone is sound of mind has a long history, but Victoria Gillick sparked a contemporary version of it in the 1980s that demonstrates how parents' and their children's wishes can conflict (David 1989). The Fraser Guidelines are the basis for guidance to health professionals today about whether a young person has the maturity to consent to medical treatment, and if deemed competent to consent they may do so regardless of age.

Standard good practice encourages young people to tell their parents about a pregnancy, a request for an abortion or for contraceptive services. When young people are reluctant, anxious or fearful about doing so, school nurses offer support, including, for instance, accompanying a young woman to disclose pregnancy to her parents if she wishes. Whilst encouraging a young person to talk to a parent/carer, nurses respect that it is the young person's own decision. The Fraser principle applies in health to ensure that young people's decisions and privacy are respected, but there is no parallel statement of principle in education. Parents may be contacted or informed of something against a young person's wishes.

The nurses believed that their professional relationship with individual pupils trumped both teachers' and parents' perceived right to know. However, the grammar of schooling (Kelly 2001) – its language, structures and hierarchies – was very powerful and sometimes overruled this. Clarity about the balance between health and education provision for SRE and hence between nurses' and teachers' roles was an urgent priority for schools. The issues of school variability, censorship of medical content and lack of consideration of pedagogy must be addressed. The nurses often felt beleaguered and that their expertise in planning and evaluating their lessons was not given parity with that of teachers. Delineation of their very specific role and responsibilities might enable their expertise to be recognised and more valued on a defined part of the school's terrain.

A key obstacle to the provision of effective SRE became the fact that schools try to deliver *health* education in an *education* environment. In an ideal world the measurement of effectiveness would not compromise aims, and educational and health aims and measures would not be conflated. Is SRE a success if it brings down the teenage pregnancy rate, if citizens agree about family values, or if it helps people articulate their feelings and values whatever they are? Is it sexual health *education* that is to be delivered in schools, or a sexual health *service*? The 2000 SRE Guidance does, in fact, make health objectives the business of schools in its ambitions for teenage pregnancy and STI rates. Some of the conflicting impulses between health and education go right back to the inception of SRE in the SEU (1999) report. Its emphasis on SRE was for health or welfare, not educational ends (Bullen *et al.* 2000).

Healthy bodies, healthy minds?

Sex is viewed negatively in education discourse, an unwelcome interruption to the refinement of the cerebral sphere, an intrusion of the body into a place of the mind. In particular, sex is 'bad' if not contained by marriage or 'stable relationships' and reproduction is bad if it occurs outside wedlock, despite the proportion of children born outside marriage reaching 42 per cent in 2004 (compared with 12 per cent in 1980) in Britain (ONS 2006b).

Health discourses do not view sex as intrinsically unhealthy, only 'unsafe' if the young person is at risk emotionally or physically. In education discourse teenage pregnancy is to be reduced by promoting particular moral values in school. In contrast, health discourse presents information and access to services as the means to reduce teenage pregnancy. Health professionals give information about 'health' and health services, whereas education professionals teach certain values and – from the public vitriol reserved for teachers who breach society's moral expectations – provide role models.

What was the National Healthy Schools Standards when the research was conducted now provides accreditation for schools meeting the criteria for Healthy Schools Status. This remarkable collaboration draws on accreditation and certification to boost its low (cross-curricular subject) status. Sport too has low status in school curricula (Hardman and Marshall 2000). That sport and health occupy such marginal places in the school curriculum, in the gaps between NC subjects or on the edges of the timetable, illustrates the relegation of the body and its health from the curriculum – the more important business of educating the mind.

Educational discourse is about the child's mind and the inculcation of desirable qualities and abilities, looking beyond 'mere' behaviour (and by implication bodily practices) to the knowledge and understanding that inform the moral subject's governance of their body. The UK's education system is predicated on such age-banding and strict developmental hierarchy that not to have age-related guidelines for contraception is a surprising interruption of the education discourse. By contrasting features of the health/information discourse we have exposed some of the peculiarities of that most powerful discourse in our schools and in society at large, education.

chapter / **six**

'Too little, too late': Young mothers, sex education and educational values

We now consider the views of young mothers about SRE and the Teenage Pregnancy Strategy and illustrate the pervasive nature of deeply held normative assumptions about masculinities, femininities and gender relations. These young women were of Government concern in the teenage pregnancy agenda, and we were interested in their perspectives on improving SRE in order to reduce teenage pregnancy rates. We therefore add their views on sex education to those of the 13–14-year-old pupils in Chapter 4. However, we conclude that these young women's views and values regarding education and adult women's lives more generally illuminate, and serve to question, some of the values assumed and promoted by New Labour.

Whilst sexual health information evidently had particular personal relevance for school-aged parents, we do not see these young people as instances of SRE having *failed*. Instead we tried to hear what they had to say about their hopes and expectations, their family and local norms regarding early childbearing. What they said impressed upon us the need to situate their views on sex education in the context of their views about education in general, and then to situate their views of education and employment within their constructions of youthful and adult femininities and masculinities. The title of this chapter reflects a commonly held view of sex education among practitioners and we agree with this sentiment – the sex education young people currently receive in school *is* too little, too late. However, we will show how our discussions with young mothers both support this conclusion, and point to an important caveat. Better SRE might have been 'good for' these young women, but not necessarily through having the effect intended by the Teenage Pregnancy Strategy. Instead their decisions about mothering and studying have to be seen in the context of gendered and class-based community norms and expectations about parenting.

The negative experiences of school that most of them recounted confirmed other research showing how experiences of school disengagement overlap with 'early' sexual activity and childbearing (SEU 1999; Swann *et al.* 2003). Assumptions about the delivery of SRE, PSHE and even pastoral care in schools are questioned when the relationships depicted between staff and pupils are not positive enough to support either sensitive discussion or relations of care. The poor treatment some of these young women received from their schools whilst pregnant leads us to consider the education of pregnant teenagers and young mothers. Sexuality is a key marker of the adult/child distinction in Western societies, with perhaps peculiarly fierce British investment and, as we have seen, makes schooling the evidently sexual pupil an apparent problem. In the final chapter we discuss whether separate educational provision helps or hinders their social inclusion, and try to think through an alternative to treating these young women as a *problem* for education. Here we see discomfort about, and for, the pregnant body in school as well as hostility directed at young mothers-to-be outside school. Being *a mother and a pupil* does not fit with educational assumptions about learners, learning or home–school relations (Pillow 2004). Again, the gender-neutral norms of policy do not suit real, gendered and embodied young people.

These young mothers' experiences in relation to schooling raise questions about current UK education policy priorities. The pressure they feel to return to education illustrates the general pro-education orthodoxy that sees education or training for young people strictly in terms of its use in gaining paid work. Paid work itself is constructed as almost a condition of citizenship (Levitas 2005). We now add another dimension to our earlier position on New Labour education policy – a feminist critique of the pro-work agenda and attendant ideas about social mobility through education that we believe leaves young women carrying the burden of gender amid gender-neutral ideals.

Not only are working-class young women at odds with the masculine model of the neoliberal subject that is imagined to be free to become, through education, whatever he wishes, some, as these young mothers illustrate, have responsibilities stemming from their gendered identities and relationships. The particular position of these young women as *mothers* is not adequately recognised in the pro-education, pro-work climate. We asked them their views on teenage pregnancy and SRE policies directly, but it is seeing their position in the broader context that informs our critique of current education policy.

School-aged mothers' accounts

We draw on the accounts that ten young mothers gave us about their views and experiences. Eight school-aged mothers, one 17-year-old mother and a soon-to-be mother and father-to-be (her partner) told us in detail about their lives in interviews either individually, in a pair or couple, or in a group of three. Five had had their babies at the age of 15, two at 16 and two at 14 years old. Another was not technically still 'school-aged', but was attending the same project and so was invited to participate, and she had been a school-aged mother with her first baby. Four were interviewed at home with their babies present, and two of these, for part of the interview, had their own mother and other family members present. The others were either at a young parents' group in a community college or at a large voluntary organisation's Parents Into Education scheme, sometimes with the project worker present. The pregnant young woman clearly expected her boyfriend would stay in the room, so we took the chance to ask him his views too, whilst noting this context for her comments.

The context in which these accounts were produced is significant: as always, interview data are a product of the interaction between researcher and researched in the specific context and moment. Their accounts were notably not generated in schools, which distinguishes them from the pupils' views presented. Moreover, the domestic setting of some of these interviews illustrated vividly the points they were conveying – other people, their needs and relationships quietly shaped and sometimes noisily intruded upon our (education research) agenda. We did not anticipate the full significance of the research's educational association, as we discuss later.

Although we do not claim to represent young mothers in general, we have no reason to believe our participants were atypical and draw on findings from other recent studies of young mothers in the UK which identify similar themes. The research account is ours and we do not know whether the participants would share our analyses. All of these young people were white and working-class, living in areas of economic deprivation, on large estates with bad reputations, on the outskirts of the city. We were shocked by how few facilities or food shops these areas had. A trip into the city was seen as a big event. When asked about what professionals saw as their 'local' sexual health clinics or maternity services, many said they did not know that area or how to get there. This obstacle to accessing services illustrated what local practitioners had told us: that this was an area of low mobility, geographically as well as sociologically.

We describe our participants as working-class, but the discourse of social exclusion (MacDonald 1997; Levitas 1998; Milbourne 2002) usefully recognises both their economic deprivation, certainly in terms of income poverty, and their cultural location, of considerable marginalisation, isolated from the formal cultural and political centres of the city. The community was often described as inward-looking and traditional in terms of its values around gender, family and gendered authority in the family. We did not discuss social class with our participants, but as a researcher with a 'good job at the university', Pam felt very aware of her relative economic privilege and cultural capital (Bourdieu 1977, 1990). This seemed particularly vivid in relation to food, and she noted feeling unable to buy 'food' on her way home from interviews, by which she meant fresh vegetables and ingredients as opposed to take-away meals. A youth worker involved with some of the young mothers corroborated this impression of the local food culture with her agenda to teach young mothers that it was possible to make healthy food themselves and for less money than a take-away.

Here, such embodied practices of class that Walkerdine *et al.* (2001) write of served to remind us of some of the differences and power relations that structure research conversations regardless of their warmth and identifications. While Pam identified closely with these young women as she talked with them in their homes and their discussion foregrounded commonalities and shared values, travelling back across the city, she felt highly conscious of her privilege, her power in the research relationship and the role of education in her own upward social mobility. Arriving back at her office, the university felt as distant from these communities as it was alien to these young women, the journey and campus itself gave her access to better-quality foods, and she felt aware of having 'taken' these women's words into a different (academic) setting to 'make sense' of them (Burman 1992; Reay 1998). Pam's own cultural capital but childlessness prompted reflection on the role of expectations and 'choices' in relation to education and fertility: a higher degree and research contract conveyed considerable capital and palpable approval from practitioners, but worrying that she had left it too late to have a child felt a high price to pay. The women she was interviewing had babies but not qualifications, and paid the price of social disapproval for this.

Young mothers' views of sex education

These young people were highly critical of what little SRE they had received. Some had conceived before the standard Year 9 SRE and some were not attending school before conceiving. Those who were attending, when asked what SRE they'd received, said 'practically nothing' or described one-off sessions disrupted by sexual banter and 'fooling around'. They were disappointed with their SRE because it was boring, too little, too biological (just about fertilisation and pregnancy) or just worksheet-based, comments which reflect those of young people in other studies, with two notable exceptions, discussed shortly. They were all strongly in favour of sex education in schools, and even though they said it had been of little help to them, they saw its potential. They said they would have welcomed more information, at an earlier age, with an increased emphasis on making them realise the risks they were taking. When asked if they had discussed sexual relationships in SRE or PSHE, one complained that they'd looked mostly at job interviews and another said the class was too disruptive and that, with everyone screaming, 'you couldn't hear a thing'.

Among the few recollections of actual SRE classes were some notably poor-sounding sessions, although admittedly we do not have the teachers' accounts of these. Three young mothers described how upset they were by an extreme anti-abortion video shown in class. They were angry that there had been no chance to discuss the issues raised, to hear alternative views or to choose to opt out of the session. We were troubled by the content of this resource and the pedagogic failure to allow a supported discussion of it. The fact that pupils from more than one of the city's schools appeared to have seen the same video suggested that an anti-abortion campaign group had sent their materials directly to schools since neither the LEA nor health authority had supplied it. We suspect that over-stretched staff may have accepted these without viewing them (free materials arriving might not be subject to much scrutiny) as it seems unlikely such materials would be approved in these schools – two having since become hosts to CIBs providing emergency contraception. We read recognition of the existence of such materials in the SEF's comments on faith, values and SRE. The SEF notes that whilst it and Ofsted recognise that outsider visitors can make valuable contributions to SRE, it cautions that: 'It is not good practice to allow visitors who try to frighten children and young people, or provide information which is factually incorrect (this often happens in relation to termination of pregnancy)' (SEF 2004: 2).

By contrast, the two most positive accounts of SRE came from young women who were proud of the fact that they *had* participated, had 'been bold' and got past their embarrassment to put condoms on a demonstrator. They prided themselves on a matter-of-fact approach and had found these sessions helpful and empowering, and they viewed their classmates as 'immature and silly' for being disruptive.

Easier access to condoms was the single most important change they all wanted. The young mothers at home each suggested condom availability and young people's sexual health clinics in schools.

They're saying it'll make [young people] have more sex, but at the end of the day they'll do it anyway and at least they've got protection.

Kids need warning. They are going to experiment and need to know what risks they're taking.

Adults need to get real about teenagers and sex.

As parents themselves they were determined to be open about 'sex and risks' with their children, they wanted good SRE in schools, and several declared they would buy condoms for their children well before they were needed. Some were well informed and very positive about new approaches in SRE such as minding 'flour babies' or carrying around dolls for 24 hours, working out the cost of providing for a baby, and having young mothers talk about their experience in school. They were critical of girls who cooed over and idealised their baby and said they wanted one too. They wanted to tell them about the crying, the broken nights and, for one, the feeling of 'being trapped indoors'. Like other young mothers, they were sometimes ambivalent about motherhood (Holgate and Murakami 2005).

They did not oppose schools talking about values, relationships or emotions, but their active concern was with sexual health information. They felt, as did the Year 9 girls, that asking a question in class would implicate them and draw negative judgements about their sexual morals – and it was judgemental responses from teachers, not other pupils that concerned them. They did not trust teachers not to gossip, and the teachers they most feared having to disclose information to were called 'gossipy', 'bitchy' or 'snidey'. They wanted their questions answered by nurses, sexual health experts, people *external* to the school. Both learning from and disclosing to teachers was unwanted, whereas for the pupils, reservations about SRE were about *disclosing* information, but seldom was there resistance to *receiving* information from teachers. The young mothers did not even want to take part in class discussions for fear of being stigmatised by teachers merely for participating.

They commonly reported having had 'no one to talk to' about sex and relationship issues when they had needed to. Their relationships with teachers meant that the nurses were by far the preferred source of sexual health information or support, and they liked the idea of nurses becoming more involved in SRE, but in practice, nurses had been a source of information for only two of them. Although they felt that schools should talk to young people about sex and relationships, many had strong reasons for schools not being appropriate sources of information or support in their case. The neat idea that better SRE will reduce the teenage pregnancy rate is undermined by the fact that more complex factors lay behind their conceptions: two had been denied the pill (by parents or their GP) and one had been sick, preventing their pill from working.

Young mothers' experiences of school: lack of respect?

All but one of these young parents had had bad experiences of school: three had been bullied, three young women mentioned getting into fights, one described graffiti at school calling her 'a slag', and most had experiences of being picked on. Moreover, they shared a strong sense that they were not respected at school by either their peers or teachers. Sometimes this was offered as a defensive explanation for their behaviour: 'If they'd have shown me respect, I'd have shown it them'. Sometimes it was a point of contrast with college where staff treated you with more respect, 'like a person'. The regimented school environment was significant because 'not being allowed to go to the toilet when you want' was experienced as controlling and infantilising. When heavily pregnant, not being allowed to leave lessons to go to the toilet was physically problematic, and a deeply unsupportive gesture, sending out a message that they should not expect concessions. Several mentioned not feeling physically safe from the rough and tumble of the playground, being afraid of tripping up and in one case still being threatened with fights. Two even reported having had things thrown at them by teachers in the past. One young mother was very touched by her learning support mentor bringing her a present of baby clothes when the baby was born and staying in touch, because otherwise she had felt completely unnoticed in school:

> None of the teachers ever spoke to me. Everyone ignored me 'til I was pregnant, then one or two teachers spoke to me and asked how I was.

The YWCA's study of 21 young mothers in another large English town found similar accounts of unhappiness or disengagement at school (Harris *et al.* 2005). Not feeling respected by teachers was a common theme here too, as was not being allowed to leave the classroom to visit the toilet. Is it the experience of a heavily pregnant belly that makes this experience so significant or is it because it is an intrusive and authoritarian wielding of power over others' bodies?

SRE requires conditions of mutual respect and emotional safety for the discussion of personally sensitive and value-based topics. Among the aims of SRE and PSHE are raising pupils' self-esteem, developing communication skills and enhancing emotional literacy, indeed ideally the pedagogic relationship will itself model the respectful communication and trust needed to explore differences and values. But what these young mothers described were experiences of feeling unsafe, emotionally and physically, and a lack of trust, respect or recognition. School was not a site in which their self-esteem was protected, let alone promoted. Without relations of trust between teachers and pupils it is hard to envisage successfully discussing controversial subjects sensitively, let alone modelling good relationships.

A problem in a couple of the schools was that 'teachers kept leaving' and PSHE was therefore frequently taught by supply teachers. This meant that staff knew neither the pupils nor what previous lessons had covered. This is far from the pedagogic ideal of SRE being delivered by teachers who know them well, but indicates the pressure some schools are under.

Young mothers and education: aspirations and priorities

In contrast with their negative views of *school*, these young mothers were mostly positive about *education*. Most had ideas, admittedly vague, of future courses at college, and four mentioned future training towards childcare or other care work. In fact, six were currently involved in some form of training (at college or through a voluntary organisation), one had had a home tutor in her final school year, and two had tried to return to school after having their babies, but without success. One was doing business studies at college, another was keen to work with children in sport, but would continue to think about how while she tried for a second child. Unsuccessful attempts to return to education for two of them highlight the potential difficulties of combining motherhood with study: one was nudged back to school 'too early', felt completely alienated from her erstwhile friends and mortified at leaking breast-milk onto her school shirt, and another began a beauty course at college, but said she was 'thrown off' for missing a few weeks when her baby was in hospital. Another wasn't expected to return to school because it was recognised that she was a carer for her own mother. These experiences illustrate the presumption on the part of education providers that young people are 'free' from care responsibilities to attend courses, as implied in the ideal model of the educable subject.

What seems significant here is that these women with young children *did* talk about college courses and future training for work, but with one important caveat: they used the *future tense*. Those with young babies thought they might continue with their education when the baby reached a year or so, and others talked about 'being free to' go to college or get a job 'after having children' which meant when their children started school at 4–5 years of age.

> I can go to college later when I've had longer to work out what I want to do.

> By the time this [unborn] baby's in school, I'll only be 22 and with all three of my children in school, I'll be able to get a job then.

For them, being with their child throughout infancy was expected and preferred. Parenting was clearly much more important to their social identities than education (or employment) had been in their past, or than employment (or education) were to their imagined futures. Mothering came first in terms of both importance and timing. It was possible to see mothering as conveying a valued social role, promoting their community inclusion and their elevation to responsible woman-hood, in contrast to the policy construction linking teenage parenthood to social exclusion (Kidger 2004). The policy link relies on a particular definition of social exclusion centring on paid work (Levitas 2005).

The YWCA study also identified this cultural norm of full-time mothering until children start school and that 'being a good mother meant staying with your baby': 'you'd be a bad mum if ... you're not with your kid at all and you're working most of the time', said one young mum in their study, and another said: 'There are young girls in my estate and they leave their babies all the time with their mums, and ... they get slagged off' (Harris et al. 2005: 11, 10). Being responsible meant being there for your child, as we found, but also, 'time spent with [the] baby was precious and rewarding' (2005: 25). Harris et al. describe how this ideal of full-time mothering dominated their interviewees' thoughts over returning to employment or training and note how important being a good mother was to young women facing stigma about their parenting. As they point out, until recently, social policy reflected this same cultural norm, which has a long tradition. Punitive responses to mothers deemed deviant are historically continuous but currently emphasise age rather than illegitimacy (Alldred 1999; David 2003a, 2003b).

Parenting carried gendered expectations and young women's role as the primary carer was invested in by young men too. Some young mothers in the YWCA study and another by Lee et al. (2004) described their partners not wanting them to work: 'He doesn't want me to work, he tells me I shouldn't have to ... he wants to look after me' (Harris et al. 2005). We found similar gendered expectations including of male breadwinning, despite the local job market offering largely 'women's work' in the lighter side of local industry. This, alongside the fact that at least three of these young women lived with and helped care for babies born to their mother or sister, shows the importance of situating their decisions about participating in education, employment or training (EET) in the actual context of their lives, and seeing them embedded in family and other gendered relationships with the interdependencies these entail.

In addition, when these young women were publicly harassed by being told they were 'too young to have a baby', they understood this to mean 'too young' to parent a child adequately, not too young to leave education. The child's – not their own – well-being was their attacker's concern. This criticism draws on a discourse of mothering that can sacrifice a mother's needs for her child; however, for now, we simply note the absence of community corroboration of the idea that motherhood was interrupting her education, her earning or her pathway to a career.

For mothers of such youngsters, when day-to-day life with a baby is so absorbing even for non-school-aged mothers (see Gatrell 2005), their consciousness of education seems notable. Notable, yet not surprising given our introduction to them via the LEA's School Reintegration Officer (SRO) who worked with all the city's school-aged mothers to help them identify and access EET. The SRO was sympathetic to their wishes, but clearly had an educational remit, albeit within a flexible framework that did not assume schooling was the only form education could take. It was on the strength of the trusting relationships she had built with young women that they agreed to talk to us, and our association with her must have shaped their perception of our interest in education. More directly, their previous conversations with her and other professionals had probably shaped their sense of their selves-to-be-educated, and their knowledge of what the local college offered.

They may have employed a discourse of education, but theirs was not an abstract education for its own sake. It was the recognition that education or training would improve their chances of future paid work. A couple drew on the notion that teenage parenting had interrupted their education, in line with the Government's concern with teenage motherhood as a route to social exclusion, when they discussed ideal ages to have babies (19 was the most frequently mentioned). One young mother said that ideally she would have waited until she was 17 and had therefore 'finished her education' before having children, a second referred to her mother's hopes that she'd have 'stayed on at school', and a third said:

> Ideally 18–20. When you've got your education so you can fall back on it later, so you can get a job afterwards.

None mentioned higher education, however, and, as these comments show, further education, after 16, was the furthest 'staying on' envisaged. None were committed to particular careers or had already identified EET pathways, which must be seen in the context of the local labour market's unemployment given the 'downsizing' of the main regional industry. When they did talk about future employment, it was clear that they saw working as heavily contoured by their status as parents. It was not some idealised fantasy of future lives in hugely improved living situations. It was motivated by pay and the desire to provide well for their children.

These young people's instrumental view of education-for-work matches the government's, but their view of work as coming *after* parenting deviates from the new expectation of paid work *alongside* parenting and subsequent need for formal childcare. This late twentieth-century development was a response to social and global transformations and the fight by feminists for women's right to (not requirement to) paid work (New and David 1985). These young parents could not assume they would find either particularly well-paid or fulfilling work since only two had completed compulsory schooling, one gaining some qualifications as a result of LEA provision of a home tutor. For some parents, unless a second income or unpaid childcare is available, it may not 'pay' to work.

Whilst being presumed single was part of the stereotype of teenage mothers that they objected to, in the sense of being unlikely to have a partner's income to draw on, young mothers' situation was similar to that of lone mothers. Partners, where they had them, whilst older, were generally caught in the same structures: unemployed, on a training project or otherwise peripheral to the household economy. It is unsurprising, therefore, that these women were not more interested in work. However, it was not simply a matter of economics that small tweaks to 'family-friendly' work or college policies could change, it was (also), we suspect, born of ideological differences.

These young mothers rarely constructed their pregnancies as interrupting plans for study or training. Indeed, in their accounts paid work and mothering were constructed as fundamentally different pathways to adulthood. Paid work was similarly constructed as clashing rather than compatible with mothering young children by the white mothers in an earlier study of ours in London (Duncan *et al.* 2003b). This same research found that African Caribbean mothers saw doing paid work as *part of* their mothering role, rather than clashing with it, because they felt it important to model managing paid work alongside mothering. This illustrates another way in which common experiences and histories (marking gender, ethnicity, class) can produce geographically situated shared sets of values. The body of work conducted by Rosalind Edwards, Simon Duncan and co-workers demonstrates that different groups of mothers have different values informing their mothering. Mothers' decisions about combining paid work with mothering or about using childcare are not simply economic decisions, but are value-based and locally situated, employing 'gendered moral rationalities' that reflect the values of the communities with which they are connected (Duncan and Edwards 1999). Government policy makes a fundamental error in expecting the model of 'rational economic man' to apply to mothers' decisions about childcare, which we found instead reflected priorities regarding the culture and values informing particular childcare provision and, for ethnic minority mothers, the ethnic origins of providers (Duncan *et al.* 2003a). This also means that Government assumptions that the childcare 'market' will operate according to market forces is flawed, although such a model is central in the neoliberal reform of education and other public services.

Local norms and values about motherhood

Like other studies of the cultural norms in teenage pregnancy 'hotspots', we found a coherence among the young mothers regarding their views of motherhood, education and employment, and an indication that community views were notably distinct from those assumed in government thinking. Our participants described as the norm: early childbearing, large families, childrearing in three-genera-tion or extended family households, financial support from and often complete dependence on parents and reliance on mothers, especially for childcare. All but one said that having babies when young was not unusual in their families. One 14-year-old said that she was the youngest mother in her family but that 16 had been common beforehand, and another described 17 as the norm 'round there' and for her family. Several of their own mothers had had their first baby at 16 or 17. Most interviewees had several siblings, and even the young woman who was one of six children and said she didn't like 'big families' was pregnant with her third child – suggesting perhaps that the local average is higher than the national average (see Land 1976). Siblings had had babies young too; at least three of the girls' parents were already grandparents. One had a 16-year-old sister who was pregnant at the same time, another's brother had had his first at 16 and had since had another three (with the same partner). The mother of one interviewee had shared her daughter's experience of an unplanned pregnancy discovered late (too late for an abortion, her initial plan) just a year earlier. This young woman was already involved in raising one small child when she realised she was pregnant.

None of their first pregnancies were planned (and, when asked, most would ideally have waited another year or two), but subsequent pregnancies were. Only one expressed anti-abortion views – fewer than we expected – but two were talked out of having an abortion and three were put off by the video they had seen in RE. More significant in ruling out the possibility of abortion was the fact that all had concealed pregnancies, typically confirmed at 5 months or later. In retrospect, most described suspecting they were pregnant but being 'in denial'. As the youngest participant put it: 'I was 13, I really didn't want to know'.

One of the overwhelming impressions we gained was of their peer group engaging in sexual activity as the norm. However, it is possible that this was amongst a particular subgroup and that, as sex educators point out, the impression that 'everyone's doing it' outstrips the reality. However, it is perception not prevalence that shapes expectations. Pam's understanding of peer pressure was quickly corrected when she asked whether girls who had sex were criticised for being 'easy':

PA: Do you get slagged off for having sex?
T: No, you get slagged off if you're not having sex! [later: 'from about 13']
PA: Did you feel under pressure to have sex?
T: No, I didn't have any 'til I was 16!
PA: Did you feel like you'd waited ages, then, before having sex? Had lots of your mates already?
T: Lots of my mates already had *babies* by the time I had sex!

This young mother said 17 was a common age to have a child in her community and her own family. Her own baby was born when she was 17, after a year at college, and was not seen as problematically early by her family. It is clear that times have changed since the post-war generation of young women had their babies in their early twenties as the norm. Now, educational and economic changes see huge numbers of especially middle-class women having babies much later, as we saw in Chapter 1, creating more of a gap between the 'young mothers' and the 'elderly primigravidas'.

Despite these culturally accepted age norms, there was not an unproblematic acceptance of teenage pregnancy and some ambivalence, even rejection by the peer group:

None of my mates stood by me, they just slagged me off as soon as they found out I was pregnant.

Another described slurs on her reputation which she felt were utterly unfair because:

They were all sleeping with different people each week and I'd had the same boyfriend for 3 years [actually since age 11].

Another young woman suspected that some of her friends were jealous of her pregnancy.

Apparent ambivalence about teenage pregnancy among the mothers themselves, when explored, came not from its clash with a New Labour expectation of further/higher education but, instead, from the painful recognition of social condemnation, sometimes reinforced by direct hostility and by their awareness that the media greeted news of a 'surprise' baby to Cherie Blair in different tones to those adopted regarding 'surprise' babies born to teenage mothers. Yet this confirmed their view that 'most babies aren't planned anyway'. Since Leo Blair's birth we have seen increasing condemnation of women conceiving 'too late' in life, with a recent furore over a woman having a baby at 63 via IVF. Contrast this, however, with the amusement at male celebrities in their 60s or beyond fathering children.

We see the values expressed in the accounts gathered in our study as reflecting the values of the local community, and therefore mothers of all ages within it, rather than being specific to *young* mothers. Lee *et al.* (2004) found a strong correlation between the proportions of under-18 pregnancies and adult pregnancies ending in abortion in different communities and concluded that young women's perceptions of motherhood were shaped by community and family views, including the extent to which having children relatively early was accepted and the importance placed on goals that are not compatible with early motherhood, and hence 'local, familial and/or gendered cultural processes' were important in young women's decisions about pregnancy.

Like Lee *et al.*, we do not wish to see teenage motherhood as simply 'passed down' through the generations (sometimes they 'don't want to make the same mistake my mum did') but are indicting particular sets of meanings and values that are drawn on in decision-making. Firstly, in areas of high teenage pregnancy rates, abortion carries more stigma than does early motherhood (Tabberer *et al.* 2000; Lee *et al.* 2004). Secondly, young women's decision-making is affected by their expectations about what can be achieved through education and success in the world of work: 'those who continued their pregnancies could perceive motherhood in a more positive light, since it did not appear to interfere with plans for the immediate future' (Lee *et al.* 2004: 4). Thirdly, in our study, as in that of Tabberer *et al.*, mothering is constructed as immensely rewarding, rather than associated with lack or loss: the chance to develop close personal relationships with a child and perhaps partner and to take up a position of responsibility.

The notion of responsibility can play either way, relating to class cultures: Harden and Osgood (1999) found that teenagers having abortions often experienced unplanned pregnancy as a sign of their 'irresponsibility', whereas young mothers we interviewed and those in Tabberer's study associated motherhood with responsibility: despite fearing parental reactions, going ahead with the pregnancy was framed as taking responsibility, and adapting to new responsibilities was a positive thing, even perhaps a marker of growing up, as Thomson *et al.* (2003) describe. It was a spur to achievement for our most educationally engaged interviewee – becoming a mother gave her a reason to seek qualifications, which before she had lacked.

Young women not in employment, education or training (NEET)

The significance of these values described is that they are distinct from those assumed in the TPS and show that when the Government implies it represents the consensus, it clearly does not. These values should not be depicted as the faulty culture of the underclass that prevents them from fully participating in work, seen in the new ideology as the route to citizenship (Bullen and Kenway 2004). In addition, the practical difficulties facing young mothers in returning to EET, and the structural factors limiting their success in the job market, must be acknowledged.

The YWCA study highlights the practical difficulties of combining motherhood with education or training:

> Only those with informal childcare, through family support, returned to EET relatively easily. Others felt childcare and a lack of support and flexibility in work or training made EET a struggle and forced them to sacrifice too much time with their children.
> (Harris *et al.* 2005: 25)

For some, 'EET was out of the question because concerns about the baby's health, not knowing what to expect and learning to manage on a limited budget, along with learning basic childcare skills, constituted a full-time job' (2005: 25). Trying to combine EET with mothering placed considerable strains on their lives.

The consensus seems to be growing that the pro-work agenda of New Labour puts too much pressure on young mothers in particular (Harris *et al.* 2005; Kidger 2004). Even research with mothers in their twenties and thirties who have the support of a partner shows that the arrival of a child can be stressful (Gatrell 2005). In addition, there are judgements reflecting values such as those discussed above:

I'd rather be poor and see my own kids, rather than like, be rich and never see them at all ... You need to be there ... if they've got problems they can talk to you.

The SEU (1999) report advocates raising girls' aspirations as the third of its three action points, but what does the job market provide for young women such as these in their communities and regions? In an area of high unemployment, low social and geographical mobility, and male breadwinner expectations, young women without academic or vocational qualifications or experience will not easily find employment, and available employment may not meet their 'raised aspirations'. Whilst women overall have increased their participation in the labour market, working-class young women may find their options restricted. The neoliberal promise of social mobility through education (Walkerdine 2003) sounds hollow in areas of multiple deprivation, social exclusion and male breadwinner expectations.

The YWCA report presents a critique of the TPS. First, the target for 60 per cent of teenage mothers to be in EET is unrealistic, given that it exceeds the employment rate among mothers in general. The British Household Panel Survey (1991–7) shows that nearly 60 per cent of all first-time mothers are not in employment when their children are 5 years old, so to expect the youngest group of mothers to achieve a 60 per cent rate whilst their children are even younger is to expect something highly exceptional. Even older mothers, of whom 70 per cent have been in full-time employment *before* having a baby, do not nearly reach the 60 per cent target for working afterwards. Second, the report questions whether the objectives were ever appropriate given the different value women attach to their mothering. It 'fails to acknowledge the starting position and the aspirations of the young women it is trying to reach' and 'instead presumes they will take a life path not necessarily suited to their needs or reflected in their families and communities' (Harris *et al.* 2005: 25):

> The Teenage Pregnancy Strategy needs to understand ... [that] social class shapes many young women's views of young motherhood as normal and respected, so strategies based on presumptions that teenage motherhood is 'a mistake', 'a problem' or 'abnormal' and that caring for children rather than paid working is a failure, are irrelevant to the lives and experiences of young mothers and are unlikely to succeed in encouraging young mothers into EET. (2005: 31)

This values differential may shed some light on another unmet TPS goal – for a 15 per cent reduction in under-18s conceptions by 2004 (ONS 2004). Closer inspection of the reported fall of 11.1 per cent shows that conceptions among under-16s have dropped by 15.2 per cent, indicating that the conception rate among 16- and 17-year-olds remains more resistant to intervention. Seen alongside these qualitative findings of (sub)cultural norms of 'early' childbearing, one interpretation is that this 'older' group of teenage mothers – having children at 17 or 18 – do not fit TPS assumptions because they are not seen as aberrant in their communities. If they reflect community norms they are less amenable to pressure.

The TPS approach to teenage pregnancy as a social ill to be tackled, an individual failure to be redeemed, further reinforces the stigma. However, there is some evidence that it is not being young but being disapproved of that creates some of the problems of early childbearing – reversing the TPS's cause-and-effect assumptions. A medical study in Jerusalem compared young mothers from an orthodox Jewish community who marry young and receive considerable social and economic support from their community, with other young mothers across the city who were mostly poor and unmarried. Even controlling for exact age, marital status, ethnicity and smoking, the young mothers who received the support of their community had a significantly lower incidence of low-birth-weight babies (Gale *et al.* 1989). Where adverse outcomes of teen pregnancies are observed, environmental disadvantage (poverty, limited pre-natal medical care, and lack of psychosocial support) may be key factors.

New Labour celebrates the 'good' old-fashioned values such as that of respect for others, but actively undermines another old-fashioned value, that of full-time mothering. When we have seen the Government explicitly seeking to promote certain values that suit its economic priorities through education policy, their recent valorisation of 'old-fashioned community values' (Sennett 2003) seems a cherry-picking of the aspects of the 'old' culture that suit its own agendas.

The ungendered 'parents' of policy

Legal, social and educational policies in the UK all now refer to 'parents', 'young people', 'employees' and avoid gendering subjects. However, as long as there remain highly gendered expectations of 'parents' to act as 'mothers' or 'fathers', to refer only to 'parents' and 'workers' as if they are not gendered obscures what is often happening in reality. In particular, it does women a disservice by failing to recognise that women's increased participation in paid work has not been matched by men's increased participation in housework or childcare (New and David 1985; Kiernan *et al* 1998; Duncan *et al.* 2003a, 2003b). Sociological studies of heterosexual couples have shown how even when both partners work full-time, women tend to do more housework than men, and where there are children, mothers tend to do more but also take more responsibility for managing care of and provision for children (David *et al.* 1994; Van Every 1995). The discourse of 'parents' therefore masks inequalities and allows them to continue unchallenged.

In this case, the difficulties 'young parents' (in policy terms) face in returning to EET are compounded by gender. The Government Equalities Review of 2006 confirmed the existence of a continuing gender pay gap, with women earning an average of 17 per cent less than their male counterparts. Commentaries revealingly lament the 'waste of talent' of women working below their abilities when the UK faces increasing competition in the global marketplace, before expressing concern for the women themselves. Rather than making pay audits compulsory, 'the answer' is seen as increasing women's employment and ending gender segregation. The review concluded that mothers are the single most disadvantaged group in the job market, with mothers of under 11s having the greatest difficulty finding work, irrespective of ethnic or social background (Smith 2006). Difficulties finding childcare and securing jobs with flexible hours are recognised as among the factors militating against mothers finding work, and refreshingly the difficulties of combining work and parenting get a mention:

> While some of these women may 'choose' to stay at home, the researchers caution against assuming those mothers do not wish to work. The choice, they said, may well be made in the light of the hurdles facing them, including the issue of the exhausting nature of trying to work and have a family (Smith 2006).

The rationales employed by mothers in decision-making about childcare must be understood as locally situated, reflecting the values of their community and the relationships within which their lives are situated, which are, amongst other things, gendered. Several of these young mothers already had responsibilities for another family member, and/or were helping to care for another child. Two were in relationships with reformed 'bad boys' or ex-drug users, for which they had the respect and gratitude of their partners' families. Their identities as 'copers' and 'survivors' embodied gendered expectations of caring and responsibility for others in a working-class female archetype which was a source of positive self-esteem. In contrast, they did not have sources of self-esteem in their identities as learners or workers. Not only are their identities formed in the context of these gendered meanings, but they may also be applying *gendered* moral rationalities (Duncan *et al.* 2003b).

Whilst gender-neutral notions of workers are intended to include women, they can unhelpfully ignore the gendered meanings that either workers themselves or employers bring to the table. The celebration of the business travel and employment opportunities brought by globalisation in Third Way policy models 'forgets' the need of many women for well-paid local work within reach of home and school which 'cuts them off from the networking opportunities of the global firm' (McRobbie 2000: 109). The very myth of unfettered social mobility through education that is central to the neoliberal discourse of education is itself a masculine ideal (Walkerdine 2003). The notion that everyone is free to be this self-directed subject is an ideal that young women find harder to attain than young men because they live among and have developed a sense of themselves through ideas about girlhood/womanhood that prioritise more relational, people-centred aspirations. Not only does mothering involve a greater clash with working than does being a father (the parallel verb, 'fathering', illustrates the point by denoting an act of procreation rather than the same ongoing commitment as 'mothering'), but some of them may be engaged in caring roles with dependents other than their own child, and selfishness is, of course, far worse a charge for women than men. There are conflicting sets of expectations of young women: to succeed as workers alongside men, to be good mothers for the children who are (culturally) worried about more than ever. Socially there is ambivalence about women's role: there are two distinct discourses with their attendant values. Women are set up to fail – and to take individualised responsibility for failing (Thomson *et al.* 2003; Walkerdine 2003) – in this ungendered discourse of social mobility through education.

The conflict between work and family life is framed as merely a matter of *managing* it all better (Bunting 2005) – the domestic equivalent of the injunction to 'work smart'. The implicit assumption is that individuals need to find their own biographical solutions to what are, structural problems. Furthermore, as Walkerdine (2003) asks: when the value of self-determination and individuality becomes a new cultural ideal of femininity, what happens to working-class girls? Gendered expectations make for contradictory messages about how they should be and when the labour market disadvantages women in general, working-class girls bear the brunt of the conflicts between these sets of values.

In recent attention to the fall in the UK's birth-rate, and the increasing bulge of women mothering in their late thirties, we see cultural anxiety circulating around the figure of the mother and scrutinising the motives of both teenage mothers and 'left-it-too-late' career women. What this opposition produced in some interviews was the dynamic by which both interviewer and interviewee were at pains to value what the other had. Both could see that the researcher, with a university job, had lots of 'education', which, in the dominant value system, carries considerable cultural capital. However, the surprised-but-happy baby-mother and the broody, childless 30-something researcher agreed that the dominant pro-education climate failed to acknowledge what really mattered to each of them and concurred in their critique of this agenda through their shared rhetorical question, 'what's important at the end of the day?'. The idea that acquiring cultural capital could compete with raising a child irritated the research team at the start of the project, but six years later the advance of pro-education ideology makes it more difficult to question, and its presumption more difficult to spot. So embedded is this ideology becoming in contemporary UK society (for instance, today's university students do not easily 'see' it) that it achieves the status of a 'mentality' – a discourse so taken for granted that only from an historical vantage-point can it fully be 'seen' (Dean 1999).

Anti-natalism: the parent as failed neoliberal subject

Contemporary British culture exhibits a curious ambivalence about maternity: heightened anxiety about the quality of parenting today's children receive at the hands of their 'self-centred', 'ill-prepared' parents (hence 'parenting education'), coexists with a fetishising of the 'freedom' and 'independence' that having children so clearly compromises. The qualities celebrated in this model of adulthood, the neoliberal subject, in fact run counter to parenthood. The orientation to another or others that defines parenthood defies the self-absorption required by the self-as-project model of adulthood. Bunting (2006) counterposes our privileged material and medical ability to make childrearing easier with the anxious questioning that greets the pregnant woman about the social conditions: Who is going to care? What will you do? She identifies the clash parents face with their worker identity, and corporate capitalism's model consumer ('you can spot the mother in the office, because she's the one in last year's fashions') and remarks that 'in a society that values consumption, choice and independence above all, it's a wonder that we have as many babies as we do' (2006: 31).

Motherhood is, anecdotally at least, when women recognise their interconnectedness and interdependencies with others: the profound dependency of a baby on its mother and often the increased dependency of mothers on their mothers/partners/kin or perhaps childminders and friends too (see Edwards 1993). It is when daughters who boldly moved away from the lands of their parents wish they lived closer. Pregnancy and parenthood go against the grain, Bunting (2006) argues, because they sabotage independence and choice – characteristics valued highly in our culture – and demand of us long-term commitment. Having 'spent much of the previous ten years attempting to eradicate any hint of dependence, either of your own or of others on you' and 'having avoided all such long-term commitment (including probably to your partner) you are, at the very least, uneasy about it', she writes.

Not only does mainstream culture fail to recognise and value motherhood, as many feminists have argued, but the qualities required are antithetical to those we are expected to aspire to and which hold an increasingly central place in intensifying neoliberalism. Bunting calls it an 'anti-natalist bias', implicit in many of the influences that shape our sense of self and purpose, our identity, our aspirations and our understanding of success and the good life: the problem with motherhood (and to a lesser extent, fatherhood) is that it comes at the cost of failure – or at least compromise – as consumer or worker, or both.

This means that the self our education system is currently preoccupied with helping us develop is little use to a new parent:

> What use is that sassy, independent, self-assertive, knowing-what-you-want-and-how-to-get-it type when you fast forward five years to the emotional labour of helping a child develop self-confidence? Once there's a baby in the cot, you need steadiness, loyalty, endurance, patience, sensitivity and even self-denial – all character-istics that you've spent the last decade trashing as dull or, even worse, for losers. (Bunting 2006)

When Bunting says that motherhood hits most women 'like a car crash', she refers to the experience of women – like Pam, Miriam and many other women academics – who approach motherhood relatively late in comparison with previous generations, but around whom a new orthodoxy has emerged. Such education-then-motherhood women have experienced adult life without ('free from'?) children; thus parenthood, if experienced, is distinct from adulthood. Whilst heterosexuality and parenthood have been almost synonymous pre-contraception, they symbolise contradictory lifestyles or models of being in the neoliberal framework, although perhaps different biographical moments in a life. However, young parents are outside this new norm. Not for them a luxurious few years to explore sex, sexuality, relationships, living independently, earning and work relationships. Instead, their first experiences of sex, a relationship, parenthood and an intensified pressure for financial self-sufficiency may come much more bunched together. If the ideal middle-class subject's twenties allow a brief period of indulgence to 'find themselves' before they get on with improving themselves (a 1970s ideal now condensed into a 'gap year' for middle-class young people), this period allows them to ground their project-of-the-self in some, albeit shifting, self-reflection, perhaps having identified 'what they want to be'. Young parents, for whom adulthood and parenthood arrive more closely together, are unlikely to have identified 'what they want to be or do' or have had long to work on a project-of-the-self (or even a CV). From this perspective it seems premature to expect them to have identified their pathway through education and training, even if their circumstances had not recently changed dramatically. Moreover, the privilege of choice applied to employment, and the idea of a career seem optimistic from locations such as that of our or the YWCA study groups. While a new generation of (mainly middle-class) women may increasingly occupy this privileged, hitherto male mode of selfhood, this may be time-limited since if they become mothers they are rudely reminded of their gender, in terms of social expectations, including those they have of themselves, and the necessity of their political analysis. It is this 'crash' that explains why it is said that some women 'get (understand) feminism' when they 'get children'.

Disciplining young mothers

Even though we sometimes shared critical comments about the TPS with our participants, in retrospect, despite seeking to question government assumptions, we possibly reinforced them. By asking young mothers about their education and employment aspirations, an unintended consequence of our research was perhaps a reiteration of the dominant message from welfare agencies and peripatetic education workers that paid work is of more importance than parenting: that young people, even those with babies, ought to orient themselves to EET. Our questions played into the expectation that they imagine themselves a project, something that can and ought to be worked on and improved. As university researchers, on an LEA-funded project, and introduced by the SRO or a training project's worker, we could not escape our positioning within education, nor the fact that they had already had practitioners ask them about their employment aspirations and discuss options for education or training.

Furthermore, our discussions provided an opportunity for them – in fact, *required* them – to give an account of themselves as lacking in education and with future plans to make educational self-improvements. This meant taking up a subject position within this *educable subject* discourse, and for those who had hated school, potentially a narration of salvation, reform or determination. Merely asking about any plans for returning to education plays into the expectation, reinforces it as a possibility and therefore increases its probability by being productive of this particular sense of self. In our interviews they narrated themselves through dominant educational discourses, coming to see and think of themselves and their lives in these terms. Whilst we asked open questions, we required them to narrate their lives through hegemonic meanings, make their hopes for the future meaningful in government terms. Our research conversations became part of the process by which young people are expected to govern themselves.

This should not surprise us. Marks (1996) found in her research with young people excluded from school that the research encounter, despite her intentions to the contrary, could function as an opportunity for contrition, acceptance of punishment, and hence for pupils to self-govern in line with disciplinary expectations, and we have ourselves argued that interviewing produces a particular version of subjecthood through implicit expectations of the reflexive, self-critical subject (Alldred and Gillies 2002). Whilst we had not assumed that our research left people in schools untouched, as positivist research does, and had relished the way action research involved us in promoting as well as studying the status of SRE, we had given less thought to what message our interviews with young mothers might carry. We had framed participation in the study of young people *not in school* as a way of not replicating their exclusion from education in education research, and involving young men as well (see the next chapter) helped us feel we were not simply problematising teenage mothers. However, we forgot to consider the distinction we make elsewhere, following Burman (1992), about the politics of research *within* and *beyond* the interview dynamic (Alldred and Gillies 2002). Our concerns with the politics of representing a particular social group in the research distracted us from focusing on the impact on the individuals taking part (Alldred and Burman 2005). We had not quite anticipated how difficult it would be to avoid being positioned, and positioning participants, within a pro-education agenda. Here the research itself illustrates a broader concern we have about the 'cost' of inclusion to young people – of accepting the terms in which it is framed.

One of the most insidious aspects of these terms, reflected in the 'can do' culture (Thomson *et al.* 2003), is the individualisation of responsibility for failure to succeed in the job market and the expectation that teenage mothers themselves must avoid their future 'social exclusion' by embarking on an education-to-employment pathway. Whilst we sought to challenge the 'epistemological fallacy' (Furlong and Cartmel 1997) that individuals are to blame for the impact of socioeconomic structures on their lives, the tacit question our interviewees adeptly perceived was about how they would take responsibility for their own education-to-earning pathway to financial independence. In response to this they narrated themselves as aspiring, educable, future returners to EET. Research interviews, far from providing a window onto pre-formed selves, helped them perform a version of self-as-project and therefore produce themselves in line with expectations of neoliberal policy. This imagined subject, as we have seen, assumes masculine norms.

Young parents' experiences of school are of note to policy-makers because the hope of schools promoting young people's social and emotional development may be seriously limited by the teacher–pupil relationships possible within the current system; and because particularly communities or peer groups may not share the values New Labour presumes or seeks to promote regarding the role of paid work for parents or the undesirability of teenage pregnancy. The place of education/training and employment in adult lives is discussed further in the next chapter, where we explore the views of another group of young people not in school, this time young men. Whilst similar themes emerge regarding the (lack of) orientation to education, there are different inflections because, as Griffin (1997, 2004) has argued, whereas young women such as these had got 'into trouble', young men tend to be seen more as 'trouble' themselves.

chapter seven

'Young people' not 'pupils': Sex, education and boys not in school

Gender again emerges as a core theme in our discussions with young men who were not in school. In groups, they described and played out in front of us the gendered expectations and local cultural norms they face. Gender is often implicit but sometimes explicit in what they told us. It is primary in our analysis and, we believe, accounts for the particular research dynamics produced among this group. The very real material limits that frame the boys' 'choices' and 'aspirations' were apparent. We felt that what these working-class young men had to say about sex education had to be understood in the context of their views about education and sexuality in general. Their ideas about education and sexuality were tightly bound up with the types of masculinity available to them and deemed acceptable in their peer group. The identity struggles and decisions they had faced or would face about education, training or employment could not, we argue, be understood outside of the locally defined and policed, gendered and class-based constructions of adulthood.

Our account is drawn from three group discussions conducted with 13–15-year-old boys, all of whom were white. All the discussions took place at training projects which were in parts of the city synonymous with 'sink' estates and areas of high multiple deprivation. We sought research participants who were not receiving school-based education, although not specifically young men. All the group participants had, in fact, either been permanently excluded from school or were long-term school non-attenders, but all were currently managing to attend small, specifically tailored alternatives to school. The LEA was proud of its efforts to support the development of alternative educational provision, which was usually in the voluntary sector. All the students on these training programmes were boys, which reflects the majority of excluded pupils in England and Wales, although the number of girls in this group is probably underestimated (Osler *et al.* 2002) and increasing (Daniels *et al.* 2003). However, the nature and culture of the projects were also significant here. Work experience in car maintenance or gardening were key attractions and the informal culture established within the groups seemed to us quite male in character. It is possible, therefore, that workers only thought to place young men on these programmes. The all-white group does not reflect those excluded nationally, among whom African Caribbean boys are overrepresented (Wright *et al.* 2000; Blair 2001), but was typical of the area.

At the start of the project, when we were commissioned to research the views of young people under 16 who were not in school, we were pleased that the LEA was adopting an inclusive approach to young people's views, but we did not foresee how central to the study's emergent themes the experience of these young people would be. It is an important reminder for those of us who have researched children and young people's views through schools that there remain groups of young people not represented in schools, and moreover, that their views may differ considerably from those within schools. Clearly these are only one of the groups of young people not in mainstream education who could have participated in the study. Their specificity and the small number of participants make this an analysis that can identify themes they raised and dynamics among them, rather than necessarily general patterns of experience.

Boys not in employment, education or training

Our original research questions included what these boys' experiences of school-based (or training project-based) SRE had been, what they thought could have improved it, whether they thought schools *should* deliver SRE, and if so, how. We anticipated they would bring a critical perspective to bear on government assumptions and imagined we would use their accounts to think critically about the social inclusion agenda informed by the experience of those who are themselves relatively excluded. How might those who experienced teachers as 'unfair' and school as threatening to their self-esteem – as we documented initially in David *et al.* (2002) – manage identifications with staff in alternative training sites? Could SRE be constructively transposed to such a project? Revisiting our data for this more detailed analysis, we found we could not answer these questions directly, but the reason we could not offered us some insight into our topic as we shall see.

Government policy constructs social exclusion and poverty as the long-term consequences of school disengagement or exclusion (SEU 1999), yet when poor, working-class and black young people are so overrepresented in school exclusions (Wright *et al.* 2000; Blair 2001), this causal analysis is hard to sustain. Government rhetoric also implies that socioeconomic class is an outmoded concept (Walkerdine 2003). However, education researchers show how social class still functions to limit 'choices' (Walkerdine *et al.* 2001; Ball *et al.* 2002) such that working-class young people often expect to leave school at 16 and more middle-class young people often expect to continue in education (Archer and Yamashita 2003; Ball 2003). Large-scale statistical analyses have recently confirmed the significance of social class in explaining patterns of educational success at secondary level (Smithers 2005; HEFCE 2006; Butler *et al.* 2007) and of drop-out from higher education (Quinn *et al.* 2005).

Young people today are 'schooled' in the individualism of neoliberal ideology (Furlong and Cartmel 1997) where responsibility falls to them as individuals for achievement, autonomy, self-regulation, self-financing and control over self-biography (Lucey 2001). Whilst New Labour rhetoric sustains the illusion of choice and agency at the individual level, structural conditions can preclude these (Wynn and White 2000). Risks and opportunities are not evenly distributed, nor are the social and cultural resources available to young people which shape their ability to respond to them (Thomson *et al.* 2003).

As Beck (1992) acknowledges, in the absence of older certainties, and of recognition of the class structures of disadvantage, common experiences are perceived as individual troubles and each person constructs an individualised 'pluralistic overall biography in transition' (1992: 115). This also creates what Furlong and Cartmel (1997) call the 'epistemological fallacy' whereby young people are likely to attribute their own failure (or success) to individual factors rather than sociopolitical ones. They therefore take responsibility for things that may in fact have structural – social and economic – causes and contributions. In addition, the 'choices' open to young people are clearly bound by strong expectations – for example, to engage in training, to enter the workforce – and services such as Connexions can function to query the decisions some young people make. Ultimately young men and women can find themselves pathologised or criminalised for not conforming to expectations and policy preferences. Young people are taught to look to education for social mobility and self-transformation, but 'it turns out that the "new social order" of the twenty-first century retains some distinctly "old order" features which even the shiniest meritocratic rhetoric of "can do", "can have" and "excellence" cannot entirely banish' (Lucey 2001: 177).

The cultural politics around social exclusion are therefore harsh.

Where inclusion represents the acceptance of the dominant values of the mainstream, dissenters can be blamed and condemned for their own marginality irrespective of their attitude towards it, and where marginality is seen as wilful, as in popular constructions of travellers, there is resentment about people 'reaping the benefits' of society whilst not sharing mainstream values. Levitas (2005) calls this the moral underclass discourse where the excluded are constructed as being so on account of their moral failings or deviant culture. The New Labour project is to promote education so that citizens are more 'employable' and hence less welfare 'dependent'. In what Levitas calls the social inclusion discourse, employment will combat social exclusion. This pejorative construction of dependency is criticised from feminist and psychoanalytic perspectives, and it reveals an individualist fantasy of independence from others and separateness from networks communities (Burman 1994a; Treacher 1989). As education is more closely linked to labour market participation, its definition becomes narrower and instrumental (Bullen *et al.* 2000).

It is in this political context – when on the national stage education is presented as the panacea and we see a return to employment training programmes and vocational education for 14–19-year-olds – that we wish to explore the identity practices of those young men marginal to the education system in a community experiencing high levels of social exclusion. Perhaps not all people seen as socially excluded by policy-makers seek 'inclusion' in the way in which it is usually presumed. Particular values and priorities are assumed in policy that not all people share, as we have seen. But as government pro-educational policies intensify the pressure on young people, and young personhood becomes increasingly defined through education, training and employment futures, what are the values of those on the margins of education?

Boys, schooling and excluded identities

White, working-class boys are the focus of the *failing boys* discourse (Epstein *et al.* 1998) and are problematised in relation to poor behaviour and discipline in schools today (Skelton 2001; Connolly 1998). Academic success – and, in particular, working hard towards attainment – is constructed as incompatible with the esteemed or hegemonic masculinities among their peer groups: it's 'uncool' to be a 'swot'. Middle-class boys sometimes manage to combine occupying positions of hegemonic masculinity (being seen as 'cool') with being academically successful provided that success appears effortless (Mac an Ghaill 1994b; Martino 1999). Mac an Ghaill (1994b) found that they could afford to reject schoolwork until the sixth form (post-16), when they could readopt academic identities just in time to pass their A levels or get a degree.

Epstein (1998) found that getting homework done signified to other pupils that one was middle-class, fey and not masculine and as a result, bullying and homophobic abuse were meted out to boys seen as swotty or academic: 'many constructions of masculinity in schools ... not only dominant ones, involve engaging in 'resistance' to schooling which is not only ... about class, as Willis (1977) suggested, but also deeply invested in compulsory heterosexuality' (Epstein 1998: 99). In addition, amongst African Caribbean boys being swotty can be seen as acting white (Sewell 1997; Frosh *et al.* 2002).

These anti-education sentiments in peer group discourse are not to the complete occlusion of other discourses or meanings, but they are enough to suspect that there may, in certain settings, be some peer kudos in being excluded from school. In addition, boys' school disengagement has to be seen in relation to the traditional anchoring of masculinities to employment identities yet erosion of the industries that provided blue-collar work for many working-class men. Many of the professionals we spoke to were gloomy about employment prospects in the area, noting the feminisation of the workforce prepared to work part-time in the service industries. In examining school disaffection and truancy in another socially deprived area, MacDonald and Marsh (2004) found a powerful (sub)cultural critique of the instrumental relevance of education. The shifting orientations to the value of schooling they found had to be seen in the light of 'the changing structures of opportunity that prevail for young people in different places and their fit with localised, class-cultural tastes and aspirations' (MacDonald and Marsh 2004: 143).

Just as we had approached the classroom as 'a site for the production of sex/gender subjectivities' (Mac an Ghaill 1994b: 2) and for the performance of particular masculinities and femininities and contests among them (Epstein and Johnson 1994, 1998; Measor *et al.* 2000; Kehily 2002), so we approached these training projects. We conducted group rather than individual discussions with these participants, making the research settings more like those for the 13–14-year-olds we researched in classrooms than the individual interviews we conducted with young mothers. This arose from a project worker's suggestion that groups would be preferable for the boys, more closely resembling their usual discussions and therefore the work of the project, and because, in her view, we would 'not get a lot out of some of the lads'. In addition, Hilton (2003) found the familiarity of boys with each other in a group discussion valuable for discussing intimate subjects in front of a stranger. We happily complied, eagerly anticipating that this would be valuable in terms of illustrating the peer group norms and some of the shared values and presumptions of the group. Indeed, would the group show a similar 'hunger for an "us"' that MacPherson and Fine (1995) identified among a small group of young women of similar age to the boys? We were convinced that we would 'get more' than from stilted conversations with potentially monosyllabic young men.

Kehily (2002: 54) writes that 'pupils' sexual cultures, often defined in opposition to teachers and the official curriculum, frequently utilise sexualised themes as a vehicle for humour in situations where teachers can be humiliated and school authority flouted'. Measor *et al.* (2000) found that this sexualised humour occurred in particular ways when sexuality itself was the topic of discussion and that it being a 'licensed' topic in SRE modifies slightly the disruption to pedagogical relations that is possible. Here, whilst the topic was 'licensed', the discussion was dominated by disruption, if what we wanted from the discussions were tapes that we could transcribe. Indeed, one tape was returned to us as 'completely impossible' to transcribe and the others produced patchy dialogue with much '[indecipherable]' and '[overlapping comments]' on the transcripts.

Of course, all research accounts are produced in particular social and linguistic contexts (Mishler 1986; Edwards and Alldred 1999) but these boys' highly animated performances left us in no doubt of this. The advocacy of focus groups to elicit data precisely through the interaction of the group (Burman 1994b; Kitzinger 1994) and discourses acceptable among the peer group (which Edwards and Alldred describe even pair interviewing as providing) had a new depth of meaning for us when the dynamics of the groups were such that few statements of views were discernable from the tapes. Just as their heterosexualised bodies interrupted the research agenda in the group discussions, so do their heterosexualising performances come to dominate our discussion here.

'Alternative' provision

Most of our participants were involved in one of the two discussion groups of five boys each that were run at the training project provided by a local voluntary organisation, the National Association for the Care and Resettlement of Offenders (NACRO). Significantly, it employed staff with youth work backgrounds, not educational ones. 'Education' was defined broadly here, to include vocational education, some organised trips to local amenities and discussion-based group work in the centre. The workers were keen to promote the boys' self-esteem and help them develop an interest in or motivation for anything. Successful participation in the two-days-a-week programme consisted of attending a minimum number of days per term. There were ground-rules for discussion and behaviour, but the boys were used to coming into an informal classroom-style room and sitting around some desks pushed together.

Important to the success of these groups was the fact that short attention spans and the need for frequent cigarette breaks were catered for. It seemed as if most or all of the project participants and many of the staff smoked and since they could be seen smoking together outside the main entrance during breaks, the project had a culture of smoking, in line with popular constructions of working-class masculinity. Pam noted in her field-notes that getting on well with the staff and enjoying the informal culture of the project meant that her body language reflected the project's culture and that she felt drawn into its agenda for the boys. She was joined by one or two project workers for most of the research sessions.

The third group of young men involved three particularly 'stubborn' long-term school non-attenders, most of whom had been excluded from school many times, and were meeting with various education and welfare professionals in a loosely defined project run by the LEA. Workers told Pam that these boys were undergoing assessments to identify explanations for their behaviour that would allow them to access additional resources to support their education. The special educational needs discourse elicits funding on the basis of needs or individual pathology. This group were less educational in orientation, although the funding sought would locate them in educational provision. For each of the groups there was an ambiguity about the nature of the setting as educational or not, because they were educational but not school-based in a context (the UK) in which the discourse of *education* is dominated by *schooling*. We decided to refer to these participants as 'young men' to reflect their position outside of school, although some were the same age as the 'boys' who were researched in school. This reflects the youth work rather than formal educational framing of the projects. However, in practice we, like some of the workers, sometimes referred to them as boys. In her field-notes, Pam noted how struck she was by the diversity among them both physically and emotionally: some seemed to be 'little boys' with particularly small bodies and others seemed sexually mature young men with much bigger bodies and, often, a bigger presence in the room.

We wondered what subject positions those excluded or self-excluding from mainstream education would find to occupy when asked about education and sex education in group discussions. We were interested in what discussions would reveal about how governmental discourses of social exclusion are seen by some of those they construct as 'at risk'. In long-term school absenteeism for reasons of either disengagement/alienation or pressing life events, we expected some opposition to the dominant discourse that constructs education as the main priority for all young people. Admittedly, we sought 'juicy' empirical material on which to hang our own critique of education policy.

School non-attenders' views of sex education

The dominant account that emerged in each of the group discussions was that the young men accepted the need for SRE and supported the role of schools in delivering it, because, as one asserted confidently: 'Parents aren't gonna tell you about it, are they?'. Extracting such views from the transcript of sessions is a hard task because they were such lively, multi-vocal and non-linear discussions, but we will draw out a few such general views before focusing on the dynamics of these groups, although as will become apparent, disentangling the two is difficult. Accounts of what sex education they had received were vague and short, although several recalled having some SRE in Year 9 at school. One boy who'd gone to school outside the area described the SRE in his school as 'crap', and several others concurred. But at least one had more positive recollections:

PA: Do you think schools *should* teach sex education?
Boy: Sex is safe … As long as you use a condom, you're safe. That's all you need to know. I put a condom on a [condom demonstrator] post [in the sex education class].

Recounting his active participation in the SRE lesson provided a chance for him to demonstrate his (hetero)sexual confidence in front of the other boys, and there followed banter about how they each felt they measured up to the size of the post.

This exchange, along with other similar ones early on in the discussions, seemed designed to test the researcher's boundaries and to see whether she would get embarrassed. It positioned this boy as the one amongst them who had lots to say, was confident on this topic, and from then on he rather dominated the group in terms of providing the most and most audible responses. A similar moment early on in one of the other discussions led to a particular boy attaining dominance in that group, after which he speaks the most often and usually first in response to questions. Often his comments serve to demonstrate that he is 'up for it'. For instance, he tells the group where he would like to have sex, rather than answering the question about where he thinks sex education would best be delivered – an easy slip to make in the excitement of suddenly licensed discussion of sex perhaps, but one that served his purpose of confirming his heterosexual interest, enthusiasm and confidence.

In line with the opinion expressed by the majority of Year 9 boys in our survey and classroom discussions, these boys said they prefer mixed rather than boys-only groups for SRE. More particularly, they said they wanted to be with the girls, and the reason given, at least in this performance, which made the other boys laugh, was one of heterosexual titillation:

PA: Just so you can flirt with them?

Boy: No not really. You just sit next to them 'til you get a stiff on!

This expression of lusty feelings and the graphic depiction of male arousal created an exuberant atmosphere. This joyfulness perhaps reflected both the topic of male pleasure, and its enhancement by the fact that they imagined it interrupted the researcher's expectation of a polite, sanitised discussion. Its shock value, which comes from the transgression of the 'private' matter of sexuality into public space, may not be as high as in school where sexual explicitness can be seen as contrasting with elaborated codes, but the training project, by virtue of its association with education, clearly counted as public in terms of this boundary. This type of comment highlights their lusty bodies, not simply enquiring minds. Some of them made multiple references to their bodies, and their physical performances drew attention to their bodies in a way that was notably different from the muted, controlled presence of the bodies of the young mothers, some of whom were interviewed in small groups. Men's bodies were key to many working-class male occupations, where 'real work' was physical labour (Mac an Ghaill 1994b), and this region had its own history centred on such industry.

Embodiment can disrupt conventional pedagogic relations, as we have argued. The focus on the body in parts of SRE felt uncomfortable and boundary-breaching for some of the teachers who found themselves delivering SRE to their forms with very little training in relevant pedagogies (Alldred *et al.* 2003). One specific incarnation in SRE of the general distancing of the intellect from the body, is the difficulty of acknowledging sexual desire. Doing so conflicts with the desexualised construction of the pupil, and it is also a topic not easily addressed in mainstream British culture. When Pam acknowledged their bodies and the potential for desire to structure their choice of learning setting, the discussion faltered. When speaking of pleasure was licensed in this way, it was either not of interest to or simply not easy for the boys. Since they had said they would 'just have a laugh' about sex education with the lads in class, she had asked if they would pick up a leaflet to read later. When one of them said they would 'chuck it back', she asked: 'What about if it is information you need to know? Say it was about different diseases or stuff that is going to improve your pleasure?' There was laughter, then a relatively long pause, which Pam eventually broke by asking another question. It is possible that they felt uncomfortable because it pointed (unkindly) to how this rejection of information might spite themselves. Or perhaps they were uncomfortable with the attempt to recognise sexual pleasure in the relatively public setting of the group. It addressed this risky topic directly, rather than it being an entertaining, transgressive aside, and it also took it out of their control. In general, this educational institution (the NACRO project) was paying more attention to bodily needs or experiences than schools might, as is evidenced by its acknowledgement of smoking and structuring of the timing of sessions around nicotine and concentration levels. But it was much easier to speak of the body's desire for nicotine than it was to acknowledge sexual pleasure or desire.

Trying to hear the conversation on the tapes of each group, we are struck by the amount of laughter, banter and heterosexual male posturing. Indeed, the conversation frequently descended into cacophony, and laughter and comments from the other boys would overlap. In the quieter, less intensely heterosexualised classroom discussions, boys in male groups occasionally gave pedagogic reasons, such as learning about the girls' viewpoints or learning from their more 'mature' or 'sensitive' questions. However, many remarks are inaudible because of laughter, and many times the researcher struggled to return to the agenda because of jokes and remarks that were sexually explicit and seemed designed to shock her and/or make the other boys laugh. Of course, when she asks as an open question, 'What would you ideally like sex education to be like?', the answer is 'A good demonstration' and, when asked to elaborate, 'A practical one where you get a woman and the whole class lines up and you get a man on that side and . . . then they take it in turns . . .'. This produces a loud guffaw of overlapping comments and laughter amongst the boys. Pam asks if before that practical experience they would need to be sure they understood about STDs and gets some agreement and is about to get the discussion back 'on track' when she says she wants to know how they want 'it' delivered, which is met with 'On top' and more laughter.

These discussions were dominated by short, emphatic statements about their school experiences and about sex. There are assertions of status on the basis of sexual experience or confidence, endowment or performance, and a conventional masculinity holds sway in the group. The boys use sexist (sometimes), homophobic (occasionally) and sexual comments (almost all the time) to shore up their own status in the peer group. Displaying their homophobia consolidates their own masculinity but at the expense of others in a process of gender norming in which other heterosexual men, women, as well as sexual Others are their foils (Nayak and Kehily 1996).

Boys' banter

So much of their peer culture banter is about confirming status that it is worrying to think how this feels to those not at the top of the peer group hierarchy (Askew and Ross 1990; Nayak and Kehily 1996). It is largely the same boys who are older, more sexually experienced, make the others laugh, interrupt the others more and dominate the discussion. We call it banter, rather than discussion, because of the considerable amount of interruption and overlap and the triumph through loudness of sexually explicit or otherwise humorous remarks. Frosh *et al.* (2002) also found that the all-boys group discussions functioned as a site for boys to jockey for position within the peer group, reproducing versions of themselves and their peers that valued hardness, appearance or capacity to subvert schooling. Competition between boys and the need to establish hierarchies have been noted by many researchers (Head 1999) and, as Willis (1977: 147) argued, 'male homophobic expression may be tightly bound up with attempts to increase status within the competitive pecking order of masculine groups'.

Kehily and Nayak (1997) described the role of humour among male pupils in school as an organising principle of heterosexual masculinity, deployed to position other pupils within differing dominant and subordinate peer group sexual cultures. We found similar processes at work in a boys-only (not just boy-dominated) group where boys' performances indirectly, and occasionally directly, positioned other individual boys as implicitly less sexually experienced/confident/less heterosexual in ways which provided for themselves a superior position. We too found that whilst boys' humour contains 'moments of subversion (to teachers, bourgeois values, compulsory education, etc.), it is also a compelling mode for sex/gender *conformity*' (Kehily and Nayak 1997: 70). We share their analysis of both continuity with and distinction from the work of Paul Willis (1977) where humour is a product of class cultural tensions, but is productive of rather than an effect of working-class masculinity.

The boys competed to hold the 'stage' and so one might initially imagine this suggests a flirtatious interaction with the young(ish) female researcher, whom the boys are competing to impress, but not so (or not only so). The bragging had the character of asides, although comments were spoken loudly and emphatically. A manufactured casualness about the comments was one hint that these young men were more conscious of each other than of the researcher as their audience, but there were others too. The quality of being an aside also conveyed a form of modesty or self-consciousness about bragging which seemed at odds with the brash comments themselves. Overall their behaviour was self-conscious and mutually surveillant, and there was much evidence of what Redman (1994) called the 'playground policing' of sexuality via awareness of others' reception of their body language, intimacy or physical proximity, joke telling and verbal abuse. As Nayak and Kehily (1997: 151) describe: 'Young men invest in masculinity in psychosexual ways where sexuality is itself a barometer for measuring male performance. Here, sexual reputation, wit, physical strength and swagger are vital ingredients'. Their displays were oriented to others, seeking external validation and recognition. But the primary audience for these overtly heterosexualised performances was their peers, not the researcher.

It is dismaying to see how significant physical size and sexual maturity seem to be in conveying social status. A male worker commented on this at the end of one session, telling Pam privately about how odd it was that the two boys from the same school both seemed physically and socially 2–3 years 'behind' the other boys of their age on the programme. These boys' embarrassment at the discussion of sex was 'obviously because it's something they've not approached yet', he said, whereas he knew that several of the other boys were sexually active. Physical performances, which the tape-recording failed to capture, also played a part in these dynamics.

Trying to 'look big in front of your mates' captures the physical quality of the verbal posturing and the significance of actual bodily size in this competitive 'play'. A conventional hegemonic masculinity drawing on physical force for power is implicit in this *big man* discourse. Barron and Bradford's (2007) notion of 'corporeal capital' captures the advantages of a bigger body for social status amongst young men. Those with deep voices and facial hair used displays of heterosexuality to their advantage, whereas for others this was a riskier performance. If their act was not credible because their sexual inexperience was known, or, worse, if their performance attracted the derision of one of the older or more experienced boys, the performance would backfire. Ranking low in the peer group hierarchy would then have been made worse by having attracted attention to it and having been seen making a bid for higher status. This behaviour might be paid for by continued put-downs for daring to compete. This shows how 'looking big' is often at the expense of others, as Nayak and Kehily (1997) and others have shown, whether those others are mates or abstract Others (like 'faggots').

School non-attenders' experiences of school

The upbeat atmosphere created by humour and sexual innuendo ebbed away and another way of doing working-class masculinity emerged when they recounted their experiences of school. These were marked by an overriding sense of injustice, and they described unfair punishments from teachers. Without exception it was the teachers, as opposed to pupils or the school regime itself, that they were critical of. They felt disliked by teachers, picked on or unfairly treated. One boy said: 'The teachers egg you on to fight with them so they can expel you'. Another said: 'They wind you up'. A third: 'One of the teachers would spark you off, then keep winding you up'. Several of them alleged physical violence from the teachers. One boy in particular who had said at the outset, 'I'm never happy at school cos the teachers try to beat you up, they do', a minute later in response to the question 'Have you generally had a good or a bad time [at school]?' replied, 'A cruel time'. A sense of injustice in relation to teachers' behaviour was also a key theme in Pomeroy's (2000) study of the views of 30 young people excluded from schools in Birmingham.

Many of them claimed to have been bullied by teachers, but none described bullying by other pupils. Several had been suspended for fighting. It is possible that they may themselves have been accused of bullying, but there was certainly no peer group acceptance of bullying. Instead they presented themselves as victims. One alleged that a teacher had thrown a chair at him, another a shoe, another that he was slapped and another 'strangled'. Like other researchers who have gathered accounts from school-excluded young people (Marks 1996; Pomeroy 2000), we found both external attributions of cause – 'I was just in the wrong place at the wrong time', 'she just needed someone to blame' – and internal ones – 'I've got a real temper on me', 'I just lost it'.

When asked what they wanted schools to be like, they talked about wanting to feel respected. They usually described feeling disrespected as individuals, but sometimes there was also a complaint about the general treatment of the class:

PA: One of you said it's about the way teachers treat you?
Boy: Yeah. People have to show me respect, then I'll show it them
PA: What should teachers do to make you feel respected?

Boy: Not shout as soon as you walk into the classroom
PA: Shouting at you or just generally?
Boy: The whole class. Mr X doesn't like me. I walk in and say 'Hey up, Sir' and he's pissed off with me!

Descriptions of school experiences unlikely to promote self-esteem characterised all three of the boys' groups. In this respect, the young men's accounts closely resembled those of the young mothers. Despite the boys' recognition of their need for sexual health information, where their experience of school had been overwhelmingly negative, few of the aims of PSHE or SRE would be likely to have been met, relying as they do on positive relationships with teachers and an atmosphere of trust. Individual interviews with these same young men may, however, have elicited differing accounts. A couple of boys did say they wanted to go back to school, one saying he would only want to go back to his previous school which he liked because it was familiar.

For all the competitiveness evident in their jockeying for position in the peer group hierarchy, there was also a sense of collectivity at play: a shared identification in having been victimised in schools. It is possible that the research encounter helped produce this, with an outsider coming into their familiar setting. In fact, their awareness of being of research interest as excluded young men might create a more cohesive sense of being 'in it together' and called upon to explain their common marginality. Seldom did an individual narrative emerge through a monologue or even several successive sentences. Their short utterances overlapped each other's, but rather than treating these as interruptions, they seemed comfortable contributing to each other's accounts of personal experience. This gave the sense that this performance was well rehearsed, these positions familiar to them, suggesting their previous sharing of and hence familiarity with each other's stories. The boys had bonded through a shared sense of injustice at teachers' treatment of them, and this victimisation mostly by men both older and with institutional power over them did not threaten their masculinity. In contrast, complaints about treatment by women teachers usually descended into derision and childish humour about them 'screeching' or passing wind. Perhaps these experiences were not dramatised in the same way because they functioned differently amongst the peer group. Trivialising them avoided a knock to male pride.

Given the negative identity of excluded or truanting pupils in dominant educational discourse, a defensive, justificatory position is not surprising (Marks 1996). Identifying against a common enemy was perhaps an important and supportive dynamic of the group. MacPherson and Fine (1995) showed how an emphasis on commonalities within a group's discussions could create a corresponding difficulty in acknowledging differences between members. Theirs was an all-girl group who similarly met over a period of time. Given that none of the boys in any group mentioned being bullied by other boys (or girls), the absence of this subject position in the groups might reflect the difficulty of 'breaking rank' and admitting power relations and abuses between boys. Occupying such a position of difference would carry certain vulnerabilities – not only bearing the weight of difference, but also implicitly undermining the victim status of the others, perhaps even implicitly accusing them, and risking consolidating a victim identity within the group with the potential for further bullying. Here is a specific issue on which other positions may have been possible in individual interviews. Less sense of a shared identification emerged among the boys in the LEA group, which could reflect the participants having spent less time together and/or the individualism of educational psychology's discourses of individual educational needs (Thomas and Loxley 2001).

School non-attenders' values, priorities and aspirations

These boys were, unsurprisingly, not educationally oriented, and the dynamics of the focus groups illustrated a bravado-rewarding peer group culture that neither valued education nor would be easy to teach. The boys were defensive about their educational experiences, especially their permanent exclusions, justifying their behaviour and rejecting educational values and identities.

However, whilst these young men were outside *mainstream* education, by virtue of being enrolled on a training project, they were still in the system as a whole. By promoting 'alternative provision', the LEA had managed to engage these young men in some form of education. Like the young mothers we interviewed, they had already talked with professionals whose agenda was to re-engage them in education with an underlying narrative of reducing social exclusion. Locally there must also have been young men who had not been 'captured' by these practices of including young people 'at risk of exclusion'. Those who participated in the groups, it must therefore be remembered, had presumably been convinced either of the value of training, that the terms of these educational schemes were preferable to school, or of the benefits of cooperating with such initiatives. Whichever, like the young mothers, they were already 'in conversation with' the government-backed discourse of education and training. Lukes (2004) argues that government participation schemes inculcate the prevailing order in participants by requiring that they internalise their logic. Enrolment on these programmes implies and engenders acceptance of the centrality of employment for citizenship and the need for individuals to take action to make themselves 'employable' or responsibility for not being so. Politically, this represents the triumph of a model of citizenship in which social support is conditional upon specified individual action over a model in which social support is an entitlement. This is New Labour's contractual model of welfare in which state support is conditional upon the individual meeting their obligations (Levitas 2005).

Our participants were not passive in adopting dominant discourses, however. Indeed, we could not draw out any comment on training or employment hopes. Whilst our research questions were about experiences of education and employment aspirations, the young men in fact only talked about sexual activity or negative relationships with teachers. Their refusal of our research agenda – or its continual disruption by references to sex – can be seen as rejecting an educational agenda and the researcher as yet another education-associated professional scrutinising them. Their ambivalence towards the research is unsurprising if it is an unwelcome reminder of how their presence in an out-of-school project needs explaining, especially to people 'from education', given Pam's introduction by workers as 'from the university'. The efforts the boys go to in order to explain their expulsion from or rejection of school, and their displacement of our agenda, show their resistance to the educational subject positions the research had unintentionally provided for them – an uncomfortable reflection on what we thought was an approach that was sensitive and open to participants' perspectives.

Their disidentification as pupils either through a discourse of injustice or of their own personality appeared to block discussion of education in any broader sense. That is, it was not possible to discuss *education* without experiences of *schooling* dominating discussion. This illustrates the monopoly that schools have on 'education'. Having been unable to occupy the role of pupil successfully apparently limited the boys' conception of themselves as educational subjects. This is a reminder of the need to, and difficulty of, challenging the conflation of education with schooling.

The fact that the boys' performance in the discussion was oriented to their peers rather than the researcher indicates the significance to them of their current *social* rather than their previous *educational* identities. Performing and re-establishing heterosexual identities when amongst their peer group was of primary importance. The hegemonic masculinities in the groups were defined through being seen as sexually experienced, sexually knowing and confident, a stud, a horny lad – (hetero)sexual identities, not pro-educational ones (swot, boffin, ear'ole, studious, future-oriented, smart, going places, ambitious). The boys took up positions as knowing about sex, knowing about safer sex, having a laugh about SRE, being bold enough, knowledgeable and confident enough to demonstrate condom use in class, having desiring bodies rather than merely listening to SRE lessons, lusting after girls in the class, etc. The significance of these is that they offered much more positive subject positions for the boys than those provided for them within the research or within dominant discourses of education. Their performances were based on their identities as sexual beings, not as learners. Their sexuality was something they could feel positive about, in contrast to their school or coursework. A heterosexual masculinity with the emphasis on sexual interest or activity provided for them an adult identity offering positive self- and peer esteem.

Valued identities and currencies: adulthood and sexuality

The two groups of young people outside of schools who participated in our research both actively positioned themselves in opposition to educational discourse: both the young mothers and the young men constructed themselves as actively sexual and, in this sense, when they said schools should 'get real about sex', they distanced themselves from the pupil identity that rests on the notion of the non-sexual child. They deployed sexualised identities to resist the identities available to them in schooling, the significance of which is its adult nature. For young men, the need to defend against being positioned as a child is intensified by its association with femininity (Burman 1995). The adult masculine subject positions to which they could aspire were primarily defined through sexual activity.

The importance of accessing these more positive, sexualised identities in discussions was possibly intensified by the research's framing as about their experiences as pupils, as learners about the very personal subject of sex and relationships, and where, in addition, most had experienced being relatively powerless pupils subject to the behaviour of more powerful teachers. Smoking also operates as a marker of adult identity, largely because cigarettes are not legally sold to under-16s. This conveyed double status benefits to those larger boys who could pass as old enough to be sold them. Working-class young women sometimes describe smoking as helping them calm down, avoid rows or deal with difficult emotions (Gillies 1999). Whether or not it plays a role in stress management for these boys, smoking, like sex, operates symbolically to consolidate an adult identity, in the absence of an employment-related adult masculinity.

Like their fathers and grandfathers perhaps, their bodies were a resource for adult male identities, though not in sustaining manual labour. Thomson *et al.* (2003: 218) describe how young people today, without the earlier markers of 'transition' to adulthood (leaving school, leaving the parental home, starting work, marrying and living in their own house) base their own adult identities on 'competence, recognition and investment'. It is not surprising that these young men's investment is in their heterosexual competence, and if their sexual bodies are their capital, their heterosexual activity is their currency.

These are the triumphant, but not the *only* discourses of masculinity at play within this peer group (Haywood and Mac an Ghaill 2003). They are notably not the institutionally sanctioned masculinities that associate social power with middle-class ways of doing masculinity, where control, rationality, deferred rewards and intellect are valued (Connell 1989), but are among the 'alternative resources that young men take up in response to being failed by schools' such as 'sporting prowess, physical aggression and sexual conquests' (Haywood and Mac an Ghaill 2003: 67). Alongside their homophobic postures and comments, these boys might have access to more positive gay identities through pop stars or TV soap characters. In this peer group 'the "meaningless" use of the term (as in 'your pencil case is gay') [probably] runs alongside the "meaningful" use to insult a fellow pupil', both of which function to marginalise non-heterosexual identities, however (Atkinson 2002: 123). Another element of the context that we cannot see here is the wider social construction of masculinity by and in opposition to local femininities (Reay 2001a, 2001b; Renold 2005) or other dimensions of locally anchored discourses of adulthood.

As well as the range of ways of 'doing boy' and values attached to them within particular gangs and subgroups (Connell 1989; Mac an Ghaill 1994b; Martino 1999), by speaking of 'subject positions' (Davies and Harré 1990; Parker 1992) we can avoid presuming that the boys' identities or feelings about their exclusion are necessarily fixed or unitary. Whilst educational engagement is despised in some peer groups and particularly penalised for boys – to the extent that MacDonald and Marsh (2004: 151) describe a culture in which 'inclusion in the formal life of school could mean effective exclusions from informal friendship groups' – some boys do manage to occupy contradictory positions. Reay (2002) describes one working-class boy's struggle to hold onto the esteem he has amongst his peers whilst being successful at school. He manages to be neither a 'lad' nor an 'ear'ole' (Willis 1977) but a self-consciously crafted concoction of the two, but at no small psychic cost.

Unlike MacPherson and Fine's (1995) group of young women who struggled to acknowledge difference within the group and strove to name similarities of experience and perspective against the odds (being of differing ethnicities and class backgrounds), the dynamics among these young men are of seeking individual differentiation more than group commonality. This individualisation brings implicit or explicit competition, which seems more overt than among young women and must take its toll.

Unfortunately, only with the benefit of hindsight can we see how the research discussion misses the chance to question the individualising ideas embedded in these discourses of masculinity and the highly individualised notion of 'young person' adopted in preference to the institutional identity 'pupil' that they shrug off. These young men were not, as crude education discourse might have it, 'educational failures'; their emotive accounts of school experiences and current success in the placement testified to their being casualties of schooling – as a particular way of organising education. In terms of wanting to help them access alternative currencies to heteropatriarchal masculinity, we also want them to see the structures that disadvantage them rather than adopt the potentially self-damaging discourse of individual choice and responsibility.

The relationship context of SRE for boys

Woods's (1976) description of laughter as a strategy for coping with the regulatory and oppressive authority of schools, and especially as a therapeutic response to the emotional scars of such institutions, resonates here despite this non-school setting. The role of these boys' humorous banter can be seen in the light of previous school experiences or educational outcomes that, if we take the boys' accounts literally, were damaging to self-esteem, even if the peer group rescues some pride in having been expelled.

The dynamics of the groups probably offer insights into the likely dynamics of conducting SRE with boys-only groups, whether in training projects or schools. Above all, we see the importance of face-saving, of appearing to know about sex, and its corollary, the unavailability of a keen learner subject position, or penalties attached to not knowing about sexual matters, not desiring, or not being heterosexual. Frosh *et al.*'s (2002) analysis shows the struggle many young men have constructing masculine identities that are socially 'acceptable' with regard to peer group values, whilst trying to hold on to intimacy and emotional contact. Of course, whilst the outward face of sexist talk is bravado, the inward face is another story: 'Insecurities lurk beneath but the stories isolate the speaker from sympathy as well as from hurt' (Wood 1984: 79, cited in Nayak and Kehily 1997: 140).

Men's displays of self-sufficiency can be seen in a different light once their vulnerability is exposed (Hollway 1989). These boys' investment in their heterosexual masculinity has to be seen in the context of their socioeconomic and educational marginality. Their social and emotional investments highlight the way overly rational approaches to anti-sexism and anti-homophobia do not work alone. It would not be helpful to challenge, in a one-off session, elements upon which their sense of self is based. This could only be done over time with a worker they trust, and it needs be more than a mere rationalist approach (Walkerdine 1990). Recognising the limits of *intellectual* commitment to wipe clean the psyche of splitting and projection onto others implies the need to work with them to reflect on their *emotional* investments and on securing alternative sources of esteem. It might be important to help them identify other currencies before devaluing their existing one.

The emotional or self-esteem risks that boys face in being asked to discuss sexualities 'publicly' in SRE or research are not to be taken lightly. They have implications for the safety of their sexual practice. As Abel and Fitzgerald (2006: 105) found among young people in New Zealand: 'The "risk" to reputation and subjectivity [of discussing condom use] overrode any "risks" that may have occurred through non-use of condoms'. By implication, SRE programmes must attend to assertiveness, communication and empowerment, they conclude. Even then, appeals to rationality can be unhelpful in promoting safer sex because 'different actions are "rational" from within different frameworks of meaning. For example, if my aim is to prove that I am committed to a particular relationship, then unsafe sex may indeed be the rational choice' (Willig 1999: 113). Indeed, fully recognising the power of emotions and of contradictory or unconscious investments and fantasies is key to avoiding being overrationalist or 'getting real' about the psychological dimensions of SRE.

Hilton's (2003) study of boys' views of SRE involved slightly older boys who were still in education in the UK (16–17-year-olds at college). These young men showed an impressive awareness of pedagogy and its relationship to personal teaching style and commented insightfully on their experiences of different approaches regarding the teacher–pupil relationship and classroom atmospheres established for SRE. Whilst they had differing views about whether women SRE teachers are preferable (because women are 'usually better at talking about relationships and stuff') or male teachers are preferable (to ask about 'men's stuff'), so too do researchers – for instance, Biddle and Forrest (1997) find boys wanting male teachers with whom they can identify. However, what is interesting is that the personal qualities of preferred teachers overlap well across studies, and indeed are a matter of agreement among Hilton's respondents, despite disagreement about their preferences regarding age and gender of SRE teachers. What was really important in teaching SRE, they agreed, was feeling comfortable with the subject, hence being approachable and not being embarrassed or 'easily fazed' by questions. They were conscious of when teachers struggled with the subject, and this made for neither comfortable nor effective learning. Echoing our findings, Hilton found the importance of a teacher engendering trust, respecting confidentiality and not gossiping or laughing in the staffroom. Disagreement about whether younger or older staff were preferred similarly boiled down to agreement about the quality required, which was empathy with young people.

What we want to highlight here is the concern young men register with the emotional tone and social dynamics of the educational setting. The young men in Hilton's group discussions expressed the 'need for a teacher who could produce a safe environment' (2003: 39). The young men in our study did not articulate this, but their concerns can be seen in the light of it. In the sense that their discussion of *education* (including future ideas) was dominated by *school* (past experiences), and their discussion of school was dominated by accounts of the problematic dynamics of their social relationships with staff and the emotional consequences of this, the importance of teachers' training in the creation of emotionally safe and supportive environments is underlined. The social dynamics of the classroom were a primary concern expressed by the Year 9 boys in our study, but these young men add a greater urgency to attending to the emotional dimension of educational relationships.

The relationship between this type of emphasis on emotional or therapeutic approaches, gender cultures and feminism is complex (Burman 2006; Parker 2006). For now, let us merely note that it does not ameliorate the need for feminist analysis of the way such modes of masculinity use and abuse power among men or between men and women. If a capitalist society is becoming more stereotypically feminine in its attention to the emotions, this is not something to celebrate uncritically (Parker 2006) and the role psychological discourses play in, for instance, attributing responsibility must be scrutinised.

chapter/**eight**

Conclusions: Getting real about sex – embedding an embodied sex education in schools

The working-class young men who participated in our group interviews, as we have seen, illustrated vividly their embodiment in youthful, lusty, male, smoker's bodies and showed how they were learning a heterosexual masculinity that mapped closely onto traditional (perhaps especially Northern) white, working-class masculinities. They had already learned the hegemonic version of masculinity in their culture and community. They had discovered its apparent conflict with educational success, their own low standing in terms of earning potential, the competitive dynamics of 'laddishness' and the social rewards from their peer group of the heterosexualising performance of being 'up for it' – confident and enthusiastic about sex with women/girls. Their schooling, their training project attendance and even their participation in the research were opportunities for learning and rehearsing heteronormative gender identities. Not exactly the impact we had imagined for our action research, but how could it be otherwise? We could not, of course, step outside of existing local and wider discourses and power relations in order to research them.

The same was true for the young women we interviewed. The discourses of adulthood through which they were negotiating their identities were gendered, classed and racialised. Social expectations of maternal and other caring roles were 'real' enough, and some of them already had care responsibilities before becoming mothers. The subject positions offered them in education and welfare policy discourses take no account of such relations. As Aapola *et al.* (2005: 7) argue: 'The neoliberal incitement of individualism, rational choice and self-realisation bump up against discourses of femininity creating contradictory and complex positions for girls'. In addition, girls from working-class families face a 'girl power' which 'tells them they can be what they want in a labour market that cruelly sets limits on any ambition, together with an education system that classifies them as fit for certain kinds of work' (Walkerdine *et al.* 2001: 21). They bear the burden of the expectation of upward social mobility and risk being constantly failing subjects with only the individualised explanations of their position provided by psychological discourses (Walkerdine 2003; Thomson *et al.* 2003). In this particular, economically deprived area, professionals' attempts to 'raise aspirations' for education or employment bump up against expectations of women as 'copers' at home, in this white, working-class mothering, unlike the way African Caribbean mothers in London expected to cope with work and mothering simultaneously (Duncan *et al.* 2003b; Reynolds 2005).

For both the young men and the young women, education was failing to recognise the reality of their relationships and their subjective investments. The expectations and aspirations for adult lives in this community were clearly gendered, and mapped onto traditional gender roles particularly around parenting and breadwinning. Yet the gender-neutral language of education policy refers to 'pupils', 'students', 'workers' and 'parents' as if we are ungendered beings. SRE needs to engage with the existing lives and loves of young men and young women, and not only as future partners and lovers, as implied by the discourse of child as person-to-be.

We now draw out our arguments from our overall findings about the contemporary politics and practices of sex education in the UK. As we do so, we emphasise the need to recognise educational subjects as embodied and gendered, to embed SRE more centrally in education and in schooling, and to embed an analysis of SRE in schools in wider cultural formations, specifically of gender and sexual normativity.

Embedding analysis of SRE in society

As Thomson (1993: 219) has argued, 'sex education both constructs and confirms the categories of "normal" and "deviant" which it regulates, monitors and controls . . . Education reflects the dominant politics of a society's institutions and sex education reflects the sexual politics of those institutions'. Our account of what teachers manage to achieve in the area of SRE is mindful of the structures they work within and pressures they are up against. Normative ideas about gender, sexuality, the role of work or of parenting in adulthood which we have glimpsed through the prism of SRE operate at the broadest societal level, anchored to social practices. This raises a dilemma for us: of wanting to argue for radical change and yet wanting at the same time to provide something of use to the teacher who has a limited domain of influence at school and is subject to national policy priorities.

Chitty (1999: 297) characterised teachers as 'caring but often frightened professionals' since they had been unable to maintain consistent teaching or policy regarding sex education over the previous ten years as the Thatcher and Major Governments meddled in order to get their right-wing politics into this area of the curriculum. Much remains unchanged since then. The Blair Government's interest in sex education shows more continuity with Conservative agendas on family values and with neoliberal economic priorities than might have been predicted. Although the pace of change, in policy and guidance, duties and legal responsibilities, and initiatives for funding or attainment targets has quickened and many teachers and head-teachers feel swamped by the burdens these impose.

The teachers' emotional state that Chitty (1999) described seems little improved. Anxiety is palpable at all levels of education, and sex education is suffused with concerns that refract bigger tensions in British society. What are our shared values, what is 'good for' children – and what is culturally specific about either presumed consensus or what is taken as fact? What is the common value-base and curriculum for sex education that will invoke the wrath of no parents? How is a values-based education to be squared with multicultural value-plurality? What is the role of the school in promoting values anyway? If it is the school's role to promote social cohesion, does this require agreeing shared values? Anxiety about what parents or governors of diverse religious and cultural backgrounds are likely to object to, in practice, blocks clear thinking about what schools ought to deliver and how. Yet research finds that anticipated parental objection to sex education far outstrips reality. A value-free education may be an impossibility, but a different starting point could be in what girls and boys are entitled to learn.

The emotionally unhealthy dynamics in many British secondary schools create cultures of blame and accusation, so that teachers are reluctant to take responsibility for, or management positions on, issues perceived as risky. They defend their subject territory against imagined intrusion of either parents or other professionals because they feel threatened and are fearful of potential moral outrage and approbation. Our research was haunted by the spectres of the angry parent convinced that the SRE teacher had corrupted their child's innocence, and the outraged journalist hounding teachers who thought they were simply doing their job.

Gender is on the public agenda now, as are certain questions of sexuality, and although passions rage about how sexual orientation is viewed (for instance, threatening to split the Christian church), the passion and connectedness of intimacy are absent from policy formulations. Even when gender differences and sexual orientation are acknowledged, recognition of difference is limited by the binary boxes offered for its containment, and responses are limited by the individualistic and pathologising models that prevail. If, for some, gender norms are becoming more flexible, they are perhaps least so around issues of sexual orientation. The compulsoriness of hetero-sexuality is a 'pervasive, silent and often denied power that permeates formal education' (Epstein *et al.* 2003: 12) and that is policed differently for (and by) boys and girls and requires they all take up a position as one or other gender. There are contradictory shifts: whilst for some it is becoming more publicly acceptable to express oneself openly about sexual matters, new risks emerge. Individualisation brings greater identity investment in sexuality and greater responsibility for sexuality as a matter of personal ethics. These investments and the moralities on which judgements are made differ for boys and for girls. As we have seen, the ungendered and desexualised official discourses of young people in schools can impact in troublesome ways. They lead to an idealised construction of the child-pupil as non-sexual, and hence to the stigmatising or pathologising of those young people whose sexuality is evident. In addition, a particular and heteronormative notion of sexuality is enforced in punitive ways. This, along with failing to challenge the silence around, fear about and resistance to 'the homosexual Other', lets down *all* pupils.

Teachers are caught in a double-bind: legally obliged not to discriminate between pupils on the grounds of gender and yet reading research findings that single-sex discussions can work better for subjects such as SRE. There is also an increasingly loud pupil preference expressed, especially by girls, for some single-sex classes. Nurses, by virtue of their concern with health and therefore the body, are 'licensed' to employ a discourse of gender differences among young people. We recognise a tension here that feminists have long agonised over – between identifying gender as a significant social construct, and yet through this analysis further reifying such normative categories.

Radically rethinking sex education points to the broader social changes needed. Sexual empowerment or autonomy would be best learnt alongside autonomy in all spheres of life, and the ethical principles behind 'many valued elements of sexual experiences (e.g. communication, trust, active consent, pleasure, flexible negotiation, equality, etc.) should also exist in the relationships that make up a healthy society' (Heckert 2005: 1). As Heckert (2005) points out, sex education in schools would probably receive more popular support if accompanied by non-directive, participatory and caring discussions about sex, sexuality and relationships in the wider community. For now, we restrict our focus to the goals we seek within educational practice. Our conclusions concern recommendations for SRE practice in class; for relationships in school; and for teacher education.

Embedding SRE in schools

By the end of our study we came to view SRE as a practice that is central to gender normativity and as key to treating young people as sexual subjects. However, it will fail in its goals and will fail young people unless schools actively and critically examine the gender, sexuality, body and beauty norms of society and specific peer group cultures. Wider social values cannot simply be ignored in the classroom, of course. Furthermore, within schools, recognition of the differing perspectives and agendas of the multiple actors is essential. Here, in addition to recognising potential differences between pupil and staff priorities, by drawing together differing professional agendas in schools and contrasting education (pupil-based) and health (client-centred) pedagogies, we can see the very different understandings of young people within these sets of professional practices. We make proposals for SRE practice on the basis of our findings and of a thought-exercise about the education of young mothers/mothers-to-be. This suggests an approach that is generalisable if we are prepared to rethink what education might look like. Finally, we bring together our arguments for rethinking priorities in education overall.

The context for learning and teaching about sex, sexuality and gender has been changing in Britain and in post-colonial societies, as the troubled implementation of the UN's (2000) Millennium Development Goals of gender equity illustrates (Aikman and Unterhalter 2005). This policy context has altered the curriculum in ways that have reduced the perceived importance of PSHE (Best 1999) and contribute to a split between different approaches to teaching or to understanding young people's development. Broadly this split is represented by an emphasis either on academic success or on personal well-being, and illustrates how the Cartesian dualism plays out in schooling today (Paechter 2006). This mind/body dualism underpins the importance attached to schools' role in society, and to the low status of health education in schools (Buston et al. 2002b). PSHE, as a 'social' rather than academic subject, and SRE, by association with the body, have been relegated to the educational sidelines as cross-curricular themes and asides to the school's main business. The mind/body split unravels when examined closely and has long attracted feminist critique for its gendered hierarchical associations. The falsity of splitting affect from the intellect also has substantial recognition within education, as initiatives such as Circle Time and programmes for emotional literacy indicate, but the particular policy agenda of the last decade has seen one particular school bully grow bigger and harder to avoid – what we have been referring to as the achievement agenda.

'School improvement' is driven forward in the name of 'raising standards', with standards reduced to the impoverished measure of success that is numbers of A*–C grade passes at GCSE. This agenda has exacerbated lack of consideration of pupils' personal development as well as trampled social justice concerns, whilst co-opting its language. The fact that this has eroded the school's welfare role, sacrificing pupil *well-being* at the altar of narrowly defined *education*, is, in practice, admitted by the compensatory development of children's centres for multi-agency welfare work. Sometimes the same building, a school, operates as a nexus for accessing services and for multi-professional surveillance and intervention. The comprehensive framework for children's services in *Every Child Matters* (DfES 2003) engenders partnership work towards shared goals, several of which support SRE. Such partnerships across health and education services are critical in SRE, but paradigmatic differences between the approaches of differing professionals must be recognised. Where partnerships produce clearly identified professional roles and responsibilities they are to be welcomed, but where they allow children and young people's needs to be compartmentalised, allowing 'education' to continue to imagine it can disregard social, emotional and physical well-being and development, it could be unhelpful.

These educational agendas are now suffused with discourses of young people's gender, in terms of academic achievement: with a new concern for boys' rather than girls' achievements in secondary schools (Epstein *et al.* 1998; Arnot *et al.* 1999; Skelton 2001; Younger and Warrington 2005). New policy and legislative frameworks are emerging around choice and personalisation under New Labour in 2006. The standards and achievement agenda has sometimes come to be interlaced with a more personal or individualising agenda, and teachers and head-teachers told us repeatedly about this as a dominant form of attending to 'the personal' within learning but which could not extend explicitly to questions of sexuality or sexual identities. The sex education now on offer in most schools takes a specific and narrow form, hidebound by the regulatory requirements of the standards and achievement agenda and the moralism of contemporary political culture.

Many commentators, as well as some of our participants, have become extremely sceptical about the New Labour project of using SRE and education more generally for its social inclusion agenda.

This social exclusion discourse propels individuals into the workforce without attending to the causes of poverty and inequality (Mizen 2004; Levitas 2005). It is a wolf in sheep's clothing, since it is not simply a slight variant on conservative family values, but something altogether more troubling. It represents the continuation and extension of the Thatcherite project of neoliberal economics and ruthless individualism but is even more insidious for its successful colonisation of everyday thought (Hall 2003). What concerns us is the power wielded by a hegemony so naturalised that its political values can barely be identified as such. As McRobbie (2000: 102) has noted, the contradiction within the New Labour project hinges on 'the celebration of individualism which cannot be comfortably reconciled with traditional family values. Hence the problems of endorsing a full free market position which ends up promoting antisocial values'.

The teachers, head-teachers, PSHE coordinators and nurses we spoke to felt restricted and compromised by the contemporary policy and legislative frameworks within which they had to work. They found the current balancing act between SRE, or PSHE generally, and the NC difficult to maintain. Committed PSHE teachers showed us how the creation of markets in education produced new obstacles to good SRE through pressure to meet the achievement agenda. Schools' fear for their reputation and their position in the local schools' marketplace and hierarchy, concretised in the schools league table, narrowed their focus and made it hard for non-attainment-related issues to win a place on school management agendas. The status hierarchy this produced between PSHE and league table subjects had direct implications for resources too. The consequences of competitive relations between schools were widespread and profound, becoming apparent in competitive thinking applied elsewhere. It established competitive relations between subjects over resources such as time or staffing, and in competitive bidding between PSHE topics for the scarce timetable collapse days. The logic of competition has made its way into many places, organisationally, where either cooperation or a coordinated overview would be preferable.

Personal learning and development were felt to be sacrificed to 'achievement' in the name of competitive advantage. Even more disturbing, we find pupils and teachers, as well as schools, expected to apply this logic to their thinking and decision-making about themselves. We are not the first to find that concerns with equity are displaced by concerns with 'school effectiveness' (Rassool and Morley 2000; Whitty 2001; Lauder et al. 2006) and we conclude that the introduction of market forces into education and the consequent competitive relations between and within schools compromised their provision of education that supported pupils' social and emotional development.

Ofsted's recent (2005) report into the delivery of PSHE was dismal, concluding that it was largely failing young people. It supported our finding of the overarching need for staff training, and ideally for the delivery of PSHE subjects by specialist teachers, experienced and trained in the pedagogic approaches required by PSHE, not form tutors teaching it 'on the side'. It endorsed our argument that PSHE requires discursive approaches – suitable for considering values, active learning for skills development and to link information with experience, and an emotionally safe (or at least caring) environment where respect and ground-rules set the tone. PSHE had only been part of initial teacher education for one of the participating teachers in our study, and the PSHE postgraduate certificate in continuing professional development was not available until after our fieldwork. Effective training could, however, have involved peer observation, shadowing or mentoring to share good practice in-house or between local schools. Good PSHE teaching is, of course, good teaching across the curriculum, and attending to the relationships upon which any teaching and learning rests is seen by some as the bedrock of an 'emotionally intelligent' – or, as we would prefer to call it, a caring – school. Organisations and training programmes exist (e.g. Antidote, Non-violent Communication, Transforming Conflict) to promote emotional literacy/articulacy and restorative justice approaches in schools as tools for improving a school's whole ethos, not just meeting the communication skills aims of the SRE curriculum. These offer a philosophy as well as a set of pedagogic tools.

The Ofsted (2006) report on citizenship education, in constructing PSHE as 'about the private, individual dimension of pupils' development' and 'citizenship on the other hand [as] concerned with the wider public dimension, educating pupils about public institutions, power, politics and community – local, national and international – and equipping them to engage effectively as informed citizens' (2006: 14, para. 57) maintains traditional views of public and private, with their conventionally gendered overlay. Producing fit citizens apparently need not address matters of sexuality, identity or ethics surrounding family and sexual relationships. These are constructed as private concerns belonging to the domestic sphere, feminised and devalued, implying that matters of power, values, justice and respect are not important here too. The problem lies in trying to draw a boundary between what is 'social' and what is 'individual'.

The relationship between PSHE and CE is complicated, and teachers can see lessons on friendship and relationships as CE because they deal with conflict resolution, an aspect of the Key Stage 3 curriculum. But pupils need to learn about negotiation and compromise, principles and pragmatism, values, consensus and difference – principles applicable at all levels from the personal to the local, national and international. Arguments about which curriculum a topic belongs to might be irrelevant in a holistic approach that rejected the logic of competition. PSHE and CE programmes can complement each other and both drugs education and SRE would seem ideally suited to study within both a social and a personal frame. Indeed, it might well help to raise the status and alter thinking about young people's sexuality to explore it within the framework of citizenship, to consider specifically their sexual citizenship (see Waites 2005).

The current statutory framework for sex education in schools, as we have seen, makes significant strides towards answering young people's call to 'get real about sex' by at least requiring that all schools provide SRE that is more than biology. However, a peculiar political constellation of conservative family values and sexual morality, alongside more 'liberal' attitudes and hypersexualised cultural images, allows for interesting moves that sometimes grant young people improved access to sexual health information and services. But this is often at the cost of adopting a medicalised approach to sexuality. Indeed, by constructing sexual behaviour primarily through a discourse of risk, the discourse of pleasure remains muted and the chance to engage with young people's own agendas is missed. In addition, the compartmentalisation of such interventions within or without school often means they do not go far towards addressing young people as embodied sexual beings in the classroom more generally.

Even commentators who welcomed and were positive about the current sex education legislation have their reservations. Monk (2001: 289) described much of the legislation in the area of sex education as 'reflect[ing] at best a democratic political compromise and at worst highly politicised "moral panics" about AIDS/HIV, homosexuality and child sexuality which have little to do with the every day needs of real young people'. Teachers in our and other studies are critical of the way SRE is not informed by and does not even particularly *seek* to meet the needs of children or young people (Corteen 2006).

In addition, the concern to meet the wishes of parents or carers about SRE rides roughshod over the wishes and values of young people themselves. One of the consequences of marketisation in education is that the 'turn to parents as consumers' produces a turn away from pupils and a consideration of their views. As others have observed (Monk 2001; Lyon 2007), the children's rights agenda, enshrined tentatively in UK but more robustly in international law, is only slowly filtering through educational practice. Resistance to this is more institutional than individual, if the practitioners we interviewed are representative of those working in schools. Schools have long been adult-run institutions embodying adult-centred approaches to the 'problem' of educating the young. Hearing and taking account of pupils' views is a profound challenge.

Schools with a faith-based ethos saw SRE as explicitly value-based and delivered it through the Family Life part of their RE curriculum. They were less comfortable with the knowledge and information strand, particularly, for some, regarding contraception and abortion. More typically, schools took refuge in the fact-based nature of part of the SRE curriculum. As we have seen, the school nurses all shared a contrasting view to that of the faith schools and a few of the other teachers. They saw giving sexual health information as a client-focused service providing medical information, whether this was on a one-to-one or whole-class basis. They were confident in their teaching – having been trained to deliver this material to this age group in class settings – were comfortable with active learning and discursive pedagogies and clear about the confidential nature of their one-to-one discussions. Their resolution to the values-versus-information formulation that caused stress for teachers was to distinguish clearly the 'facts' they imparted from the moral decisions young people would make about their own behaviour. They attributed young people moral agency, as their clients, and saw them as legitimate sexual subjects. This contrasted with schools' sense of accountability and orientation to parents, governors, the LEA, the DfES, and finally to pupils. This is what we call a paradigmatic difference between health and education approaches to SRE in schools.

Head-teachers, on the whole, were more engaged with the achievement agenda than with how to implement the SRE Guidance. This seemed yet another resource-intensive initiative they could ill afford, and their sense of 'initiative overload' meant they had little energy to think creatively about links between academic and personal education. Some head-teachers saw the potential of personal and social education to contribute to pupils' personal development and to more effective learning across the curriculum, but in practice their agendas were full with attainment and financial concerns. Most were relieved to delegate SRE as a discrete topic. It is SRE's combination of being low status but high 'risk' that makes it particularly problematic and hence an ideal candidate for anxiety-managing processes such as compartmentalisation or abjection. Some schools were committing to self-efficacy or emotional literacy programmes, and these tended to be the ones doing poorly in the schools' league tables. These may be appropriate responses, but unfortunately can reinforce the idea that social and emotional learning is more basic than academic learning and is prioritised only as a remedial strategy to serve the achievement agenda.

When we asked head-teachers questions about SRE and its relationship to the achievement agenda, they sometimes seemed disconcerted about the intrusion of sexuality onto the school's management agenda. This reminded us that addressing sexuality in education disrupts the uneasy balance between public and private life (Epstein 1994a). Broaching the topic of sexuality in the mainly male head-teachers' offices felt like 'taking the lid off a can of worms'. This feeling, like the urge to restrict classroom discussions of sexuality, stems from a construction of sexuality as in need of controlling and containing, repressing or civilising that feminists and others have criticised. It invokes a hydraulic metaphor of pressure and release, such as that underpinning the male sex drive discourse (Hollway 1989). This view of sexuality and the model of power implied in the metaphor or classroom response are questioned by the discursive approach we have adopted.

Feminist post-structuralist writers, such as Deborah Britzman, Bronwyn Davies, Valerie Hey, Patti Lather and Erica McWilliam, have written about the implicit but important role of sexual desire and eroticism in education, but the potentially sexual dimension of adult–pupil relations is not readily acknowledged in the popular sphere. Recently an education researcher wrote an academic article about heterosexual desire and relations between male teachers and female secondary school pupils in which she revealed her own attraction to one of her teachers whom she went on to marry after they had both left the school. The proposed publication of the article led to a sexual scandal and prurient interest from the press (Sikes 2006a and 2006b). It is revealing of the cultural attachment to the desexualised pupil discourse that more scandal attaches to a teacher and pupil who later marry than to the sexual gyrations of teenage pop stars or the sexual violence in some young boys' computer games.

What does it mean that studies such as ours find that teachers' professional views about what is good for pupils, schools or the education system differ from what the Government thinks? It appears that teachers' and head-teachers' views are sidelined by governments that increasingly centralise education policy, seeking such control over what teachers do that they stipulate not only what curriculum to deliver, with what pedagogy, but even how to divide up the minutes of the literacy hour. Paradoxically perhaps, we agree with the FPA that SRE should be made statutory. However, we would not want to see teachers handed a script since that would undermine the responsive pedagogies SRE requires.

PSHE coordinators highlighted the contradictions they felt in discussing sexual desire, sexual bodies and sexual practice with young people when, in the classroom context, they are positioned as pupils who can or should be educated into certain values. They found it hard to acknowledge 'publicly' (in the classroom) that pupils already had considerable sexual knowledge, feelings and some experience with partners. They were frustrated by the treatment of SRE and PSHE at school and national policy levels as separate from and subordinate to the academic NC subjects.

We conclude that there remain troubling contradictions between educational policies at the national level and the ways in which they are being implemented at the school level, despite some of these issues now reaching public agendas such as in discourses of human rights, inclusion and citizenship (Osler 2005; Mirza 2006). There remains a mismatch between young men and women's needs and wishes for sexualities education and the sex education that exists on the margins of the curriculum, where it reflects an economic agenda and attempt to enforce 'work ethic' norms. Not surprisingly, then, it fails to reflect what young men and women have told many studies they want from sex education – more attention to desire, emotions and the techniques and practicalities of sexual pleasure.

Embodied young women and education

We want to make constructive suggestions for improving SRE and to try to imagine a feminist SRE that does not subjugate the body. We use insights generated about the education of that most problematically embodied of pupils – the pregnant schoolgirl. If an approach can fit her body, it must surely allow more room than the usual. Adopting a female and pregnant model of the pupil disrupts the naturalised masculine and desexualised default. Centring our thinking on the pregnant or mothering pupil might also help shift the 'problem' mentality about her.

Education policy problematises young motherhood because it conflicts with the Government's economic priority of work, so it is refreshing when Graham and McDermott (2005: 21) turn the tables to ask what potential role policies could play in '*supporting* the identities and resilient practices young mothers develop in the face of social and material disadvantage'. How could education policy better support the education of young mothers? Teenage pregnancy may have been treated as having *implications for* education, but education policy has not been developed *for* pregnant and mothering teens. Even discussions of implications have progressed no further than the debate over *where* to provide such education, in mainstream or separate, 'special' provision (Pillow 2004).

For the majority of young mothers in our study and in others, schools did not feel secure or positive places to be. Harris *et al.* (2005: 25) write: 'Once they were pregnant they were often rejected and stigmatised, reinforcing messages that they were not welcome in the education system ... a feeling that appears to have remained with them over time'. Even for those who did not have negative school experiences beforehand, pregnancy could bring feelings of intense vulnerability. The physical vulnerability felt by pregnant young women points to a broader problem of violence within British schools today (see Duckett *et al.* 2007). Their struggles to move around the school safely, comfortably and to eat or visit the toilet when necessary, highlight just some of the bodily normative and regulatory aspects of schools.

Even without specific experiences of rejection or vulnerability, a young mother's increasing distance from education might not surprise us. Her perception is of the school's irrelevance to her new set of needs and growing priorities, and we would support her 'primary maternal preoccupation' (Winnicott 1956) as wholly legitimate for a mother-to-be or mother of a small child and highly important for her child. Her concerns and the school's concern with her educational progress towards examinations operate in different registers. Furthermore, the construction of the non-sexual, ungendered child pupil and the school's business of their cerebral development leaves schools ill-equipped to deal with the physically changing, sexual body and potentially emotionally labile young woman experiencing pregnancy, or young mother with real, not just role-play, relationships to build, sustain or mend. She is not really, of course, a special case: all pupils have real relationships and emotions, but the image of her bulging body and perhaps tearful outbursts highlight the naturalised absence of emotion and the body from the dominant pupil discourse, and the imagined interruption of the 'intellectual' by the 'emotional'. Despite schools' concern with 'children', they can seem remarkably disengaged from the embodied processes of family life and, indeed, are founded on an institutional devaluing of emotion and subjective experience.

Arguments about physical safety or relevant curriculum can imply the desirability of separate educational provision, as was previously the case in Britain and elsewhere, although earlier homes for unmarried mothers and their babies were more concerned with containing shame and rescuing respectability than with education (Hudson and Ineichen 1991). Educational provision now tries to be inclusive and meet pupils' differing needs in a common setting. In the USA, there are still specific educational programmes for pregnant and mothering teens. Luttrell's (2003) ethnographic study of one such programme focused on the identity work done by working-class teenagers to manage their shamed identities. The setting differs but the cultural politics described is similar to that in Britain (Phoenix 1991; Wilson and Huntington 2005).

Stigma and individualising blame are attached to non-approved sexualities or fertility pathways. Teenage mothers' motives are scrutinised in class-blind, sometimes racialised ways. They are accused of 'looking for love' in a pathological way that other mothers are not. It is possible to eschew such psychological focus on the individual (to the neglect of socioeconomic factors), whilst still keeping in mind a concern for individual young women. These girls are painfully aware of being scrutinised and judged by others and are hurt by their depiction as lazy or irresponsible. With this grief comes insight too, however, and Luttrell describes them becoming more self-aware, tentatively expressing fears or mixed feelings. An emotionally engaged environment would, of course, attend to and support them in this.

Luttrell's analysis of this programme echoes the findings of previous studies and offers cautions for the education of young mothers and pregnant young women. The first feature of their curriculum she identifies is the representation of education as a responsibility of the girls, indeed a responsibility they bear for others: the teachers' mantra is 'your child needs you to be educated' and 'if you won't do it for yourself, do it for your child', and unsurprisingly this 'educated motherhood' discourse featured in the girls' accounts: 'I wouldn't be here if it wasn't for my baby' (Luttrell 2003: 23). Second, there were striking 'absences and silences' especially around sexuality, bodies and pleasure. Ironically, female sexual desire was not only absent from the official curriculum, it was even more suppressed in this specialist provision than in mainstream education. If and when it was discussed, it followed the 'education as responsibility' line that 'as girls, *they* were responsible for practicing "safe sex" or abstaining, and not that, as girls, they were entitled to an education that would provide them with a sense of their own sexual desires and power vis-à-vis boys' (2003: 23; emphasis in original). The third feature was the social redemption messages which included strict behaviour rules such as how the girls ought not to 'parade themselves' and should be 'respectable' and 'discrete' because by being pregnant they were already setting a 'bad example'. Education was the road to redemption, and the girls were delivering themselves from their 'fallen' status as teenage mothers. The 'education as responsibility' approach, whether related to pregnancy, motherhood or sexuality, framed education in terms that could limit a girl's sense of self-regard, rather than support or enhance it.

The white girls' attendance dropped off in each cohort she studied, so that from being a minority at the outset, they disappeared completely from the programme, withdrawing from classes in favour of home study. The remaining girls were convinced this was because they 'don't want to be associated with us' (2003: 17). As a result, in spite of race equality legislation, black and white working-class pregnant teenagers were being educated separately. Luttrell explored the historical framing of white girls as redeemable, but black girls as irredeemably unruly and deviant, and the tradition of black supplementary schools. We can see how this pattern plays into the inaccurate depiction of teen motherhood as a black problem in the USA and the differential representations of white 'good girls who made a mistake' and black 'Welfare Queens' (Pillow 2004).

The girls' accounts of how the programme differs from mainstream school show gratitude for the most measly of concessions, such as being allowed to take time off for medical appointments or to eat when hungry. Such basic requirements for pregnant women point to the unreasonable inflexibility of the school regime and the firm hold that 'school' has on 'education'. Why need their education be in the form of old-style schooling which some of them had rejected anyway? The very normality of schools restricting eating and drinking can be questioned anew when the body in question draws attention to itself by 'showing' and revealing that it is a pregnant body that is being so disciplined. Human rights discourse applies to the treatment of pregnant women in prison, but not to school-age mothers-to-be where the punitive control is by virtue of their age and the school's 'normal' disciplining of pupils' bodies.

The pregnant body itself provided a site for some teachers to convey negative messages to the girls, albeit implicitly. 'Showing' was a recurrent theme in the conflict described by both teachers and students. When a pregnancy begins to *show*, the pupil's body no longer conforms and, moreover, it flaunts their sexual activity. When the girls *show* their pregnant bodies they are deemed to have a 'bad attitude'. Negative messages were communicated indirectly by the physical setting itself, which was inadequate and unsuitable. Housed in a long-standing temporary adjunct to the school, it had no heating or lift for the two flights the girls had to climb to reach it. When relocated to where there was heating, it was on the periphery of the school grounds with no educational facilities, such as a library, in reach. The desks were of the old-fashioned, wooden type with desk and bench joined, and therefore completely inflexible and barely big enough for some girls to get their pregnant bellies behind. Not only have they 'done wrong', but they themselves, their bodies, *are* wrong.

Pillow (2004) describes a young woman perching uncomfortably for a whole session on the edge of one of these same chair-desks because her three absences that month meant she didn't dare miss another class. This was a classroom specifically for teen mothers, yet her body still didn't fit. From this, Pillow develops her analysis of how pregnant/mothering teens do not 'fit', either literally or figuratively, into educational research, theories, policy and practices. Paradoxically, these US programmes, established under anti-discrimination legislation to provide equal access to education for pregnant teens, end up further marginalising them: they are excluded from mainstream education, geographically and socially isolated. Furthermore, instead of providing education 'as a right', the culture of these programmes can present it as 'a responsibility' towards their child.

For an earlier generation of women forced to leave education when they became pregnant the problem was not being pregnant, but the school's response (Luttrell 1997), as in Britain. 'Special' provision has not eradicated the problem, but has merely shifted it insidiously onto psychological grounds. Luttrell found this new generation of young women painfully aware of the hierarchies of class, race, gender and age framing their lives and the stigma of teenage pregnancy. Now, however, they are bound into meanings of education which claim to offer their only chance of improvement and redemption whilst at the same time delivering punitive, derogatory messages. Our participants did not seem as politically informed as their US peers, strengthening the hold that individualising discourses of responsibility for economic success might have over them.

Embodied young people and SRE

We now apply these insights to help imagine feminist educational principles for young men and young women that take account of gendered, lusty bodies. Firstly, education need not be in a school or modelled on schooling. Provision could start afresh, learning from the experience of the mother-to-be and not trying to squash her pregnant body and interests into the pupil mould. A model of education might be devised that is flexible enough to fit a young man or woman's life, values and physical health, and attend to local cultures and opportunities rather than assuming the naturalised but particular values of the neoliberal subject. A negotiated curriculum would focus on topics that students themselves identified as relevant. Luttrell calls for more chance for young people to play and to explore moral and identity issues. Attendance could be voluntary and flexible, and life events would be acknowledged and supported, not greeted with frowns for 'interfering with' education. Policy that allowed for this might avoid seeing pregnant or mothering pupils as 'a problem' for education, and an approach to education that lost the baggage of 'schooling' would benefit many pupils, not just those 'at risk of exclusion'.

Physical location, timing, structure and co-presence could be rethought, certainly to allow the changing requirements of the pregnant – or any other – body to be accommodated. For the young men we interviewed, rethinking the school's strict regulation of the body would be an essential component of an education that worked for them. Lusty and/or pregnant bodies might enjoy moving around more freely for comfort and in the interest of concentration. Reflecting *with* young people on the disciplining of bodies in schools could be an insightful exercise regarding the operation of power.

The mind might not be seen as split from the body, and the body might not be relegated to curricular or cross-curricular margins. This might enable sexuality and nutrition, say, to be high-status topics, integrating academic and practical knowledge. The relative status of academic studies and social and personal education could be rebalanced. Financial and practical knowledge might be valued without lapsing into cooking-cos-you're-girls and car-maintenance-cos-you're-boys or being limited to 'training'. Indeed, devising a relevant curriculum for today's young people could allow the study of social and environmental justice issues and movements to be prioritised appropriately. Dominant social values they may already be aware of negotiating could be scrutinised, including sexual double standards, the cultural ambivalence regarding motherhood and sexuality, and the tension between parent and worker identities. Boys and girls could be encouraged to think openly and critically about whether and what types of parenting, partnership and friendship relationships they value and aspire to.

Sexualities education would, of course, challenge normative assumptions about families and parenting that position teenage mothers as marginal and stigmatised and occlude or pathologise same-sex relationships. A proactive approach would create – not merely wait for – opportunities to disrupt heteronormative presumptions and stereotypes and to acknowledge alternatives, and education for a multi-sexual society would recognise and celebrate sexual diversity as part of the formal *and* informal curriculum (Atkinson 2002). The idealisation of 'good mothers' and denigration of 'bad mothers' could be challenged, as could the 'good girl/bad girl' construction of young women who are active in relation to or conceal their sexual desires, and the 'stud'/'wimp' constructions of young men according to their perceived sexual experience, prowess or endowment. Relational rather than performance aspects of sexual practice could be emphasised. Feminist insights into sexual obligations, duties and heteropatriarchal institutions have much to offer men as well as women (hooks 2000). Sensitivity would be needed to help some working-class young men identify other currencies to avoid devaluing their only or most prized currency.

Struggles over representation could be explored by pupils and self-representation activities employed reflexively/therapeutically so as to 'break the gaze' of those who judge, belittle or 'Other' them. Self-representational work could allow young men to think critically about their own investments, their peer group's celebration of hegemonic and denigration of other masculinities and the cost of continually competing with each other, as well as the gendering of power. It could provide an important opportunity for young mothers to manage the self-esteem damage done by the stigmatising of young motherhood. It would engage all young people in reflecting on the identity work they do around race and gender, for instance, including their own Othering practices.

Our main argument about the gendering of social reality – which is a problem when gender-neutral expectations are asserted in education and welfare policies – and the need to regender classroom practices and pedagogy are about making policy or classroom practices better match the real world – that is, reflect more accurately socially prevalent ideas about the world that we live by. We recognise the progressive intentions behind attempts to change the world through changing language, and are broadly part of that movement. But we are arguing that interventions need not only to construct aspirational categories as they critique existing ones, but also to recognise that people are already subjects, our hopes and aspirations *produced* through the gendered discourses of our home and local cultures. Feminist critiques of earlier anti-sexist work in schools (Walkerdine 1990; Arnot *et al.* 1999) argued that rationalist approaches were not enough and for the need to engage with the gendered ideals of our unconscious fantasies too: the princess and superhero images populating our imaginations despite any conscious rejection of them. Where so more than in our fantasies about relationships and sex? We need to avoid being overrationalist in our approaches to promoting safer sexual practice and truly engage with the nature of fantasy in desire if we are ever to 'close the gap' between young people's knowledge and practice of safer sex. Adding in the missing 'discourse of erotics' that young people have asked for will help raise the status of sex education for young people by relating it more closely to their lived experiences (Allen 2001).

Even if policy cannot, practitioners must engage with boys' talk and girls' talk as the only way to hear and try to meet their agendas and convince them to make our concerns (with STIs or with sex that is later regretted) theirs. The gap between peer culture and SRE practice risks leaving assumptions and myths unchallenged. The young people we spoke with were 'worldly wise' yet admitted they or their friends had believed that 'you can't get pregnant the first time' or that having intercourse standing up prevents conception. When we omit to teach something, we let playground whispers become louder and uncontested (King and Schneider 1999, cited in Atkinson 2002).

What does 'getting real about sex' mean for SRE? Direct, explicit and honest discussions of sexual practice, behaviour, feelings and safety that answer young people's questions and respond to their request that SRE is more than 'plumbing and prevention' (Lensky 1990) are essential. This means breaching the niceties of 'polite' culture in public educational settings that in practice evade responsibilities towards young people. All the young people we spoke to saw SRE as 'important as academic subjects', and were concerned with the quality of teaching, valuing confident, trained, specialist teachers and external speakers for the particular relationship they would develop with them and the confidence this instilled regarding confidentiality. Many studies have now reported that young people want more and earlier SRE and a more detailed and explicit coverage of sex, sexual anatomy, desire and feelings (Measor *et al.* 2000; Kehily 2002; Hilton 2003; Allen 2005). Sexual health services that are effective in attracting young people are those that start from young people's needs and wishes rather than from trying to get them into established, adult-centred institutions – schools, hospitals or clinics. What young people repeatedly tell researchers about wanting privacy and confidentiality is taken as axiomatic, so, for instance, it is not necessary to announce publicly a name and reason for attending as is required at family planning clinics and NHS walk-in centres. Instead a young person is greeted and invited into a consulting room before being asked to disclose personal information.

What this successful health-derived model and some of the nurses we interviewed managed to do, which analysis of young people's complaints about sex education identifies (Allen 2005), is construct young people as sexual subjects. This means granting them and encouraging them to develop a sense of sexual agency of the kind that is necessary in order to make decisions likely to promote their sexual health and well-being (Holland *et al.* 1998). Within this concept are implicit many of the strands of improved SRE practice that we have highlighted: the recognition of embodiment in differentiated and differently esteemed bodies; of existing knowledge; of varied amounts and types of sexual experience; of varying desires, pleasures and identifications; of varying emotional responses and experiences. If education could do this, then young people's sexuality would be seen as a positive part of youthful identity rather than be framed as a problem (Bay-Cheng 2003; Allen 2005), and therefore as legitimate and important business rather than as impeding the proper academic business of the school (Paechter 2004).

Good practice in SRE already has young people comparing the gendering of sexual insults, comparing lists of qualities seen as desirable in a boyfriend and a girlfriend, and comparing the qualities they seek in a friend with those they seek in a lover (Cohen 1999; FPA 2004; Heckert

2005). The result of the latter is usually the valuing of personal qualities such as sensitivity, intimacy, respectfulness, showing care, the reciprocated sharing of joys and vulnerabilities in each case. This brings into focus the psychological qualities of relationships, which helps value them more and decentres or critiques the superficial, appearance-based 'relationship' culture epitomised in music videos. Comparing the fantasy sex-lives projected through the commodification of relationships with findings of the National Survey of Sexual Attitudes and Lifestyles or the ID Research Sexualities Survey would surely be a useful exercise, even allowing teachers under the present system to tick boxes for maths, science, SRE and CE. Of course, avoiding compartmentalising relationships and sexuality in SRE could see them explored through literature or discussions of social change, etc., and illustrate the range of ways of thinking about them.

The real challenges lie in making responsible teaching about STI risks still 'sex positive' and making sex positivity sensitive to the pressures it can create (Glick 2000), helping young women and young men question some of the gendered 'rules' governing sexual pleasure (Storr 2003), and in making SRE more practical (Wilson 2003). In a thought-provoking discussion of whether SRE can and should include ' "hands on" experience rather than only the transmission of biological information and moral precepts' (2003: 23), Wilson proposes an 'erotic education' that could apply approaches familiar to PSHE such as role-play to avoid leaving young people 'to struggle with their own sexuality in isolation' (2003: 26). What this highlights is the step back taken from 'realistic' SRE when compared with other subjects on the curriculum, despite the existence of useful pedagogies that are practical yet 'safe' emotionally and physically (or at least careful). Allen (2004) points to toilet training as another 'private' bodily matter that we do not leave children to learn by trial and error. However, the very notion of 'the private', which sustains liberal society's devaluation of the feminine and exploitation of home-makers and workers under capitalism, can itself be questioned. As Heckert (2005) argues, if young people are encouraged to respect their own desires, listen to those of others, negotiate emotionally charged relationships, challenge coercion and domination, could not these same ethics be applied to all relationships and to question all hierarchies, including, for example, in the family or the workplace?

Each of the young mothers and the young father we interviewed would have liked better SRE, but not necessarily to prevent their 'early' parenting. Reasons to improve SRE include so that young people may better protect their health, and so that they may respectfully negotiate pleasurable experiences and question norms and pressures, including the gendered expectations of pleasure and performance that young men and women still report (Holland *et al.* 1998). Young people's views and experiences of school in general are important for envisaging an education 'otherwise', or else the wish to promote young people's social and emotional development and their radical empowerment may be seriously limited by the current education system. Young parents' and school non-attenders' experiences of school are of particular note to policy-makers because they reveal how the use of schools to implement a sexual health strategy or reach social inclusion goals may be limited by the teacher–pupil relationships possible within a resource-pressured, attainment-focused system. This evidently does not support the self-esteem of all pupils; and local or peer group cultures may not share New Labour values regarding the role of paid work for parents or the undesirability of teenage pregnancy.

Governing young people and their sexuality

Drawing on feminist post-structuralist approaches, we have developed an understanding of the experiences of young people in relation to education and located their sometimes gendered aspirations in the context of neoliberalism. Young people do not just *learn* about gender and sexuality as 'out there' in the social world, but the meanings and values they have access to are those through which they *produce themselves.* Their expectations, aspirations, desires and their sense of self are formed through constructions, including classroom and peer group vogues, regarding sexual attractiveness and desirable masculinities and femininities. This highlights the need for the curriculum to support young people in examining critically the normative and alternative discourses of gender, sexuality and relationships available for and already producing their subjectivities.

Interviewing someone indeed invites them to narrate a particular version of subjectivity or personhood. Researchers provide implicit expectations of a self-critical subject who identifies their own failings, but resolves to make good of them (Alldred and Gillies 2002). The research encounter can function as an opportunity for contrition and the acceptance of punishment, and hence for governing the self in line with disciplinary expectations (Marks 1996). The old binary of the educable/ineducable subject echoes in current Government rhetoric, transformed through the discourse of training, from which no one is exempt, but our discomfort with this and our intention that the research questioned such constructions were irrelevant to the way the research encounter may have functioned for young people. Merely asking young men and women whether they had plans for returning to education or training mobilises the expectation that they ought to. It reinforces the construction of work as central to adult identities. This offered the chance to occupy the position of 'educable subject' which is productive of a sense of self through education discourse. For those who had 'failed' at school, it offered the chance to position themselves as reformed characters redeeming themselves. This was not our intention, but who were we to think we could step outside the dominant discourse of education and training, or gather accounts 'before' or 'beyond' power (Butler 1990)?

Interviewing can be a tool of disciplinary gaze, then, and sometimes a means of censure: going to see the head-teacher means 'having a talk about it' rather than the cane these days. Central to the work of Connexions is interviewing young people 'towards' employment or training, where the interview is the chance for them to make 'appropriate' choices.

Sex education lessons for professional educators?

Specific, high-quality professional training on SRE is essential, as others have argued (e.g. Biddle and Forrest 1997; British Medical Association 1997; Measor *et al.* 2000), and indeed the Teenage Pregnancy Report (SEU 1999) urged the then Teacher Training Agency to consider whether the initial teacher education curriculum needed changing to reflect this. Specialist PSHE teachers are needed, in our view, to improve the knowledge base, the pedagogic skills base, the status of and to help meet young people's requests for more and better SRE. However, this is not enough. Questions from pupils about sexuality and relationships can crop up in any timetable slot and with an ever-lowering age of puberty and sexual experimentation, as Hilton (2003) has argued, SRE needs be on the curriculum for initial teacher education across the board, not only on the curricula for those who expect to teach it (e.g. science, for SRE, and social science, for PSHE). We propose comprehensive input on SRE for all trainee teachers and youth workers so that confidence in responding to young people's questions and interest becomes good practice across all preparation for working with young people. Updates through in-service training could help staff further develop their own communication and self-awareness to the benefit of all their relationships.

We draw from our study the need for education to place more emphasis on the emotions and on the relational aspects of teaching and learning and less on economic and employment agendas. Indeed, we see a need for educational researchers and teacher educators to find ways to discuss, without raising the emotional temperature, interpersonal teacher–pupil relations, pleasure in teaching, and ways to prioritise emotional, physical and sexual well-being, not just educational 'success'. Education is not only about academic achievement, but also about developing people's sense of themselves and their identities and values, linking learning and reflection with biographies and feelings, and enabling the development of personal identities and affective states that learning and academic identities rely on. Such issues need to be integrated within the substantive curriculum in individual lessons, as well as informing a rethink of the whole achievement agenda. We are arguing for a more reflective approach to learning and teaching, conscious of the role of education in society, focusing on what learners want and could gain from education, and in which all teacher education attends to social and emotional issues. The New Labour commitment to personalised learning might be seen by some as the vehicle for such a transformation, but its focus on 'choice' and the 'employable subject' would need serious critical scrutiny before and within any such attempt. Two areas of contention would be the reduction of choice to the options current policy provides for choosing, and the material constraints different individuals face.

The mental health pressures faced by young people today are reaching the agendas of educators, for instance, through concerns over the increasing suicide rate amongst young men, even those who appear to be coping well with academic pressures. Academic, sporting or peer group successes do not ensure they are not struggling with personal or emotional issues. This is where educators must pay close attention to individualised risks and vulnerabilities which young men and women, in their different ways, bear. The need to develop curricula around self-efficacy, self-esteem and emotional literacy is increasingly apparent, as is the need to make more publicly accessible critiques of the 'heterosexual matrix' identified by Judith Butler – and used convincingly in recent education research (Renold 2005, 2006; Nayak and Kehily 2006; Rasmussen 2006) – and to theorise masculinities/femininities in relation to subject achievement (Davies 2006; Hey 2006). It is here that broader attention to PSHE in initial teacher education will have its second advantage – in the greater confidence all teachers will have in being able to create emotionally supportive environments and hold sensitive discussions with young people about intimate or charged issues.

We want, therefore, to urge that, in future, education prioritises emotional well-being: it is not 'effective' for schools to produce young people with strings of qualifications at an emotional cost that leaves some of them on the verge of breakdowns. We want also to insist that education is for social and environmental justice too. Indeed, it should be about trying to make the world a better place, not just about processing individuals and inculcating qualities useful to the economy or capitalism. We have seen how the heavy emphasis on paid work and the current preoccupation with employment or training, even for new parents, plays out in young people's lives. Combining paid work and parenting is a juggling act at the best of times, and the emotional investment in parenting only ever increases with the intensification of psychological discourses of childhood (Burman 1994a; Beck and Beck-Gernsheim 1995), so we wholeheartedly support young mothers in wishing to focus on mothering before trying to carry the burden of individual financial self-sufficiency too. Indeed, shouldn't all young people be supported in thinking critically about the normative expectations about their lives in policy discourse or their own peer group?

In any case, the gender-neutral worker model neglects the actualities of much parenting, and the normative expectation for these working-class young people that mothers stay at home to look after their children. In the debates we have charted we see the politics of individualism in the extreme: personalised learning for the normative young woman in the classroom; punitive welfare cutbacks for needy young women who are seen as socially irresponsible for not being financially self-sufficient; and financial levers to coerce young men and women onto training courses or into jobs they will flow out of as quickly as they were shunted into. The lives of young mothers cajoled back into education or employment without listening to their preferences or views about their children's needs contrast with those young women who are outperforming boys at GCSE. But even these academically successful young women are later admonished for their overzealous commitment to work if they do not leave the workforce to have babies at the socially approved time. Policy debates neglect the work of feminist scholars and activists on the pressures of the 'double shift', the forgotten demand for 24-hour available childcare (Attar 1992; David 2003a), and that women should be able to choose if, when and how to have children. Even feminist success in adding the issue of the work–life balance to the policy agenda has been forgotten, and is constructed as a logical response to the labour market's need to increase the number and reliability of its 'workers' – constructed as gender-neutral again. Feminist work in making gender visible is still necessary, despite the selective uptake and sometimes co-option of feminist discourse.

Finally, we want to question the acceptable role for schools in implementing government policy concerning contested values, in particular to prioritise welfare budget reduction over education. We make a plea for a more compassionate schooling that values relationships above all and therefore questions the reliance on market forces to improve education. A supportive environment would allow committed educators to facilitate young people to see themselves as sexual subjects, to recognise the pressures of a culture awash with profit-driven sexual imagery, and to resist the extension of capitalist logic to emotional and sexual relationships. Students learn from the culture of a school as much as from the curriculum content. Schools are delivering their most powerful lessons about relationships and sexuality in the degree to which they respect the diverse bodies, desires and emotions of both teachers and pupils. The real challenge in schools lies in the practice of compassionate relationships that are both sustaining and sustainable.

References

Aapola, S., Gonick, M. and Harris, A. (2005) *Young Femininities: Girlhood, Power and Social Change*. Basingstoke: Palgrave Macmillan.

Abel, G. and Fitzgerald, L. (2006) 'When you come to it you feel like a dork asking a guy to put a condom on': is sex education addressing young people's understandings of risk? *Sex Education*, 6(2): 105–19.

Aikman, S. and Unterhalter, E. (eds) (2005) *Beyond Access: Transforming Policy and Practice for Gender Equality in Education*. Oxford: Oxfam.

Ainley, P. (1999) *Learning Policy: Towards the Certified Society*. Basingstoke: Macmillan.

Alanen, L. (1990) Rethinking socialization, the family and childhood. In P.A. Adler, P. Adler, N. Mandell and S. Cahill (eds) *Sociological Studies of Child Development: A Research Manual*, Vol. 3. Greenwich, CT: JAI Press.

Ali, A. (2006) Gay and Muslim: Perspectives on childhood, sexuality, faith and culture. Paper for the Invisible Boundaries: Addressing Sexualities Equalities in Children's Worlds ESRC Seminar Series, University of Nottingham (17 February).

Alldred, P. (1996) Whose expertise? Conceptualising resistance to advice about childrearing. In E. Burman, G. Aitken, P. Alldred, R. Allwood, T. Billington, B. Goldberg, A.J. Gordo Lopez, C. Heenan, D. Marks and S. Warner, *Psychology, Discourse, Practice: From Regulation to Resistance*. London: Taylor & Francis.

Alldred, P. (1998) Ethnography and discourse analysis: dilemmas in representing the voices of children. In Ribbens, J. and Edwards, R. (eds) *Feminist Dilemmas in Qualitative Research: Public Knowledge and Private Lives*. London: Sage.

Alldred, P. (1999) 'Fit to parent?' Psychology, knowledge and popular debate. Unpublished PhD thesis, University of East London, London.

Alldred, P. and Burman, E. (2005) Analysing children's accounts using discourse analyis. In S.M. Greene and D.M. Hogan (eds) *Researching Children's Experience: Approaches and methods*. London: Sage.

Alldred, P. and Gillies, V. (2002) Eliciting research accounts: Re/producing modern subjects? In M. Mauthner, M. Birch, J. Jessop and T. Miller (eds) *Ethics in Qualitative Research*. London: Sage.

Alldred, P., David, M. and Smith, P. (2003) Teachers' views of teaching sex education: pedagogy and models of delivery, *Journal of Educational Enquiry*, 4(1): 80–96.

Allen, I. (2005) 'Say everything': exploring young people's suggestions for improving sexuality education, *Sex Education*, 5(4): 389–404.

Allen, L. (2001) Closing sex education's knowledge/practice gap: the reconceptualisation of young people's sexual knowledge, *Sex Education*, 1(2): 109–22.

Allen, L. (2004) Beyond the birds and the bees: constituting a discourse of erotics in sexuality education, *Gender and Education*, 16(2): 151–67.

Archer, L. (2003) *Race, Masculinity and Schooling*. Maidenhead: Open University Press.

Archer, L. and Yamashita, H. (2003) Knowing their limits: identity, inequality and inner city school learners post 16 aspirations, *Journal of Education Policy*, 18(1): 53–69.

Aries, P. (1962) *Centuries of Childhood*. London: Cape.

Aries, P. and Bejin, A. (eds) (1985) *Western Sexuality: Practice and Precept in Past and Present Times*. Oxford: Blackwell.

Armstrong, H. (2006) Government Policy Update: Social Exclusion, *Youth Policy Update*, National Youth Agency (June).

Armstrong, L. (1995) *Of 'Sluts' and 'Bastards': A Feminist Decodes the Welfare Debate*. Monroe, ME: Common Courage Press.

Arnot, M., David, M. and Weiner, G. (1999) *Closing the Gender Gap: Post War Education and Social Change*. Cambridge: Polity Press.

Ashley, M. (2000) Chill winds and the spiritual visions of Maria Montessori and David Blunkett. Paper presented at the British Educational Research Association Annual Conference, Cardiff University (7–10 September).

Askew, S. and Ross, A. (1990) *Boys Don't Cry: Boys and Sexism in Education*. Milton Keynes: Open University Press.

Atkinson, E. (2002) Education for diversity in a multisexual society: negotiating the contradictions of contemporary discourse, *Sex Education*, 2(2): 119–32.

Attar, D. (1992) The demand that time forgot, *Trouble & Strife*, 23: 24–9.

Ball, S.J. (1994) *Educational Reform and Policy Sociology*. London: Routledge.

Ball, S.J. (2003) *Class Strategies and the Education Market: The Middle Class and Social Advantage*. London: RoutledgeFalmer.

Ball, S.J., Reay, D. and David, M.E. (2002) 'Ethnic choosing': minority ethnic students, social class and higher education choice, *Race, Ethnicity and Education*, 5(4): 333–57.

Banks, O. (1976) *The Sociology of Education*. London: Batsford.

Barna, D., McKeown, C. and Woodhead, P. (2002) *Get Real: Sharing Good Practice in the Provision of Sexual Health Services for Young People*. London: Save the Children.

Barrett, G. and Harper, R. (2000) Health professional attitudes' to the deregulation of emergency contraception (or the problem of female sexuality), *Sociology of Health and Illness*, 22(2):197–216.

Barron, M.M. and Bradford, S. (2007) Corporeal controls: violence, bodies and young gay men's identities. *Youth and Society*. To appear.

Bay-Cheng, L.Y. (2003) The trouble of teen sex: the construction of adolescent sexuality through school-based sexuality education, *Sex Education*, 3 (1): 61–74.

Beck, U. (1992) *Risk Society: Towards a New Modernity*. London: Sage.

Beck, U. and Beck-Gernsheim, E. (1995) *The Normal Chaos of Love*. Cambridge: Polity Press.

Best, R. (1999) The impact of a decade of change on pastoral care and PSE: a survey of teachers' perceptions, *Pastoral Care* 17(2): 3–13.

Biddle, G. and Forrest, S. (1997) Supporting sex and relationships education for boys in secondary school. In G. Lenderyou and C. Ray (eds) *Let's Hear It for the Boys!* London: National Children's Bureau.

Blair, M. (2001) *Why Pick on Me? School Exclusion and Black Youth*. Stoke-on-Trent: Trentham Books.

Blake, S. and Katrak, Z. (2002) *Faith, Values and Sex and Relationships Education*. London: National Children's Bureau.

Blakey, H., Pearce, J. and Chesters, G. (2006) *Minorities Within Minorities: Beneath The Surface Of South Asian Participation*. York: Joseph Rowntree Foundation.

Boden, R. and Childs, M. (1996) Paying for procreation: the Child Support Agency in the UK, *Feminist Legal Studies*, IV(2): 131–57.

Boden, R. and Corden, A. (1998) *Self-employed Parents and Child Maintenance*. London: HMSO.

Bourdieu, P. (1977) *Outline of a Theory of Practice*. Cambridge: Cambridge University Press.

Bourdieu, P. (1990) *In Other Worlds: Essays Towards a Reflective Sociology*. Cambridge: Polity Press.

Brannen, J. and O'Brien, M. (1995) Childhood and the sociological gaze: paradigms and paradoxes, *Sociology*, 29: 729–37.

British Journal of Sociology of Education (2006) Troubling identities: Reflections on Judith Butler's philosophy for the sociology of education (Special issue), *British Journal of Sociology of Education*, 27(4): 421–534.

British Medical Association (1997) *School Sex Education: Good Practice and Policy*. London: BMA.

Bullen, E. and Kenway, J. (2004) Subcultural capital and the female 'underclass'? A feminist response to an underclass discourse, *Journal of Youth Studies*, 7(2): 141–53.

Bullen, E., Kenway, J. and Hey, V. (2000) New Labour, social exclusion and educational risk management: the case of 'gymslip mums', *British Educational Research Journal*, 26(4): 441–56.

Bunting, M. (2005) *Willing Slaves: How the Overwork Culture Is Ruling Our Lives*. London: Harper Perennial.

Bunting, M. (2006) Behind the baby gap lies a culture of contempt for parenthood, *The Guardian*, 7 March: 31.

Burman, E. (1990) Differing with deconstruction: a feminist critique. In I. Parker and J. Shotter (eds) *Deconstructing Social Psychology*. London: Routledge.

Burman, E. (1991) Power, Gender and Developmental Psychology, *Feminism & Psychology*, 1(1): 141–53.

Burman, E. (1992) Feminism and discourse in developmental psychology: power, subjectivity and interpretation, *Feminism & Psychology*, 2(1): 45–60.

Burman, E. (1994a) *Deconstructing Developmental Psychology*. London: Routledge.

Burman, E. (1994b) Focus groups. In P. Bannister, E. Burman, I. Parker, M. Taylor, and C. Tindall, *Qualitative Methods in Psychology*. Buckingham: Open University Press.

Burman, E. (1995) What is it? Masculinity and femininity in the cultural representations of childhood. In C. Kitzinger and S. Wilkinson (eds) *Feminism and Discourse*. London: Sage.

Burman, E. (1996) *Challenging Women: Psychology's Exclusions, Feminist Possibilities*. Buckingham: Open University Press.

Burman, E. (2006) Emotions and reflexivity in feminised educational action research, *Educational Action Research*, 14(3): 315–32.

Burman, E. (2007) Beyond 'emotional literacy' in feminist and educational research, *British Educational Research Journal*. To appear.

Burman, E. and Parker, I. (eds) (1993) *Discourse Analytic Research: Repertoires and Readings of Texts in Action*. London: Routledge.

Burman, E., Smailes, S. and Chantler, K. (2004) 'Culture' as a barrier to service provision and delivery: domestic violence services for minoritized women, *Critical Social Policy*, 24(3): 332–57.

Buston, K. and Wight, D. (2004) Pupils' participation in sex education classes: understanding variation across classes, *Sex Education* 4(3): 285–302.

Buston, K. and Wight, D. (2006) The salience and utility of school sex education to young men, *Sex Education*, 6(2): 135–50.

Buston, K., Wight, D. and Scott, S. (2001) Difficulty and diversity: the context and practice of sex education, *British Journal of Sociology of Education*, 22: 353–68.

Buston, K, Wight, D. and Hart, G. (2002a) Inside the sex education classroom: the importance of context in engaging pupils, *Culture, Health & Sexuality*, 4: 317–35.

Buston, K., Wight, D., Hart, G. and Scott, S. (2002b) Implementation of a teacher-delivered sex education programme: obstacles and facilitating factors, *Health Education Research*, 17(1): 59–72.

Butler, J. (1990) *Gender Trouble: Gender and the Subversion of Identity*. London: Routledge.

Butler, J. (1993) *Bodies that Matter*. London: Routledge.

Butler, J. (2004) *Undoing Gender*. New York: Routledge.

Butler, T., Hamnett, C., Ramsden, M. and Webber, R. (2007) The best, the worst and the average: secondary school choice and education performance in East London, *Journal of Education Policy*, 22(1) 7–29.

Chambers, D., Van Loon, J. and Tincknell, E. (2004) Teachers' views of teenage sexual morality, *British Journal of Sociology of Education*, 25(5): 563–76.

Chitty, C. (1999) Sex education. In D. Hill and M. Cole (eds) *Promoting Equality in Secondary Schools*. London: Cassell.

Clegg, S. and David, M.E. (2006) Passion, pedagogies and the project of the personal in higher education, *21st Century Society: Journal of the Academy of Social Sciences*, 1(2): 149–67.

Cohen, J. (1999) *Safe and Sound: 11–16 Sex and Relationships (SRE) Education Pack*. Liverpool: Healthwise.

Connell, R.W. (1989) Cool guys, swots and wimps: the interplay of masculinity and education, *Oxford Review of Education*, 13: 291–303.

Connell, R.W. (1995) *Masculinities*. London: Polity Press.

Connolly, P. (1998) *Racism, Gender Identities and Young Children*. London: Routledge.

Corteen, K. (2006) Schools' fulfilment of sex and relationship education documentation: three school-based case studies, *Sex Education*, 6(1): 77–99.

Corteen, K. and Scraton, P. (1997) Prolonging 'childhood', manufacturing 'innocence' and regulating sexuality. In P. Scraton (ed.) *'Childhood' in 'Crisis'?* London: UCL Press.

Cowie, C. and Lees, S. (1987) Slags or drags? In Feminist Review (ed.) *Sexuality: A Reader*. London: Virago.

Daniels, H., Cole, T., Sellman, E., Sutton, J., Visser, J. with Bedward, J. (2003) *Study of Young People Permanently Excluded from School*. London: Department for Education and Skills.

David M.E. (1980) *The State, the Family and Education*. London: Routledge & Kegan Paul.

David, M.E. (1985) Motherhood and social policy: a matter of education? *Critical Social Policy*, No. 12 (Spring): 28–43.

David, M.E. (1986) Moral and maternal: the family in the right. In R. Levitas (ed.) *The Ideology of the New Right*. Cambridge: Polity Press.

David, M.E. (1989) Prima donna inter pares: women in academic management. In S. Acker (ed.) *Teachers, Gender and Careers*. London: Falmer Press.

David, M.E. (1990) 'Looking after the cubs': Women and work in a decade of Thatcherism. In I. Taylor (ed.) *The Social Effects of Free Market Policies*. London: Harvester Wheatsheaf.

David, M.E. (1993) *Parents, Gender and Education Reform*. Cambridge: Polity Press.

David, M.E. (1997) Family roles from dawn to dusk of the new Elizabethan era. In G. Dench (ed.) *Rewriting the Sexual Contract*. London: Institute of Community Studies.

David, M.E. (2003a) *Personal and Political: Feminisms, Sociology and Family Lives*. Stoke-on-Trent: Trentham Books.

David, M.E. (2003b) 'Teenage parenthood is bad for parents and children': A feminist critique of family, education and social welfare policies and practices. In M.N. Bloch, K. Holmlund, I. Moqvist and T.S. Popkewitz (eds) *Governing Children, Family and Education: Restructuring the Welfare State*. London: Palgrave Macmillan.

David, M.E., Alldred, P. and Smith, P.S. (2002) *Get Real about Sex: Linking Sex and Relationship Education to the Achievement Agenda*. Report to the Stoke-on-Trent LEA and DfES. Department of Education, Keele University.

David, M.E., Davies, J., Edwards, R., Reay, D. and Standing, K. (1996) Mothering and education: reflexivity and feminist methodology. In L. Morley and V. Walsh (eds) *Breaking Boundaries: Women in Higher Education*. London: Taylor & Francis.

David, M.E., Edwards, R., Hughes, M. and Ribbens, J. (1993) *Mothers and Education: Inside Out? Exploring Family-Education Policy and Experience*. London: Macmillan.

David, M.E., Weiner, G. and Arnot, M. (2000) Gender equality and schooling, education policy-making and feminist research in England and Wales in the 1990s. In J. Salisbury and S. Riddell (eds) *Gender, Policy and Educational Change*. London: Routledge.

David, M.E., West, A. and Ribbens, J. (1994) *Mother's Intuition? Choosing Secondary Schools*. London: Falmer Press.

Davies, B. (2006) Subjectification: the relevance of Butler's analysis for education, *British Journal of Sociology of Education*, 27(4): 425–38.

Davies, B. & Harré, R. (1990) Positioning: the discursive production of selves, *Journal for the Theory of Social Behaviour*, 20(1): 43–63.

Dean, M. (1999) *Governmentality: Power and Rule in Modern Society*. London: Sage.

Dearing, Sir R. (1994) The National Curriculum and its Assessment: final report. London: School Curriculum and Assessment Authority.

Department for Education and Employment (2000) *Sex and Relationship Education Guidance*, Circular 0116/2000, DfEE.

Department for Education and Skills (2001) *SRE & Parents*. DfES 0706/2001.

Department of Health (1992)

Department for Education and Skills and Department of Health (2006)

Dollimore, J. (1991) *Sexual Dissidence: Augustine to Wilde, Freud to Foucault*. Oxford: Oxford University Press.

Douglas, M. (1966) *Purity and Danger*. New York: Praeger.

Douglas, N., Kemp, S., Aggleton, P. and Warwick, I. (2001) The role of external professionals in education about sexual orientation – towards good practice, *Sex Education*, 1(2): 149–62.

Driver, S. and Martell, L. (1999) New Labour, culture and economy. In L. Ray and A. Sayer (eds) *Culture and Economy after the Cultural Turn*. London: Sage.

Driver, S. and Martell, L. (2002) *Blair's Britain*. Cambridge: Polity Press.

Duckett, P., Sixsmith, J., and Kagan, C. (2007) Researching pupil well-being in UK secondary schools: community psychology and the politics and pressures of researching in the education sector, *Childhood*, 14(4).

Duncan, S. and Edwards, R. (1999) *Lone Mothers, Paid Work and Gendered Moral Rationalities*. Basingstoke: Macmillan.

Duncan, S., Edwards, R., Reynolds, T. and Alldred, P. (2003a) Mothers and childcare: policies, values and theories, *Children & Society*, 18: 254–65.

Duncan, S., Edwards, R., Reynolds, T. and Alldred, P. (2003b) Motherhood, paid work and partnering: values and theories, *Work, Employment and Society*, 17(2): 309–30.

Durham, M. (1991) *Sex & Politics: The Family and Morality in the Thatcher Years*. London: Macmillan.

Edwards, R. (1993) *Mature Women Students: Separating and Connecting Family and Education*. London: Taylor & Francis.

Edwards, R. and Alldred, P. (1999) Children and young people's views of social research: the case of research on home–school relations, *Childhood*, 6(2): 261–81.

Ellis, V. and High, S. (2004) Something more to tell you: gay, lesbian and bisexual young people's experiences of secondary schooling, *British Educational Research Journal*, 30(2): 213–225.

Epstein, D. (1993) *Changing Classroom Cultures: Anti-racism, Politics and Schools*. Stoke-on-Trent: Trentham Books.

Epstein, D. (1994a) Introduction: lesbian and gay equality in education – problems and possibilities. In D. Epstein (ed.) *Challenging Lesbian and Gay Inequalities in Education*. Buckingham: Open University Press.

Epstein, D. (ed.) (1994) *Challenging Lesbian and Gay Inequalities in Education*. Buckingham: Open University Press.

Epstein, D. (1998) Real boys don't work: 'underachievement', masculinity and the harassment of 'sissies'. In D. Epstein, J. Elwood, V. Hey and J. Maw (eds) *Failing Boys? Issues in Gender and Achievement*. Buckingham: Open University Press.

Epstein, D. and Johnson, R. (1994) On the straight and narrow: the heterosexual presumption, homophobias and schools. In D. Epstein (ed.) *Challenging Lesbian and Gay Inequalities in Education*. Buckingham: Open University Press.

Epstein, D. and Johnson, R. (1998) *Schooling Sexualities*. Buckingham: Open University Press.

Epstein, D., Elwood, J., Hey, V. and Maw, J. (1998) (eds) *Failing Boys? Issues in Gender and Achievement*. Buckingham: Open University Press.

Epstein, D., O'Flynn, S. and Telford, D. (2003) *Silenced Sexualities in Schools and Universities*. Stoke-on-Trent: Trentham Books.

Firestone, S. (1972) *The Dialectic of Sex*. New York: William Morrow.

Foucault, M. (1977) *Discipline and Punish*. London: Allen Lane.

Foucault, M. (1980) *Power/Knowledge: Selected Interviews and Other Writings 1972–1977*. Brighton: Harvester Press.

Foucault, M. (1987) *History of Sexuality III: The Use of Pleasure*. Harmondsworth: Penguin.

Fox Harding, L. (2000) *Supporting Families/Controlling Families? Towards a characterisation of New Labour's 'family policy'*. Working Paper 21, Centre for Research on Family, Kinship & Childhood, University of Leeds.

Family Planning Association (2004) *Girls Out Loud*. London: FPA.

Family Planning Association (2005) *Agenda for the New Parliament*. London: FPA.

Francis, B. (2000) *Boys, Girls and Achievement: Addressing the Classroom Issues*. London: RoutledgeFalmer.

Francis, B. and Skelton, C. (2005) *Reassessing Gender and Achievement: Questioning Contemporary Key Debates*. London: Routledge-Falmer.

Franklin, J. (2000) What's wrong with New Labour politics? *Feminist Review*, 66: 138–41.

Fraser, N. (1989) *Unruly Practices: Power, Discourse and Gender in Contemporary Social Theory*. Cambridge: Polity Press.

Frosh, S., Phoenix, A. and Pattman, R. (2001) *Young Masculinities: Understanding Boys in Contemporary Society.* London: Palgrave.

Furlong, A. and Cartmel, F. (1997) *Young People and Social Change: Individualisation and Risk in Late Modernity.* Buckingham: Open University Press.

Gaine, C. (1995) *Still No Problem Here.* Stoke-on-Trent: Trentham.

Gale, R., Seidman, D., Dollberg, S., Armon, Y. and Stevenson, D.K. (1989) Is teenage pregnancy a neonatal risk factor? *Journal of Adolescent Health Care,* 10: 404–8.

Gatrell, C. (2005) *Hard Labour: The Sociology of Parenthood.* Maidenhead: Open University Press.

Gewirtz, S., Ball, S. J. and Bowe, R. (1995) *Markets, Choice and Equity in Education.* Buckingham: Open University Press.

Giddens, A. (1998) *The Third Way.* Cambridge: Polity Press.

Gillies, V. (1999) An analysis of the discursive positions of women smokers: implications for practical interventions. In C. Willig (ed.) *Applied Discourse Analysis: Social and Psychological Interventions.* Buckingham: Open University Press.

Glick, E. (2000) Sex positive: feminism, queer theory and the politics of transgression. *Feminist Review,* 64: 19–45.

Graham, H. and McDermott, E. (2005) Qualitative Research and the evidence base of policy: insights from studies of teenage mother in the UK, *Journal of Social Policy,* 35(1): 21–37.

Graham, D. and Tytler, T. (1993) *A Lesson for Us All: The Making of the National Curriculum.* London: Routledge.

Griffin, C. (1997) Troubled teens: managing disorders of transition and consumption, *Feminist Review,* 55: 4–21.

Griffin, C. (2004) Representations of the young. In J. Roche, S. Tucker, R. Thomson and R. Flynn, *Youth in Society.* London: Sage.

Hall, S. (1998) The great moving nowhere show, *Marxism Today* (Nov./Dec.).

Hall, S. (2003) New Labour's double-shuffle, *Soundings,* 24: 10–24.

Halsey, A.H. (1972) *Educational Priority.* London: HMSO.

Halsey, A.H., Heath, A. and Ridge, J. (1980) *Origins and Destinations: Family and Class.* Oxford: Clarendon Press.

Halstead, J. M. and Reiss, M. (2003) *Values in Sex Education: From Principles to Practice.* London: RoutledgeFalmer.

Harden, A. and Osgood, J. (1999) Young women's experiences of arranging and having abortions, *Sociology of Health & Illness,* 21(4): 426–44.

Hardman, K. and Marshall, J. (2000) The state and status of physical education in schools in international context, *European Physical Education Review,* 6(3): 203–29.

Harris, J., Howard, M., Jones, C. and Russell, L. (2005) *Great*

Expectations: How realistic is the Government's target to get 60 per cent of young mothers into education, employment or training? Oxford: YWCA Report.

Haywood, C. and Mac an Ghaill, M. (2003) *Men and Masculinities: Theory, Research and Social Practice.* Buckingham: Open University Press.

Head, J. (1999) *Understanding the Boys.* London: Falmer.

Hollway, W. (1989) *Subjectivity and Method in Psychology.* London: Sage.

Heckert, J. (2005) Radically reimagining sex education: power, ethics & relationships. Paper for the Sex Education Conference, Institute of Education, London (31 May).

Henriques, J., Hollway, W., Urwin, C., Venn, C. and Walkerdine, V. (1984) *Changing the Subject: Psychology, Social Regulation and Subjectivity.* London: Methuen.

Hey, V. (1997) *The Company She Keeps.* Buckingham: Open University Press.

Hey, V. (2006) The politics of performative resignification: translating Judith Butler's theoretical discourse and its potential for a sociology of education, *British Journal of Sociology of Education*, 27(4): 437–57.

Hey, V., Creese, A., Daniels, H., Fielding, S. and Leonard, D. (2001) 'Sad, bad or sexy boys': girls' talk in and out of the classroom. In W. Martino and B. Meyenn (eds) *What About the Boys? Issues of Masculinity in Schools.* Buckingham: Open University Press.

Hilton, G.L.S. (2003) Listening to the boys: English boys' views on the desirable characteristics of teachers of sex education, *Sex Education*, 3(1): 33–46.

Higher Education Funding Council for England (HEFCE) (2006) Review of the widening participation research: addressing the barriers to participation in higher education. A report to HEFCE by the University of York, Higher Education Academy and Institute of Access Studies.

HM Treasury (2006) *Budget 2006. A Strong and Strengthening Economy: Investing in Britain's Future*, HC 968, session 2005–06. London: Stationery Office.

Holgate, H. and Murakami, K. (2005) Young mothers: struggles with ambivalence. Paper for the First International Society of Cultural and Activity Research Conference, Universidad de Sevilla and Universidad Pablo de Olavide, Seville (20–24 September).

Holland, J., Ramazanoglu, C., Sharpe, S. and Thomson, R. (1998) *The Male in the Head: Young People, Heterosexuality and Power.* London: Tufnell Press.

hooks, b. (2000) *Feminism is for Everybody: Passionate Politics.* London: Pluto Press.

Hudson, F. and Ineichen, B. (1991) *Taking it Lying Down: Sexuality and Teenage Motherhood*. London: Macmillan.

Ingham, R. (2005) 'We didn't cover that at school': education against pleasure or education for pleasure? *Sex Education*, 5(4): 375–88.

Isherwood, L. (2004) Learning to be a woman: feminist theological reflections on sex education in church schools, *Sex Education*, 4(3): 273–84.

Jackson, S. (1982) *Childhood and Sexuality*. Oxford: Basil Blackwell.

James, A. and Prout, A. (eds) (1990) *Constructing and Reconstructing Childhood: Contemporary Issues in the Sociological Study of Childhood*. London: Falmer Press.

Jenks, C. (2005) *Childhood* (2nd edn). London: Routledge.

Jennett, M. (2004) *Stand Up for Us: Challenging Homophobia in Schools*. DfES/Health Development Agency.

Jones, K. (2003) *Education in Britain, 1944 to the Present*. Cambridge: Polity Press.

Kehily, M.J. (2002) *Sexuality, Gender and Schooling: Shifting Agendas in Social Learning*. London: Routledge.

Kehily, M.J. and Nayak, A. (1996) 'The Christmas kiss': sexuality, story-telling and schooling, *Curriculum Studies*, 4(2): 211–27.

Kehily, M.J. and Nayak, A. (1997) 'Lads and laughter': humour and the production of heterosexual hierarchies, *Gender and Education* 9(1): 69–87.

Kelly, D. (2001) *Pregnant with Meaning: Teen Mothers and the Politics of Inclusive Schooling*. New York: P. Lang.

Keogh, P., Henderson, L. and Dodds, C. (2004) Growing up gay: family, church and education. In *Ethnic Minority Gay Man, Redefining Community, Restoring Identity*. London: Sigma Research.

Kidger, J. (2004) Including young mothers: limitations to New Labour's strategy for supporting teenage parents, *Critical Social Policy* 24(3): 291–311.

Kiernan, K., Land, H. and Lewis, J. (1998) *Lone Motherhood in Twentieth Century Britain: From Footnote to Front Page*. Oxford: Clarendon Press.

Kitzinger, J. (1988) Defending innocence: Ideologies of childhood, *Feminist Review*, 28: 77–87.

Kitzinger, J. (1994) The methodology of focus groups: the importance of interaction between research participants, *Sociology of Health and Illness*, 16: 103–21.

Lafrance, M. (1991) School for scandal: different educational experiences for females and males, *Gender and Education*, 3: 3–13.

Land, H. (1976) Women: supporters or supported? In D. Leonard Barker and S. Allen (eds) *Sexual Divisions and Society: Process and Change*. London: Tavistock.

Lauder, H., Brown, P., Dillabough, J-A. and Halsey, A.H. (eds) (2006) *Education, globalization and social change*. Oxford: Oxford University Press.

Lawton, D. (1996) The changing context: the National Curriculum. In S. Hodkinson and M. Jephcote (eds) *Teaching Economics and Business*. London: Heinemann.

Lee, E., Clements, S., Ingham, R. and Stone, N. (2004) *A Matter of Choice? Explaining National Variations in Teenage Abortion and Motherhood*. York: Joseph Rowntree Foundation.

Lees, S. (1986) *Losing Out: Sexuality and Adolescent Girls*. London: Hutchinson.

Lees, S. (1993) *Sugar and Spice: Sexuality and Adolescent Girls*. London: Penguin.

Lenderyou, G. and Ray, C. (1997) *Let's Hear It from the Boys! Supporting Sex and Relationship Education for Boys and Young Men*. London: National Children's Bureau.

Lensky, H. (1990) Beyond plumbing and prevention: feminist approaches to sex education, *Gender and Education*, 2: 217–30.

Levitas, R. (1998) *The Inclusive Society? Social Exclusion and New Labour*. Basingstoke: Palgrave Macmillan.

Lewis, J. and Knijn, T. (2002) The politics of sex education policy in England and Wales and the Netherlands since the 1980s, *Journal of Social Policy*, 31(4): 669–94.

Lingard, B. and Douglas, P. (1999) *Men Engaging Feminisms: Pro-feminism, Backlashes and Schooling*. Buckingham: Open University Press.

Lucey, H. (2001) Social class, gender and schooling. In B. Francis and C. Skelton (eds) *Investigating Gender: Contemporary Perspectives in Education*. Buckingham: Open University Press.

Lukes, S. (2004) *Power: A Radical View*. Basingstoke: Palgrave Macmillan.

Luttrell, W. (1997) *Schoolsmart and Motherwise: Working-class Women's Identity and Schooling*. New York: Routledge.

Luttrell, W. (2003) *Pregnant Bodies, Fertile Minds: Gender, Race, and the Schooling of Pregnant Teens*. New York: Routledge.

Lyon, C. (2007) Interrogating the concentration on the UNCRC instead of the ECHR in the development of children's rights in England, *Children & Society*, 21: 147–53.

Mac an Ghaill, M. (1994a) (In)visibility: sexuality, race and masculinity in the school context. In D. Epstein (ed.) *Challenging Lesbian and Gay Inequalities in Education*. Buckingham: Open University Press.

Mac an Ghaill, M. (1994b) *The Making of Men: Masculinities, Sexualities and Schooling*. Buckingham: Open University Press.

MacDonald, R. (ed.) (1997) *Youth, the 'Underclass' and Social Exclusion*. London: Routledge.

MacDonald, R. and Marsh, J. (2004) Missing school: educational engagement, youth transitions and social exclusions, *Youth & Society*, 36(2): 143–62.

MacIntyre, S. and Cunningham-Burley, S. (1987) Teenage pregnancy as a social problem: a perspective from the United Kingdom. In A. Lawson & D. Rhode (eds) *The Politics of Pregnancy: Adolescent Sexuality & Public Policy*. New Haven, CT: Yale University Press.

MacPherson, P. and Fine, M. (1995) Hungry for an us: adolescent girls and adult women negotiating territories of race, gender, class and difference, *Feminism & Psychology*, 5(2): 181–200.

Marks, D. (1996) Constructing a narrative: moral discourse and young people's experiences of exclusion. In E. Burman, G. Aitken, P. Alldred, R. Allwood, T. Billington, B. Goldberg, A.J. Gordo Lopez, C. Heenan, D. Marks and S. Warner, *Psychology, Discourse, Practice: From Regulation to Resistance*. London: Taylor & Francis.

Martino, W. (1999) 'Cool boys', 'party animals', 'squids' and 'poofters': interrogating the dynamics and politics of adolescent masculinities in school, *British Journal of the Sociology of Education*, 20(2): 239–63.

Martino, W. and Meyenn, B. (eds) (2001) *What about the Boys? Issues of masculinity in schools*. Buckingham: Open University Press.

McCarthy, C. and Dimitriadis, G. (2000) Governmentality and the sociology of education: media, educational policy, and the politics of resentment, *British Journal of Sociology of Education*, 21(2): 169–86.

McCulloch, G. (1998) *Failing the Ordinary Child? The Theory and Practice of Working-Class Secondary Education*. Buckingham: Open University Press.

McDermott, E. and Graham, H. (2005) Resilient young mothering: social inequalities, late modernity and the 'problem' of 'teenage' motherhood, *Journal of Youth Studies*, 8(1): 59–79.

McNamara, Y. (2006) The social construction of young people's political engagement. Unpublished MPhil thesis, Brunel University, London.

McNess, E. Broadfoot, P. and Osborn, M. (2003) Is the effective compromising the affective? *British Educational Research Journal*, 29(2): 243–57.

McRobbie, A. (2000) Feminism and the Third Way, *Feminist Review*, 64: 97–112.

Measor, L. (2004) Young people's views of sex education: gender, information and knowledge, *Sex Education*, 4(2): 153–66.

Measor, L., Tiffin, C. and Fry, K. (1996) Gender and sex education: a study of adolescent responses, *Gender and Education*, 8: 275–88.

Measor, L. with Tiffin, C. and Miller, K. (2000) *Young People's Views of Sex Education*. London: Falmer.

Milbourne, L. (2002) Life at the margins: education of young people, social policy and the meanings of social exclusion, *International Journal of Inclusive Education*, 6(4): 325–43.

Miller, T. and Bell, L. (2002) Encouraging participation: ethics and responsibilities. In M. Mauthner, M. Birch, J. Jessop and T. Miller (eds) *Ethical Dilemmas in Qualitative Research*. London: Sage.

Mirza, H. (2006) *Tackling the Roots of Racism*. Bristol: Policy Press.

Mishler, E.G. (1986) *Research Interviewing: Context and Narrative*. London: Harvard University Press.

Mizen, P. (2004) *The Changing State of Youth*. Basingstoke: Palgrave Macmillan.

Moi, T. (1985) *Sexual/Textual Politics: Feminist Literary Theory*. London: Routledge.

Monk, D. (1998) Sex education and the problematisation of teenage pregnancy: a genealogy of law and governance, *Social and Legal Studies*, 7(2): 239–59.

Monk, D. (2000) Health and education: conflicting programmes for sex education. In E. Heinze (ed.) *Of Innocence and Autonomy*. Aldershot: Dartmouth Press.

Monk, D. (2001) New guidance/old problems: recent developments in sex education, *Journal of Social Welfare and Family Law*, 23(3): 271–91.

Nayak, A. and Kehily, M.J. (1996) Playing it straight: masculinities, homophobias and schooling, *Journal of Gender Studies*, 5(2): 211–30.

Nayak, A. and Kehily, M. J. (1997) Masculinities and schooling: why are young men so homophobic? In D.L. Steinberg, D. Epstein and R. Johnson (eds) *Border Patrols: Policing the boundaries of heterosexuality*. London: Cassell.

Nayak, A. and Kehily, M. J. (2006) Gender undone: subversion, regulation and embodiment in the work of Judith Butler, *British Journal of Sociology of Education*, 27(4): 459–72.

New, C. and David, M. E. (1985) *For the Children's Sake: Making Child Care More Than Women's Business*. Harmondsworth: Penguin.

O'Donnell, M. and Sharpe, S. (2000) *Uncertain Masculinities: Youth, Ethnicity and Class in Contemporary Britain*. London: Routledge.

O'Flynn, S. and Epstein, D. (2005) Standardising sexuality: embodied knowledge, 'achievement' and 'standards', *Social Semiotics*, 15(2): 185–210.

Oakley, A. (2005) *The Ann Oakley Reader*. Bristol: Policy Press.

Office for National Statistics (2004) Conceptions in England & Wales 2004, *Health Statistics Quarterly*. London: HMSO.

Office for National Statistics (2006a) Office for National Statistics website (www.ons.co.uk), accessed 30 May 2006.

Office for National Statistics (2006b) *Social Trends 36.* Basingstoke: Palgrave Macmillan.

Office for Standards in Education (2002) *Review of SRE*, HMI 433. London: Ofsted.

Office for Standards in Education (2005) *Personal, Social and Health Education in Secondary Schools*, HMI 2311. London: Ofsted.

Office for Standards in Education (2006) *Towards Consensus? Citizenship in Secondary Schools*, HMI 2666. London: Ofsted.

Osler, A. (2005) (ed.) *Teachers, Human Rights and Diversity.* Stoke-on-Trent: Trentham Books.

Osler, A., Street, C., Lall, M. and Vincent, K. (2002) *Not a Problem? Girls and school exclusion.* London: National Children's Bureau/ Joseph Rowntree Foundation.

Packer, C. (2000) Sex education: child's right, parent's choice or state's obligation. In Heinze, E. (ed) *Of Innocence and Autonomy: Children, Sex and Human Rights.* Aldershot: Dartmouth Press.

Paechter, C. (1996) *Educating the Other: Gender, Power and Schooling.* London: Routledge.

Paechter, C.F. (2000) *Changing School Subjects: Power, Gender and Curriculum.* Buckingham: Open University Press.

Paechter, C. (2004) Mens sana in corpore sano: Cartesian dualism and the marginalization of sex education, *Discourse: Studies in the Cultural Politics of Education*, 25(3): 309–20.

Paechter, C. (2006) Reconceptualising the gendered body: learning and constructing masculinities in school, *Gender and Education*, 18(2): 121–35.

Park, J. (2000) The dance of dialogue: thinking and feeling in education, *Pastoral Care in Education*, 18(3): 11–15.

Parker, I. (1992) *Discourse Dynamics: Critical Analysis for Social and Individual Psychology.* London: Routledge.

Parker, I. (2005) *Qualitative Psychology: Introducing Radical Research.* Buckingham: Open University Press.

Parker, I. (2006) Emotional illiteracy and masculinization: margins of resistance. Keynote paper at the Qualitative Methods and Marginality Conference, University of Leicester (4 May).

Phoenix, A. (1987) Theories of gender and black families. In G. Weiner and M. Arnot (eds) *Gender under Scrutiny.* London: Hutchinson.

Phoenix, A. (1991) *Young Mothers?* Cambridge: Polity Press.

Pillow, W. S. (2004) *Unfit Subjects: Educational Policy and the Teen Mother.* London. New York: RoutledgeFalmer.

Plowden, B. (1967) *Children and Their Primary Schools.* London: Central Advisory Council for Education (England).

Pomeroy, E. (2000) *Experiencing Exclusion.* Stoke-on-Trent: Trentham.

Powell, R. (1997) *Raising Achievement*. Stafford: Robert Powell Publications.

Power, S. (1996) *The Pastoral and the Academic: Conflict and Contradiction in the Curriculum*. London: Cassell.

Pyke, N. (2003) Faith schools: Your weekly guide to a whole-school issue, *Times Educational Supplement*, 10 January.

Quinn, J., Thomas, J., Slack, K., Casey, L., Thexton, W. and Noble, J. (2005) *From Life Crisis to Lifelong Learning: Rethinking Working-Class 'Drop Out' from University*. York: Joseph Rowntree Foundation.

Rasmussen, M.L. (2006) Play School, melancholia, and the politics of recognition, *British Journal of Sociology of Education*, 27(4): 473–87.

Rassool, N. and Morley, L. (2000) School effectiveness and the displacement of equity discourses in education, *Race, Ethnicity and Education*, 3: 237–58.

Reay, D. (1998) Insider perspectives or stealing words out of women's mouths: interpretation in the research process, *Feminist Review* 53: 57–73.

Reay, D. (2001a) 'Spice girls', 'nice girls', 'girlies' and 'tomboys': Gender discourses, girls' cultures and femininities in the primary classroom, *Gender and Education*, 13(2): 153–66.

Reay, D. (2001b) The paradox of contemporary femininities in education: combining fluidity with fixity. In B. Francis and C. Skelton (eds) *Investigating Gender: Contemporary Perspectives in Education*. Buckingham: Open University Press.

Reay, D. (2002) Shaun's story: troubling discourses of white working class masculinities, *Gender and Education*, 14(3): 221–34.

Redman, P. (1994) Shifting ground: rethinking sexuality education. In D. Epstein (ed.) *Challenging Lesbian and Gay Inequalities in Education*. Buckingham: Open University Press.

Renold, E. (2005) *Girls, Boys and Junior Sexualities*. London: RoutledgeFalmer.

Renold, E. (2006) 'They won't let us play ... unless you're going out with one of them': girls, boys and Butler's 'heterosexual matrix' in the primary years, *British Journal of Sociology of Education*, 27(4): 489–509.

Reynolds, T. (2005) *Caribbean Mothers: Identity and Experience in the UK*. London: Tufnell Press.

Richards, B. (1994) What is identity? In I. Gaber and J. Aldridge (eds) *In the Best Interests of the Child: Culture, Identity and Transracial Adoption*. London: Free Association.

Rorty, R. (1980) *Philosophy and the Mirror of Nature*. Oxford: Blackwell.

Rose, N. (1989) *Governing the Soul: The Shaping of the Private Self*. London: Routledge.

Rose, N. (1993) *Inventing Ourselves*. London: Routledge.

Sawicki, J. (1991) *Disciplining Foucault: Feminism, Power and the Body*. New York: Routledge.

Seidler, V. (1995) Men, heterosexualities and emotional life. In S. Pile and N. Thrift (eds) *Mapping the Subject*. London: Routledge.

Sennett, R. (2003) *Respect: The Formation of a Character in a World of Inequality*. London: Penguin.

Sewell, T. (1997) *Black Masculinities and Schooling: How Black Boys Survive Modern Schooling*. Stoke-on-Trent: Trentham.

Sex Education Forum (2003) Forum Factsheet 30: *Sex and Relationship Education Framework*. London: Sex Education Forum.

Sex Education Forum (2004) Forum Factsheet: *Faith, Values and Sex and Relationships Education*. London: Sex Education Forum.

Sex Education Forum (2005) Forum Factsheet 34: *Effective learning methods: Approaches to teaching about sex and relationships within PSHE and Citizenship*. London: Sex Education Forum.

Sharp, P. (2000) Promoting emotional literacy: emotional literacy improves and increases your life chances, *Pastoral Care in Education*, 18(3): 8–10.

Shaw, J. (1976) *Single sex education*. In R. Deem (ed.) *Single Sex or Co-education?* London: Routledge.

Sikes, P. (2006a) 'Suppressing innocence: difficulties in researching "false" accusations of sexual misconduct made against school-teachers', *Research Intelligence, BERA (British Educational Research Association) Newsletter*.

Sikes, P. (2006b) Scandalous Stories and dangerous Liaisons: when Male teachers and Female Pupils fall in love, Sex Education 6(3) 265–80.

Simon, B. (1992) *Studies in the History of Education*. London: Lawrence and Wishart.

Singer, L. (1993) *Erotic Welfare: Sexual Theory and Politics in the Age of Epidemic*. London: Routledge.

Skeggs, B. (1991) Challenging masculinity and using sexuality, *British Journal of Sociology of Education*, 11 (4): 127–40.

Skelton, C. (2001) *Schooling The Boys: Masculinities and Primary Education*. Buckingham: Open University Press.

Smith, L. (2006) Situations vacant but mums need not apply, *The Times*, 21 March.

Smithers, A. (2005) Education. In A. Seldom and D. Kavanagh (eds) *The Blair Effect 2001–5*. Cambridge: Cambridge University Press.

Social Exclusion Unit (1999) *Teenage Pregnancy*, Cm. 4342. London: The Stationery Office.

Stambach, A. and David, M. E. (2005) Feminist theory and educational policy: how gender has been involved in home school debates about school choice, *SIGNS: Journal of Women in Culture and Society*, 30(2): 1633–59.

Storr, M. (2003) *Latex & Lingerie*. Oxford: Berg.

Strange, V., Forrest, S., Oakley, A. and the RIPPLE study team (2002a) Peer-led sex education – characteristics of peer educators and their perceptions of the impact on them of participation in a peer education programme, *Health Education Research*, 17: 327–37.

Strange, V., Forrest, S., Oakley, A. and the RIPPLE study team (2002b) What influences peer-led sex education in the classroom? A view from the peer educators, *Health Education Research*, 17: 339–49.

Strange, V., Oakley, A., Forrest, S. and the RIPPLE study team (2003) Mixed-sex or single-sex education: how would young people like their sex education and why? *Gender and Education* 15(2): 201–14.

Stronach, I., Frankham, J. and Stark, S. (2006) Sex, science and educational research: the unholy trinity, *Journal of Education Policy*, Autumn/Winter.

Swann, C., Bowe, K., McCormick, G., Kosmin, M. (2003) *Teenage Pregnancy and Parenthood: A Review of Reviews*. London: Department of Health.

Tabberer, S., Hall, C., Prendergast, S. and Webster, A. (2000) *Teenage Pregnancy and Choice: Abortion or Motherhood: Influences on the Decision*. York: Joseph Rowntree Foundation.

Taylor, M. (1994) Action research. In P. Bannister, E. Burman, I. Parker, M. Taylor and C. Tindall, *Qualitative Methods in Psychology*. Buckingham: Open University Press.

Thomas, G. and Loxley, A. (2001) *Deconstructing and Constructing Inclusion*. Buckingham: Open University Press.

Thomson, R. (1993) Unholy alliance: the recent politics of sex education. In J. Bristow and A. Wilson (eds) *Activating Theory*. London: Lawrence and Wishart.

Thomson, R. (1994) Moral rhetoric and public health pragmatism: the recent politics of sex education, *Feminist Review*, 48: 40–60.

Thomson, R. (2000) Dream on: the logic of sexual practice, *Journal of Youth Studies*, 3(4): 407–27.

Thomson, R. and Blake, S. (2002) Editorial: Two steps forward and one step back, *Sex Education*, 2(3): 187–93.

Thomson, R., Henderson, S. and Holland, J. (2003) Making the most of what you've got? Resources, values and inequalities in young women's transitions to adulthood, *Educational Review*, 55(1): 33–46.

Tomlinson, S. (2001) *Education in a Post-Welfare Society*. Buckingham: Open University Press.

Treacher, A. (1989) Be your own person: dependence/independence, 1950–1985. In B. Richards (ed.) *Crises of the Self: Further Essays on Psychoanalysis and Politics*. London: Free Association.

Van Every, J. (1995) *Heterosexual Women Changing the Family: Refusing to Be a 'Wife'!* London: Taylor & Francis.

Waites, M. (2005) *The Age of Consent; Young People, Sexuality and Citizenship.* Basingstoke: Palgrave.

Walkerdine, V. (1981) Sex, power and pedagogy, *Screen Education,* 38: 14–24.

Walkerdine, V. (1984) Developmental psychology and child-centred pedagogy. In J. Henriques, W. Hollway, C. Urwin, C. Venn and V. Walkerdine, *Changing the Subject: Psychology, Social Regulation and Subjectivity.* London: Methuen.

Walkerdine, V. (1990) *Schoolgirl Fictions.* London: Verso

Walkerdine, V. (1997) *Daddy's Girl.* London: Routledge.

Walkerdine, V. (2003) Reclassifying upward mobility: femininity and the neo-liberal subject, *Gender and Education,* 15(3): 237–48.

Walkerdine, V., Lucey, H. and Melody, J. (2001) *Growing Up Girl: Psychosocial Explorations of Gender and Class.* Basingstoke: Palgrave.

Warner, S. (1996) Constructing femininity: models of child sexual abuse and the production of 'woman'. In E. Burman, P. Alldred, C. Bewley, B. Goldberg, C. Heenan, D. Marks, J. Marshall, K. Taylor, R. Ullah and S. Warner, *Challenging Women: Psychology's Exclusions, Feminist Possibilities.* Buckingham: Open University Press.

Warwick, I. and Douglas, N. (2001) *Safe for All: A Best Practice Guide to Preventing Homophobic Bullying in Secondary Schools.* London: University of London.

Weedon, C. (1987) *Feminist Practice and Poststructuralist Theory.* Oxford: Blackwell.

Weeks, J. (1981) *Sex, Politics and Society.* Harlow: Longman.

Weiner, G. (1994) *Feminisms in Education.* Buckingham: Open University Press.

Wellings, K., Nanchahal, K., Macdowall, W., McManus, S., Erens, B., Mercer, C.H., Johnson, A.M., Copas, A.J., Korovessis, C., Fenton, K. A. and Field, J. (2001) Sexual behaviour in Britain: early heterosexual experience, *Lancet,* 358: 1843–1850.

Whitty, G. (2001) Education, social class and social exclusion, *Journal of Education Policy,* 16(4): 287–95.

Willig, C. (1999) Discourse analysis and sex education. In C. Willig (ed.) *Applied Discourse Analysis: Social and Psychological Interventions.* Buckingham: Open University Press.

Willis, P. (1977) *Learning to Labour.* Farnborough: Saxon House.

Wilson, H. and Huntington, A. (2005) Deviant (m)others: the construction of teenage motherhood in contemporary discourse, *Journal of Social Policy,* 35(1): 59–76.

Wilson, J. (2003) Can sex education be practical? *Sex Education*, 3(1): 23–32.

Winnicott, D. W. (1956) *Primary Maternal Preoccupation: Through Paediatrics to Psychoanalysis*. London: Karnac Books.

Wood, J. (1984) Groping towards sexism: boys' sex talk. In A. McRobbie and M. Nava (eds) *Gender and Generation*. Basingstoke: Macmillan.

Woods, P. (1976) Having a laugh: An antidote to schooling. In M. Hammersley and P. Woods (eds) *The Process of Schooling: A Sociological Reader*. London: Routledge.

Woollett, A. and Phoenix, A. (1991) Psychological views of mothering. In A. Phoenix, A. Woollett and E. Lloyd (eds) *Motherhood: Meanings, Practices and Ideologies*. London: Sage.

Wright, C., Weeks, D. and McGlaughlin, D. (2000) *'Race', Class and Gender in Exclusion from School*. London: Falmer Press.

Wyness, M. (1992) Schooling and the normalization of sex talk, *British Journal of Sociology of Education*, 13(1): 89–104.

Wynn, J. and White, R. (2000) Negotiating social change: the paradox of youth, *Youth and Society*, 32(2): 165–83.

Wyss, S. (2004) 'This was my hell': the violence experienced by gender non-conforming youth in US high schools, *International Journal of Qualitative Studies in Education*, 17(5): 709–30.

Yates, L. (2004) *What Does Good Education Research Look Like? Situating a Field and its Practices*. Maidenhead: Open University Press.

Younger, M. and Warrington, M. (2005) *Raising Boys' Achievement in Schools*. Cambridge: Polity Press.

Žižek, S. (1999) Preface: Burning the bridges. In E. Wright and E.L. Wright (eds) *The Žižek Reader*. Oxford: Blackwell Publishers.

Index